MW00629915

HAVE BAT, WILL TRAVEL

EVAN MEAGHER

DEDICATION

For my Smarrito, who makes all adventures possible

And

For Jude, so that he may have adventures of his own.

Swing hard just in case you hit something, kid.

CONTENTS

FOREWORD

When you're a stranger in a strange land, you often misunderstand what people are saying, and people misunderstand what you are trying to say. The occasional silliness created by imperfect translations across the language barrier was an ongoing theme in the Have Bat, Will Travel story, and to capture this, I have used *italics* to indicate words originally spoken in French that I have translated (to the best of my understanding *at the time*) for English readers. I feel that it's important to clarify that the *italicized text* in this book therefore represents my *perceived* translation of statements made in French, both by me and by actual native francophones. As a result, some of the French speakers sometimes sound silly because my brain translated their words imperfectly and/or literally into English. Those French speakers were not simpletons, but my understanding of what they were saying was simplistic, limited by my French language skills, which improved over my time in France but never reached a native level of proficiency. I include those translations in this book not in spite of their imperfections, but rather because of them, to convey just how lost and confused I felt at times as an American abroad. Meanwhile, readers will note that my speech in French seems to translate perfectly; it is because that is, of course, how I perceived it, not because I spoke French with native fluency. (If Eric or Aldo were to write a book about my time in France, I feel confident the themes would be the same, but my dialogue would not be quite so eloquent.) In reality, I know I mangled pronunciation and grammar with regularity, but I don't speak French well enough to describe just how badly and in what manner I did so. Such is the hazard of writing a book based on one man's perception of what he and others have said in a language other than his own, so I caution readers to remember that all conversations in this book – *especially those in italics* –

are but my perception of what was said.

The English is word for word, though.

CHAPTER 1: ACHILLES LAST STAND

I toed the rubber on that monstrosity of a cement pitching mound and peered in at Pierrick's signal, twisting the ball clockwise in my glove to rotate through my various pitch grips. I had developed the ritual years before, in an effort to avoid tipping off the hitter as to whether a fastball or breaking ball was coming next. Pierrick asked for a fastball inside, and I grimaced. I had been missing my spots all day, hanging curveballs, bouncing my Yellow Hammer, and leaving pitches out over the plate when I wanted to jam hitters inside. My elbow was in 'four alarm fire' mode, screeching incessantly at my brain that it had thrown too many pitches already, that it needed to be dunked in an ice tub and drowned with Aleve and whiskey. All in all, not a recipe for success… yet with no outs in the final inning, I found myself with an insurmountable lead, seven strikeouts in the books, and no baserunners allowed after two first-inning walks.

The hitter was a scrawny fella, all knees and elbows, and looked young enough that he didn't need to shave. Hitting from the left side, he had a lefthander's goofy countenance, his flat-brimmed hat sitting at a jauntily cockeyed angle. I had struck him out earlier in the game with a Yellow Hammer – my go-to 12-to-6 breaking ball, the pitch I threw when I needed a swing-and-a-miss – and I wanted to go back to it, but Pierrick wanted a fastball, and so a fastball he was gonna get. That deference to Pierrick's call didn't make a whole lot of sense given how short our pitcher-catcher relationship would be, but I always liked to show catchers that I respected their opinions.

Groaning quietly, I unleashed a fastball that rode up and in on the lefty, tying him in knots. He tried to check his swing well after he had turned halfway to the visiting first base dugout, and recognizing this, didn't bother trying to argue with the 'arbitre' (umpire). My eighth strikeout; one down.

The elbow didn't like that.

I fell behind the next hitter 2-0, both fastballs that I was trying to steer. The elbow pain had begun distracting me, making me reluctant to let it fly with everything I have. I gave silent thanks when their #7 hitter tapped my next offering – a 'get-me-over' curveball with very little snap to it – softly to the second baseman. Yann handled it easily and flipped to first, leaving us one out away.

The elbow throbbed again.

The #8 hitter lumbered into the batter's box, big and barrel-chested, with a bushy moustache and a twinkle in his eye. He took a batting practice fastball down the middle for strike one – lucky he didn't offer at that, I thought; I remembered his ugly-ass swing from his first at-bat, but he looks strong as a goddamn ox – and then after missing with a breaking ball, I ran him to 1-2 with a two-seam fastball that tailed off the outside corner. Probably my best of the game, I thought, not that it mattered. The twinge in my forearm and elbow had reached habanero levels of spiciness, and I resolved not to throw any more curveballs. Of course, Pierrick called for a Yellow Hammer, by far the pitch that was hardest on my now tattered elbow.

"Screw it," I thought. "Last pitch in France. Snap off a good one."

"This is gonna hurt," I added mid-delivery, and broke off a nasty Hammer that started just above the waist before snapping earthward. The hitter waved haplessly at it, like a man trying to hit a butterfly with a car antenna, and the ball nestled gently into Pierrick's glove – resting upturned on the ground at his feet – for the last out of the game. Old habits die hard; I gave an enthusiastic fist pump despite the absurdity of the situation and the lopsided score. My elbow howled in agony. One measly game, I thought, as I lined up for the handshake line. A no-hitter, sure... but one lousy, meaningless, slaughter-rule shortened game.

And with that, my professional baseball career was over.

CHAPTER 2: THE WILDERNESS YEARS

"There are baseball teams in Europe, you know," Chuck began, grinning and leaning in conspiratorially as he sipped his third or fourth illicit Sierra Nevada Pale Ale, resting his elbows on his splayed knees like a pirate discussing a map of buried treasure. "Professional teams. And they're not very good."

Still a freshman, Chuck was eighteen years old and underage, but we hadn't let that stop us. A few friends and I rolled Chuck out of his dorm room to celebrate his selection as Stanford's Tree mascot at Zott's, a beer garden just west of campus. After a few pitchers, the conversation turned to baseball.

"They've got developmental teams over there,

because they're just learning the sport. I've always wanted to try to play in, like, Italy or Czechoslovakia or something." He chuckled. "You wanna come?"

It was the kind of breezy, anything-is-possible conversation that college students have every night of every week of every year, everything promised, nothing delivered. In this case, however, my life changed the moment those words escaped his lips. My story begins there, on a warm spring night in Portola Valley, drinking beer and joking about my life's directionlessness during my final semester at college. To track the *true* beginnings of this adventure, one must travel further back, not years but decades, to explain why anyone would chase a dream as goofy as the one born that night.

For as long as I could remember, I only truly loved one thing, and that was baseball. (Mom, barbecued ribs, and the U-S-of-A; that stuff's a given.) All my life, all I wanted to do was play baseball, and unlike the other fleeting pastimes of youth, the game's hold on me grew stronger with time. I wish I could say that the most important thing in my life was the advancement of racial equality, or curing cancer, but we can no more choose our passions than our eye color; the luck of the draw left me with a boy's game played on a pizza slice-shaped field.

I saw baseball as an exacting, relentless meritocracy, one that rewarded excellence as consistently and utterly as it punished mediocrity. As Sandy Koufax said, "The game has a cleanness. If you do a good job, the numbers say so. You don't have to ask anyone or play politics. You don't have to wait for reviews." I liked how the game's clarity cut through all the bullshit, even as I intuitively understood its occasional cruelty. 'The line drives get caught, and the squibbers go for hits', as Mets' third baseman Ron Kanehl mused, making it, in the end, a lot like life.

Or maybe I just bought the cards for the chewing gum. What difference does it make? In the end, all I ever wanted was to be a 'ballplayer': a professional. The fame and lucrative contracts were of secondary importance; I hungered far more for the emotional validation that a baseball paycheck would provide than for its actual pecuniary value.

There was one problem: baseball is a game of talent. No amount of reading on the subject could help me throw strikes or hit them. The difference between a gloriously long home run and an ignominiously short pop up is a scant sixteenth of an inch, mysteriously located somewhere down the barrel of the bat, on the 'sweet spot' more mysterious and elusive than Jimmy Hoffa's resting place. As puberty dawned on me and my classmates, the Talented Guys tended to be on the right side of that sixteenth of an inch difference far more often than the rest of us. Only now, as a forty-one-year-old washed-up never-was, have I overcome my resentment of Those Guys... But as an eight, ten, even twelve-year old, I convinced myself that I *was* one. Though dimly cognizant of baseball's ruthless ways of dispensing with the imperfectly skilled, I succeeded at each level of Little League, and saw no reason why that success would not continue on into a professional career. How could it not?

Life probably would have been easier if I hadn't been so close, if the delineation between the talented haves and have-nots had been more obvious. Having no talent whatsoever probably would have spared me the long, drawn-out process of finding out I just wasn't good enough to play in the major leagues or even college. I could have avoided banging my head against the ceiling of my own athletic inadequacy, instead of being just good enough to make failure disappointing.

In the meantime, I went about playing baseball the only way I knew how: with a barely controlled fury. Lacking sheer physical gifts, I needed hustle and unrelenting aggressiveness to stand a chance. Over the years, I saw hundreds, maybe thousands of Talented Guys play baseball better than me, but I never saw anyone play harder.

In Reading, Massachusetts, in the late 1980s, Steve Langone was the resident Talented Guy. He was the prototypical superior youth athlete, whose presence fundamentally changes the game from a team contest to a one-man show. He hit the puberty escalator sooner than everyone else, and had more talent to boot, a combination that proved overpowering, particularly in the final year before moving up to full-length mounds and infields. Against a 13-year-old Steve Langone on a 45-foot mound, most kids – hell, most adults – had a better chance trying to hit a bullet from a sniper rifle.

Bill James advanced an interesting theory on players' varying impressions of the hardest throwers they have ever seen. For example, Honus Wagner swore that Cy Young threw harder than Walter Johnson. James attributes this to the fact that Wagner faced Young in the 1890s, as a baby-faced 18-year-old, but saw Johnson after years of seeing major-league caliber fastballs; Young threw no harder, probably, but made a stronger impression on a less experienced Wagner. I'm familiar with James's theory, and for the most part, agree... but I know one thing. I have watched in person the hardest throwers of our time: Pedro Martinez, Roger Clemens, Nolan Ryan, Justin Verlander. I have faced former division-1 NCAA starters and guys who pitched in the College World Series, and I know with absolute certainty that there never has been and never will be a pitcher who throws as hard as Steven Langone did at age 13. When you do the arithmetic to convert a 45-foot mound to a major league mound and carry the one, Langone threw approximately 820 million miles per hour, with a knee-buckling curveball. He may have had a changeup, but there was never any point in throwing it.

When Langone pitched, everyone knew he would pitch all six innings and strike out 15 or 16. Any bat-on-ball contact would be accidental and/or largely symbolic. My Dodgers were second-best in the league, due entirely to Langone and his Braves; when he moved up a level the following year, we won the championship with ease. However, during his final year, we put up a valiant and ultimately unsuccessful challenge for the title. Early in the season, I faced Langone in an at-bat that subsequently proved the subject of more discussion in the Meagher household than any presidential election before or since.

I fell behind quickly 0-2 (what else?) to Langone and began fouling off pitches, fastball after fastball after fastball, some eight or nine in all. I barely got a piece of the first few, tipping them to the backstop or off the catcher's chest. Langone bore down, less like a champion rising to the occasion than a man waving at an exasperating mosquito, but I started to zero in. I got more and more wood – aluminum, really – on each successive pitch, each foul ball creeping closer to the right field line than the last. (My father's version of the story differs; to hear him retell it, the number of foul balls approaches one hundred, and the last dozen or so hit the chalk in right field before one-hopping the fence, but such is the poetic license to which fathers are entitled.)

I remember the last three pitches vividly: the first, a weak ground ball, bounced just to the right of the coach's box, the second, a legitimately well-struck grounder, missed the first base bag by about a foot and a half. Again, in my father's version, the entire dugout, the parents (of both teams, in a *Rocky IV*-like moment) in the bleachers, and a passing regiment of soldiers all stood cheering at the incredible tenacity of this overwhelmed underdog. Langone couldn't throw the fastball past me, it seemed, and it was only a matter of time before I caught up to one and put it in play.

Steve was no dummy. Seeing each successive fastball end up closer and closer to the right field line, he did what any pitcher worth his salt would: he spun me a curveball, probably the first I had ever seen, and I missed it by three-and-a-half feet.

My father recalls fans cheering a courageous effort as I jogged back to the dugout, while Langone grinned goofily, embarrassed that he had to resort to such trickery against someone a year younger. I remember storming back to the dugout fighting back tears, devastated by my catastrophic failure. The strikeout was proof of a possibility I refused to consider: that I might not go on to a Hall of Fame career in professional baseball. My father and the coaches considered the at-bat a success for the right reasons. Realizing the slim likelihood that anyone but Langone would ever play professional baseball[1], they recognized it as one of youth athletics' invaluable lessons: sportsmanship, determination, grace in defeat. At the time, I wasn't interested.

Pride compels me to point out the story's happier postscript. Later in the season, in the last inning of a 9-3 Braves win that Langone closed out with ruthless efficiency, I took a defensive swing at one of his fastballs up-and-away. Powered far more by Langone's

---

[1] Langone, for his part, went on to compile a 2.68 ERA in 339.2 innings spread across six seasons in the minor leagues.

arm than by my bat, the ball took off, a towering flyball that soared over the right fielder's head and cleared the right field fence by 20 feet. I believe it to be the first home run Langone ever allowed in a career much longer and vastly more impressive than my own. To a 12-year-old desperate to believe he belonged among the athletic elite, it offered a seductive reprieve from the humbling strikeout.

After an unremarkable high school and Babe Ruth League career, I left for college. I had decided on Stanford long before high school, on an achingly cold New Year's Day at the age of seven. My father and I were watching college football. As the television trumpeted the names of college after college, I made one of the most important and impulsive decisions of my life. Looking out the frosted windows at the bleak, snow-covered landscape, I decided it was time I thought of my education.

"Dad? Are there any good colleges in warm places?" (Certainly, they had to be "good" colleges: a straight-A student at Alice M. Barrows Elementary School – penmanship excepted – would accept nothing less.)

"Well," he thought. "Stanford." A long pause. "And Rice, I suppose." The decision was already half-made. Had he inverted the order, I might have worked harder in science courses and become a world-class engineer, and I might today work in aerospace or software design, with a distinctly more rational view of the world. But no. "Stanford... and Rice."

"Are they any good at baseball?" I asked, knowing I would need an athletic program of a sufficient caliber to launch my certain professional career.

"Oh, sure. Stanford's in the College World Series every year."

I graduated from Stanford in June of 2001 with a BA in Economics and an MA in Sociology. Those first months out of college remain a dark memory. I had expected to receive my degree in the California sun, raise my diploma triumphantly above my head, hug my parents and hot girlfriend (whose presence in the fantasy likely stems from my graduation from an all-male high school), and hop into some suitably sporty roadster to drive off into the sunset of an exciting, high-paying job.

Reality proved different. On my fifth day at Stanford, I blew out my shoulder crashing to the ground in a pickup ultimate Frisbee game, requiring surgery that put a titanium screw in my shoulder for eight weeks and made my efforts to walk on to the Stanford baseball team an exercise in futility. Four years later, upon receiving my diplomas, I found myself unemployed, alone, and physically and professionally damaged. The startup software firm I had helped found underwent a power struggle just four months before graduation, leaving me without a job in the smoldering crater of Silicon Valley, post-dot-com implosion. In a stunning example of symbolism and exquisitely bad timing, the week I began looking for employment coincided with the cancellation of on-campus recruiting efforts at Stanford's Career Development Center... because it burned down. As the cherry topping on my postgraduate angst sundae, a routine doctor's checkup revealed that I had been walking around on a torn knee ligament for roughly sixteen months.

Alone, unemployed, and limping is no way to go through life. At my absolute nadir, four weeks after graduation, I found myself subletting a UCLA dorm room in Westwood, wondering how it had all gone so terribly wrong. Amidst a haze of self-pity, my emotions ranging from cheerfully hopeless to bitterly resentful, I found salvation in the unlikeliest of places: Chavez Ravine.

My friend Jacob worked in LA for a major production company. My contact with him that summer was limited to parties where would-be actors and producers determined within 45 seconds that I couldn't help their careers, eliminating any incentive for the empty gesture of further conversation. Jacob was a good friend, however, and recognizing my unusually sullen mood, called me one weekend to offer me his boss's Dodgers tickets.

"Come on, man, it'll be fun. It'll get you out of the house," he said. "They're great seats. Plus, it's the Fourth of July. There's fireworks."

I demurred.

"It's not like you have anything better to do."

He had me there. Besides, I had never been to Dodger Stadium, so my roommate Biggs and I joined Jacob on

July 4, 2001 to watch the Dodgers battle the Giants. In the ninth, we maneuvered our way toward the third baseline and the left field exit to the parking lot. When a pinch-hitting Shawon Dunston lined out to second to end the game, something miraculous happened.

A ten-year-old kid wearing a Dodgers jersey and clutching a pillow hopped the fence and took off on a beeline for center. This couldn't possibly end well, I thought, and I scanned the field for the security personnel that would take him down. Instead, I saw another child follow suit. Then another. Children started streaming onto the field, clutching blankets and pillows and rushing out towards centerfield, where an impromptu Hooverville began to grow. I turned to the scoreboard for explanation: "The Los Angeles Dodgers Welcome You to Family Night – Come Sit on the Outfield Grass and Watch the Fireworks!"

Mesmerized by the sight of children storming a previously forbidden ground, we got caught up in the momentum of the throng, which pushed us away from the exit and toward the field. "So, we're parked over by..." I heard Jacob beginning, his voice trailing off as I stared out at the MacGuffin. I took a few steps onto the outfield grass, which met the infield dirt with military precision in a crisp right angle before arcing towards second base in a perfect semicircle. I had visited a dozen MLB parks, but had never set foot on the diamond itself. Its visceral beauty knocked the wind out of me. It was like encountering Charlize Theron only to discover that she was actually more dazzling in person than on film.

Here, a shortstop would go in the hole for the backhand; there, a runner would dance off third trying to distract the pitcher; out there, a left fielder would dive for a sinking line drive. I realized at once that these visions springing to life weren't stock photographs of generic ballplayers, but rather images of me. *I* was going in the hole; *I* took care not to get picked off third. These images had lain dormant for five years, the heat of the Southern California sky instantly reawakening them, vivid as ever.

As the first Roman Candle burst over our heads to the "oohs" and "ahhhs" of the adoring crowd, my mind reeled. The light bulb had gone off. Something was missing, and those few moments on the field clarified what. A few hours and Google searches later, I found the Men's Adult Baseball League (MABL), a national organization of individuals who realized that baseball shouldn't end after high school. I looked up the local teams' contact information, and soon a gruff voice on the other end of the line gave me directions to my first baseball game in five years.

"You got gray baseball pants?" he asked.

"Sure," I said. (I did not.)

"And a blue cap?"

"Absolutely." (Not even close.)

That Sunday, I played for the East Los Angeles Monarchs. Between the team's name – the Monarchs had been a prominent Negro League team, with a roster featuring Jackie Robinson and James "Cool Papa" Bell – and location in East LA, I wondered whether I might break a reverse color barrier as the only white member of the team. Come Sunday, that proved true, and my new African American teammates watched as a rusty, out-of-shape white boy with an as-yet-unrepaired knee tear struck out badly in his first three at-bats, all on curveballs that echoed my great defeat at the arm of Steve Langone.

Of all the baseball skills that erode during a long layoff, hitting a curveball is the hardest to regain. People catch and throw things all the time, but nothing in the average day maintains the visual acuity necessary to identify a baseball's spin to determine whether it will curve. Our opponent's heavyset Mexican pitcher had a pretty good curveball, one that I couldn't have hit with a tennis racket, and after recognizing that fact, he threw me nothing but breaking balls all day. I ended the eighth with a particularly ugly flail at a curve a good foot outside the strike zone.

The Monarchs trailed by five, and a chance at redemption seemed unlikely until the same pitcher tired and lost his control, walking three hitters, hitting one, and giving up a double, bringing us within two. As I entered the on-deck circle, the gruff-voiced coach pulled me aside, and ordered "Take a first strike." The message was clear. *Don't screw this up.*

Having shown no ability to make contact, I couldn't blame him for hoping that I might extend the rally without swinging the bat. I entered the batter's box with the bases loaded and two outs, representing the winning run. I called time and pretended to adjust my batting gloves, trying to straighten out my thoughts. All day, the pitcher had gotten ahead in the count with the fastball before burying me with curveballs. The glint of recognition in his eyes suggested that he had no intention of abandoning this thoroughly successful strategy. He licked his lips, like the wolf staring down Little Red Riding Hood.

Few moments in life resonate so vividly that I recall them in slow motion. I remember the pitcher releasing a fastball on the inside half of the plate. I remember my hands whiplashing through the hitting zone, dragging 32 ounces of Louisville Slugger along with them. I remember feeling the impact and watching as the ball rocketed down the left field line, a booming fly ball that kept slicing away, away, away from the sprinting left fielder. As I jump-stepped towards first, I remember the pitcher's head snapping to his right, tracking the ball's trajectory, trying to will the ball foul just as I tried to will it fair.

It one-hopped the wall about eighteen inches inside the foul pole as the dugout exploded in cacophonous cheers. I held up at second as the tying run scored from first. Our leadoff hitter promptly doubled into the gap in left, and I scored the winning run standing up, mobbed by teammates at home.

I drove home euphoric, feeling complete for the first time I could remember. I had no job, no girlfriend, and no functional ligaments in my knee, and it didn't matter; I could still hit. That one at-bat – that one swing – seemed to break the slump and turn things around. I finally found a job, teaching 7th- and 8th-grade math and science back in the Bay Area, where I underwent successful ACL reconstruction surgery and began aggressive rehabilitation.

It was a small thing, but at the time, I attributed my change in fortune to that one swing. I sometimes wonder where I would be now if I had fouled it off. Destitute and on the lam, perhaps. Instead, I found myself on the right side of that sixteenth of an inch, and it seemed to redirect my life as suddenly and forcefully as I had redirected that thigh-high fastball.

When I needed it most, baseball wiped my brow and put the salts to my nose.

CHAPTER 3: ENTER THE PITCHBOOKS

I hated teaching. Hated every minute of it. To this day, I cannot imagine a more perfect mismatch between job requirements and personality traits. Despite occasional successes - a few students still send me notes thanking me for convincing them that they could and should succeed at mathematics – my year in Palo Alto felt like a prison sentence.

Only baseball kept me sane.

By December, I was already planning my escape from the world of chalkboards, parent-teacher conferences, and blank acne-ridden stares. I carpet-bombed San Francisco's financial district with résumés. With the economy still in shambles, I received few responses, but when one invited me to interview on a Saturday, I was desperate enough not to decline even though it overlapped with the tryout for the Bay Area MABL. Fortunately, my friend Dunagan tried out at my urging, and got drafted by a new team in need of bodies. He put in a word with their manager, and within days I was a San Francisco Red, with a scrimmage scheduled for that Sunday. My aggressive knee rehab paid off when I tripled in my first at-bat, earning the starting shortstop position that I would not relinquish for four years.

In our first year, the Reds won four games and lost 20, often in heartbreaking fashion. We played 18-inning doubleheaders in the hot sun, driving for hours to play in Vallejo, Solano, or Santa Ana, waking up so stiff the next day that merely getting out of bed had to occur in stages, like the construction of the Golden Gate Bridge. To anyone else, it seemed crazy: why put yourself through that? To me, it felt like the first gasp of air after being held underwater for five years.

As we slogged through those first difficult seasons, a funny thing happened; funny, because one rarely improves at age 23 after major shoulder surgery at 18. I could still hit, slap it on the ground and use my speed to cause trouble, and I could still wield a glove. My pitching, however…

Suddenly, and without warning, I started throwing *hard*. Real hard, by MABL standards, harder than I ever threw in high school. My breaking stuff improved too; the slip curve I had tinkered with in high school became my 'out pitch', a nasty 12-to-6 curve that dove at home plate like an apple falling off a table. It was so effective that I figured it needed a name. To my delight, I learned that noted BoSox wild child Oil Can Boyd had referred to throwing his own 12-to-6 curve as "dropping the Yellow Hammer." I adopted the name immediately.

Either way, I suddenly had "good stuff," and an attitude to match it. I had grown up, gotten over my resentment of "those guys." At this level, I *was* one of "those guys," and I entered games as a power closer, shutting everyone down for one or two innings every week. One preseason game at Golden Gate Park, I struck out five of six batters to close out the win, throwing flat-out gas and mixing in a nasty Hammer. After the game, Dunagan pulled me aside, exclaiming "Holy Shit, Ev, you were dealing today!" I had arrived. No finesse, just power and an attitude of "here it is, hit it if you can."

Most guys in the league couldn't. I racked up some impressive stats in the MABL, averaging 1.5 strikeouts per inning with a miniscule ERA. Between my occasional conversations with Chuck about Euroball, my rejuvenated passion for the game, and the unexpected new mustard on my fastball, the pieces were falling into place... but inertia is heavy, and the status quo is sticky. In order to make a drastic leap of faith and try to find someone, anyone, to pay me even a dime to play baseball, I needed a little something extra to light a fire under me and get me over the tipping point.

Enter the pitch books.

Like most class of 2001 graduates facing the one-two punch of the dot-com bubble and September 11th, I spent several years under-employed. When I saw an advertisement for a position in the venture capital placements group of a large bank, I jumped at the opportunity. Despite my underwhelming résumé, I landed an interview, and thanks to an endorsement from a family friend, I started as a first-year analyst in January.

I loved the job. It was exciting, sexy, and lucrative. I loved the feeling of being 'in on the deal,' of overcoming my initial terror and growing confident dialing up venture capitalists and pitching them transactions. I loved the networking, the sumptuous closing dinners, and above all, I loved the paycheck.

Unfortunately, I hated the life, and a steady diet of 90- and 100-hour weeks made my job and my life virtually indistinguishable. For every celebratory closing dinner, there were a hundred greasy late-night takeout meals eaten hunched over a computer, and a dozen weekends spent poring over PowerPoint decks... all took a toll. I had arguably the cushiest gig in all of banking, working for genuinely good people, but I couldn't avoid it; I loved my job, but I hated my life.

If this seems like a tangent, it is not. Had I landed one of the other thousand jobs to which I applied, something less intense and more lifestyle-friendly, the inertial drag might have kept me in the 9-to-5, building-a-career orbit. God Bless Banking, I say, because without such a burnout-intensive job, those conversations with Chuck might have remained sound and fury, signifying nothing. Instead, my passion for baseball intensified because *it was all I had.* All my other hobbies lapsed, I failed dismally at maintaining a relationship with any girl I met, and my hygiene slipped badly, but I held fast to one rule: I never missed Reds' games, even if that meant sleeping in my office and working 18 hours in my uniform after Saturday's doubleheader in order to meet a Sunday deadline.

Everyone burns out, and I did too. One sleep-deprived morning, I wondered how long it would take them to find me if I hung myself in the bathroom, and decided that no amount of money was worth it. It became even easier after I made a mistake during a particularly arduous transaction. I respected my managing directors and liked working for them, but when one exploded on the phone, tearing me a new asshole over a fairly trivial screwup, it was time to go.

"Screw this," I thought, "I'm out of Dodge. Life's too short."

And with that, the Rubicon was crossed.

Those first conversations with Chuck morphed from a running inside joke into a nascent idea, and then a half-serious plan for some indefinite future. By 2003, the possibility became real enough that I convinced my roommates to rent an enormous double-lot house in the distant Sunset district, possibly the only house in San Francisco whose backyard stretched more than 60 feet, 6 inches. I installed a full-length batting cage and a professional caliber pitching machine. It remains unquestionably the best $1,500 I have ever spent.

Along the way, Chuck fell by the wayside. We exchanged emails all fall and into the winter, and though I always thought of it as *our* project, *our* story to tell, I could tell he was wavering. I kept my fingers crossed, hoping that one day I would wake up to Chuck's email on my Blackberry saying that he'd come to his senses and was 100%, without-a-doubt 'in', but it never came. In the spring, he confirmed that he wasn't ready. I was on my own. On July 26, 2005, I sent the following email to my closest friends.

Dear Friends,

Congratulations! (And, "I'm sorry.") Your inclusion on this list indicates that I am presumptuous enough to think that you care about what's going on in my life. The upside is a potentially interesting story; the downside is a longwinded, rambling email, the gist of which is that I'm quitting my job to try to play professional baseball in Europe. Because this may come as a shock, I've set up a FAQ to answer any questions.

Q: You're quitting your job? Why the hell are you doing that?

A: Because I want to go play baseball in Europe. Seeing as that will require overcoming minimal talent with superior physical conditioning, and my current job makes even inferior physical conditioning a pipe dream, it had to go.

Q: You realize you're giving up what could have been a great career for you.

A: Yeah, well, not really. For all my cracks about being a corporate drone, I'm something of a free spirit, and banking, while lucrative and occasionally stimulating, made me feel neither free nor spirited. Don't get me wrong- the bank treated me well, and I don't regret having worked here. I just don't want to stay.

Q: Who cares? Minor league baseball? In Europe? Does that even exist?

A: Well, I care. They do have professional baseball in Europe, and it's varying degrees of not-so-good. The Italians are very good; the Spanish are good; the Croatians are terrible. I don't care where I play, I just want to get paid, even if it's 15 rubles a week. I want to be able to say, on my deathbed, that at one point, I was good enough that someone paid me to play baseball.

Q: That's insane. This is a terrible, self-indulgent,

crazy idea, and in the meantime, you're flushing away a perfectly good job.

A: Don't piss in my flowerpot. Or, "You no live-a-my-life, you no choose-a-my-dreams."

Q: Are you even good enough to do this?

A: No. Certainly not now, as the ravages of 90-hour weeks have rendered my physical form, ahem, Pillsbury-esque. And possibly not ever. Therein lies the inherent beauty: ever wondered how good you could be at something if you focused on it exclusively for six months? Just threw everything up in the air and devoted yourself to it completely? That's what I'm doing. Whatever my absolute ceiling is as a baseball player, I'll find it.

Q: Will that be good enough?

A: Maybe. Possibly- even probably- not. I'd put my odds at about 25%. But in a sense, this isn't even about baseball. It's about recognizing when you have only one opportunity to do something that will make you happy, when you have your mid-20s strength, speed, and stamina, no job, no wife, and no mortgage to tie you down, and either the courage or foolishness (or both) to take a shot at it. To die knowing that at the very least, you took a shot when you could.

Q: How do you get signed? Is there a tryout?

A: If need be. I'll try to get introductions from friends who have played over there or are playing there now. If not, there are other options, like getting a report written up by a friendly MLB scout (which would hopefully contain the words "five-tool athlete" and "uncanny hand speed") and peddling that to teams abroad. Worst case scenario, it's a barnstorming tour when I arrive in Europe: Have Bat, Will Travel. So, if you know anyone who runs a team in Europe, let them know I'm available.

Q: And?

A: And I'm excited. Sure, this could be the worst decision of my life, but I doubt it. For the first time in a long while, I'm truly excited about something- in fact, I think this is as excited as I've ever been about anything.

Q: Wow. Any last things to mention?

A: Yes. I may grow a moustache.

Peace,

Ev

CHAPTER 4: THE QUIET STORM

I began training full-time in September, rising before dawn to work with a crazed Marine drill sergeant named Sergeant Ken to shed the 25 pounds I picked up from the investment banker's veal cow workout regimen. I purchased a lathe and made my own wooden bats, engraving them with elaborate Latin names, and emailed the baseball coaches of local universities in the hopes of observing their training programs. Knowing that the Stanford coaches would respond the same way they responded to my attempt to try out – as if I had requested permission to dropkick a small child – I didn't even bother with my alma mater, sticking to San Francisco-based programs like SF State,

UCSF, and USF. UCSF's lack of a team streamlined the process significantly.

To my delight, Troy Nakamura of the USF Dons responded immediately, inviting me to watch a practice, where he, pitching coach Greg Moore, and recent alum/Padres first baseman Tag Bozied explained their workout philosophy. Later, Troy made a critical recommendation.

"You should talk to Velocity Sports," he said. "Tag uses them. They train a bunch of MLB guys, some NFL players too."

Two days later, I visited Velocity's impressive facilities about 40 minutes south in San Carlos, where a trainer named Andrew led me through a grueling 45-minute workout that nearly made me vomit. The hefty price tag for four months of twice-a-week personal training sessions gave me pause, but I left Velocity feeling both nauseous and impressed with the staff's knowledge of baseball-specific training techniques. After some deliberation, I cut the check, pushing my chips to the center of the table.

Andrew pushed me to my limit with expensive, complicated training aids that looked like they belonged in Ivan Drago's gym from Rocky IV. My training regimen followed the one that Velocity provided to college football players preparing for the NFL combine events like the 40-yard dash and the three-cone drill, and they posted the top ten in each event by age on huge white boards hanging on the wall, a sort of pecking order showing who was the most macho in each age group. About a month into my time at Velocity, another athlete started showing up to work out at the same time, so we shared the gym for 90 minutes on Mondays and Thursdays. As we were both over 18 years of age, our scores were listed in the 'Elite Athlete' bracket on the wall, marking the first time I had ever been referred to as such.

Anyone observing the two of us would immediately recognize that we existed at entirely different levels of athleticism. He stood 6'4", maybe 225 pounds, cut from marble. His chiseled frame sported a multitude of tattoos, most notably the Olde English-style font "QUIET" and "STORM" running down the back of his triceps, and his running form conjured up the image of a locomotive rolling down the track. By contrast, I had spent the last two years eating takeout Chinese food and slaving over pitchbooks. Always more student than athlete, I was *not* the one you'd identify as the NFL prospect, mostly because I lacked cornrows and muscle definition.

Curious, I asked Andrew about him one day.

"His name is Marques," Andrew replied. "He's a wide receiver from Hofstra, but he's got a girlfriend at Stanford, so he's working out here before the combine."

"Ah." I grunted. What's one more superior athlete around me, I thought? Anyway, doesn't matter. A wide receiver from Hofstra? He'll probably never make it.

Months passed in a blur. Each day, I either hit the gym or the track at Kezar Stadium for Andrew's assigned sprinting homework. After an hour of backyard batting practice, I'd force down a repulsive primordial shake made of raw eggs, protein powder, celery, carrots, brewer's yeast, and soy, relying on a childish notion that the worse it tasted, the better it was for me.

And then there were the supplements. I became a GNC salesman's wet dream, seeking any (legal) edge to put myself in the best physical condition possible. Xenadrine, creatine, glutamine, glucosamine. NoX2 for vasodilation, lutein for vision, ZMA for muscle recovery... Eight pills at breakfast, six at lunch, a few more throughout the day, and six more at night, for an eye-popping total of around 40 per day. I noted my own hypocrisy; as a baseball fan, I rooted against juiceheads like Bonds, McGwire, and Sosa, but as a player, I recognized their temptation. I was desperate to make an unknown European team that would pay me pennies; they stood to make or lose millions on baseball's grandest stage. Despite – or, arguably, because of – my almost comically low position on baseball's athletic totem pole, I can't deny the inclination to take any pill, drink any shake, do absolutely anything to make myself a better ballplayer... and I just wanted to play in *Spain.* At the end of the day, had someone told me that I could either take steroids and succeed in my quest to play professionally, or not take steroids and fail... well, I guess I wonder what I would have done. Fortunately, it never came to that, because I didn't know anyone who could score steroids, and would have been too squeamish to stick myself with a needle even if I had. Relying on legal supplements, working out six days a week, and dieting fastidiously, I got into the best shape of my life. My bat got quicker, until I could dial the pitching machine up to 90, and my fastball added even more zip. But the real story was my footspeed.

In my initial workout, Andrew timed me at 5.12 seconds in the 40-yard dash. That seemed terribly slow until he explained that Velocity used a laser-timing system that identified the precise millisecond that a runner left the starting gate and crossed the finish line, producing vastly more accurate times than the hand timers used at the NFL combine. Each NFL team thinks that their guy is the most accurate on the stopwatch, giving them a perceived informational edge over other teams, so despite the league's obsession with science and quantifiable data, they use that over a laser system that would put every team on a level playing field.

Andrew further explained that humans are good at timing the runner's departure from the starting gate, but typically anticipate him crossing the finish line by two- to three-tenths of a second, producing faster times than a laser system would, which explains the ludicrous 4.2 and 4.3 second 40 times run by no-name wideouts at the Combine.

In January, I had my mid-term evaluation at Velocity, showing impressive gains in the shuttle run, vertical jump, and 3-cone drill, but I was most curious about the 40. I came tearing out of the gate, zipping down the track so fast I struggled to slow down before the padded wall in Velocity's converted warehouse. I turned eagerly back to Andrew.

"What was it? How did I do??"

Andrew checked the laser timer, paused for dramatic effect, and grinned.

"4.81."

I looked up at the "Velocity Top 10" dry erase board marking the top scores by active customers, finding the Quiet Storm listed first, at 4.86. Marques was getting bumped to second place! Sometimes the smart money loses, I thought, and sometimes the oddsmakers take a bath. Sometimes the indomitable Russian national team loses to a bunch of amateurs on a slapshot by some kid from Winthrop, and apparently, sometimes a white ex-banker with a fat ass outruns a skill position player invited to the NFL combine. Who knew?[2]

[2] A few days later, the Quiet Storm ran a 4.76 in his final run at Velocity Sports of San Carlos. At the NFL Combine in Indianapolis, he ran a 4.50 or 4.54 (depending on whose hand timer you trust), prompting the New Orleans Saints to draft him in the seventh round of the 2006 NFL Draft.

In a ten-year NFL career, Marques Colston caught 711 passes for 9,759 yards, scoring 72 touchdowns and earning a championship ring in 2010. Considered more of a possession receiver than a speedy deep threat, he is nevertheless the New Orleans Saints' all-time franchise leader in receiving yards, yards from scrimmage, receiving touchdowns, total touchdowns, and total receptions.

CHAPTER 5: DON'T BELIEVE THE HYPE

Speed and strength were great, but they didn't solve the mystery of how I would contact a European baseball team, convince them of my skills, and finagle a paycheck out of the deal. Fortunately, I had relevant experience.

My job at the bank entailed cold-calling notoriously arrogant venture capitalists and convincing them to invest in the latest company we were flogging down Sand Hill Road. At first terrified to talk to a real live VC, I came to make more than 1,000 cold calls. None of them ever resulted in an investment in our client, but it got me over the fear of rejection. In the end, that proved the secret to selling European teams on my viability as a ballplayer; I cold called them.

I scoured websites purporting to list European teams looking for players, which provided its own entertainment. Players entered their own statistics and experience, and clearly, they thought very highly of themselves. My favorite was an outfielder from California who claimed to have hit 59 doubles in his previous season and listed his 'home-to-first' time as 3.1 seconds... from the righthanded batter's box. For comparison's sake, Ichiro Suzuki was at the time acknowledged as the fastest man in baseball at 3.6 seconds to first base... and as a lefthanded hitter, Ichiro had a two-step head start on Mr. 3.1. Anyone who could best Ichiro by a full half second after spotting him a two-step head start isn't looking to play in Hamburg or Prague, he's looking at Atlanta or LA and probably running anchor in the Olympic 4x100. How could I compete with that?

After brief deliberation, I chose not to. I posted my stats from the Reds without embellishment, with one exception; my 82-83mph fastball hopped up to 84-85. I justified my guilt by reasoning that if my workout regimen could take me from fatass banker to outrunning an NFL Combine invitee, it could probably add a few more clicks to my fastball by the time I got overseas.

To this day, it remains the only lie I ever told a European baseball team. Mea culpa.

I answered ads on sites like eurobaseballconnection.com; one from Sweden, two from France, several from Germany and the Czech Republic. For the French teams, I tried to demonstrate my five years of French study. They ignored me for months, until one day in late November. My heart skipped a beat as I opened an email replying to mine with the familiar "re: French Baseball" subject heading. It read in part,

Hello Evan,

My name is Chris and I'm the manager of the Elite team.

I understood what you wrote in french and if you want you can write in french it's a good exercice for you. It's really good that you speak french and that you want to coach. Because we need a player who can do the practice of the players and maybe coach this year. Last year I did everything alone because I hgonna have time to do this year, and I will need an assistant coach.

That's why we are intersted in you to come here to play.

-Christophe

My roommates streamed down to the kitchen to see what all the fist-pumping, whooping, and jumping around was about. “The Lions, man!!!” I explained. “The Savigny-Sur-Orge Motherfucking Lions!!! I'M GONNA BE A LION!!!” Then we listened to AC/DC's Thunderstruck at what is generally considered an ‘unneighborly’ volume, excited at the prospect of me playing in France. I spoke the language, and besides, it was 2006; with George W. Bush in the oval office, Americans were *beloved* overseas, particularly in France, the birthplace of Freedom Fries.

Christophe put me in touch with the team's general manager Fermin, launching a correspondence lasting several months, punctuated by long stretches of radio silence on their end. We chatted on MSN messenger, where I explained that I had been a closer, but would continue training to build the arm strength to pitch more innings as a starter, and that I could fly out as early as February. In mid-December, Fermin reported that the team's board of directors loved that I could speak French and coach while helping with their junior developmental teams. Talks escalated, and they offered me a salary of 300€ per month plus an apartment and a public transportation pass. At my father's urging, I pointed out that a friend from the Reds had received 400€ a month in Belgium. Frankly, I would have accepted 10€ a month, but the allure of saying I had negotiated my first (and hopefully last) professional baseball contract proved irresistible.

December 20, 2005 gave me the best Christmas present of my life: an email from Christophe announcing that the board had unanimously voted to hire me as a player/coach for 300€ a month (so much for holding out) and purchased my flight to France. For the first time in my life, I could honestly call myself a Professional Baseball Player.

Much merriment ensued.

Time accelerated out of control. After years of waking up in darkness and working 18-hour days only to return home in darkness, suddenly the future looked bright. I booked my flight for Thursday, March 2nd, which would get me into Paris just 24 hours before my first big test: a preseason tournament against Savigny's biggest rival, the defending champion Rouen Huskies; eager to earn my Lions bona fides, I hated them already. I would have to walk off the plane, and as one friend put it, "immediately start mashing."

After booking my flight, Christophe surprised me by asking that I bring some American chewing tobacco, which apparently the French could find only in Amsterdam.

"Sure," I responded via instant messenger. "I'll pick up a package or two. Any particular kind?"

"Cherry," Christophe typed immediately. "Bring a whole log (10 tins)." I chuckled.

"Uh, sure. Cherry it is." I reminded myself that this wasn't exactly the Cape Cod League. I changed the subject, asking Christophe to apologize to the guys in advance for my lousy

French.

"Don't worry, you'll be fine," he replied. "Besides, you're an American ballplayer, they'll all hail you as Jesus."

Uh oh, I thought. I better bring extra Skoal.

As my departure date neared, I felt my enthusiasm tempered with regret, because the move would separate me from my girlfriend of eight months. Becky and I met at a friend's wedding in May, and had been inseparable ever since, making it the longest I had ever dated anyone. Despite her joking that I had pulled a bait-and-switch – wooing her as a clean-cut investment banker before becoming a goateed, out-of-work wannabe professional baseball player – she supported me from day one, even throwing me a going away party at a local bar complete with a cake with a photo of my face superimposed on the head of the surprisingly effeminate Savigny Lions mascot logo.

Our relationship flourished in the fall, when we began seeing each other almost every night, and exchanged our first I love yous over Christmas. Becky was different than any girl I had dated, and I knew as much from our first date, when I brought her to a friend's party. I knew everyone, and she knew no one, but she won over everyone there within moments with her sense of humor and thousand-watt smile. She was beautiful, smart, kind, and caring... and I was leaving for France.

For months, I subconsciously avoided the topic, because the present was too good to worry about the future. I had a loving girlfriend and a team willing to pay me to play *baseball.* It seemed like tempting fate to discuss how our lives would diverge the moment we got into different graduate schools. Selfishly, I was content to remain idling in the glorious present, whistling past the graveyard of our doomed future.

We decided to stay together, at least until we knew where we would end up for grad school. I'm tempted to joke that it wasn't 'we' who decided, but that would be unfair. I knew that I loved Becky more than any woman I had ever met, and it seemed that this whole 'falling in love' thing required the occasional impractical leap of faith. I took one, buying time for a relationship that I wanted to be 'the one' despite potentially serious obstacles.

Meanwhile, my impending acid test drew nearer by the day. At the bank, Thursdays had meant that I was but 24 hours from the sweet relief of the weekend. This Thursday meant a 9-hour flight, and Saturday meant having to slug and pitch my way onto a team, jetlagged and disoriented by my arrival in a new country.

CHAPTER 6: IN ANOTHER LAND

By Wednesday night, my head was spinning from all the last-minute tasks that had gone unaccomplished. I had to cancel my last dinner with Becky (to the maitre d' still cursing that empty two-top at Café Kati on March 1, 2006, I send my sincerest apologies) and struggle through the final bring/store/discard decisions.

Leaving any other girl behind might have been awkward, but Becky had already booked her first flight to France, arriving just three weeks after me. We passed my final evening in a sense of delirium, fueled equally by denial of our impending separation, giddiness over my good fortune, and stupefaction at it all finally happening. Just after midnight, Becky forcibly interrupted my near-manic packing, grabbing my arm and insisting that I sit on my bed to deliver a series of gifts that made our parting even more bittersweet. First, she produced a pair of CDs: one from the Rebirth Brass Band, our first serious date, and one from R.J. Mischo, whose concert on Fisherman's Wharf served as the prelude to our first kiss.

Finally, she produced the piece de resistance; a Renzo Special sandwich from Molinari's, my favorite deli in North Beach. Usually, a homemade crusty Italian loaf replete with prosciutto, hot coppa, fresh moozadell and sun-dried tomatoes would be pretty nice. If you get one of those from a girl, she's probably pretty special. But if she shows that she has been listening all along, and remembers that one of the few things that kept you sane during those brutal 100-hour work weeks was walking up Columbus Street on sunny Friday afternoons for a Renzo Special, a stick of pepperoni, and a few hot peppers stuffed with provolone and prosciutto, and delivers all of these things to you in a brown bag with your name on it encircled by a heart?

Call me sentimental, but it almost brought a tear to my eye. We made love for a final time in the United States, and lay together for hours, talking about the silliness of life. It seemed that after years of struggling, I had found the answer; simply disregard everything everyone has ever told you, and go do whatever makes you happy. Idealistic? Certainly. Unrealistic? Perhaps. But it made sense as Becky lay her head on my chest in a room full of luggage and empty jars of creatine powder.

Finally, at around 3:00 AM, we slept the sleep of kings, or at least the fitful, semi-inebriated sleep of kings who have decided to polish off that bottle of champagne they've been saving for a special occasion before abdicating the throne. I woke up and shaved the center of my now-impressive goatee, leaving only a ghastly Fu-Manchu moustache in homage to the original late-innings intimidator, Goose Gossage.

A rare western breeze passed over our house on 16th Avenue as I left for the final time. Usually, Karl The Fog crept up the hill from the ocean, shrouding the house in a veil of mystery, but that day it was crystal clear from Pacifica to Marin. Encumbered by my two massive duffel bags of baseball bats, protein powder, and baseball jerseys, I stepped outside, grinning confidently at a world about to receive my nascent professional baseball career. Turning left, I found my cocksure stare returned disinterestedly by the Golden Gate Bridge. *I've seen ballplayers come and go*, it seemed to say. I ignored it and lugged my bags to the car, interrupted by an unexpected smooch from Becky.

"Okay," I gasped, trying to make it as painless as possible. "Let's do this."

We loaded the borrowed Camry and set off for the airport, occasionally glancing at each other in silent disbelief. As we took the airport exit, I struggled to ignore my mind's exhortations to stay, to throw away this silly dream and remain in a comfortable Bay Area life with the woman I loved. I glanced over at Becky, quietly tense, radiant in a black pinstriped suit, and sighed.

We shared a final embrace outside the terminal, as the taxis flew past us.

"I love you," I began, choking back tears as I

glanced over Becky's head at the San Mateo hills in the background. "I'll see you soon."

"I love you too."

I spent 13 of the next 15 hours on flights to New York and then Paris, chatting with the older woman next to me. She was a banker too, and when she asked what I did for a living, I could not resist.

"I'm a professional baseball player."

I opened up, gushing gleefully at my current situation and all the people to whom I felt thankful. We talked about Skipper Ben and Dunagan on the Reds, Andrew from Velocity Sports, and Chuck. Of course, we talked about Becky, how much I would miss her, and how despite the distance, I was sure that we would come through it together.

I touched down at Charles De Gaulle at 11:30 AM, worried that 15 wooden baseball bats, 10 tins of Skoal, and a tub of suspicious white protein powder would raise eyebrows at customs. After handing in my national entry card, I proudly uttered my first words of French: E*xcuse me- no, I do not want to* *interruptificationalismimo* (I mangled the pronunciation)- *oh, thank you. Where are the toilets?*[3]

Quite the international traveler, I thought.

Paris is lovely in the spring, or so I thought until confronting the freezing drizzle outside CDG. Perhaps I had gone soft from my time in the Bay Area, but it was cold. Freezing, bone chilling, see-your-breath-freeze-in-front-of-you cold.

Heeding Fermin's advice to 'dress like a real American,' I sported a pair of blue jeans, snakeskin boots, a white dress shirt with silver baseball cufflinks, a green blazer, black kangol hat backwards, and dark aviator sunglasses. After I stood outside nervously for an hour, a slender man with curly hair approached me and asked if I was Evan. Fermin introduced himself, saying he had seen me walk past, but for whatever reason didn't think it was me. We hopped in his car and sped south until we were stopped by a traffic jam of

---

[3] Again, because so much context comes from whether the conversation is relayed as spoken in English or as I translated it from French, I have italicized any translation from French throughout. This naturally creates a bias, as everything translated from my voice makes perfect sense, while the translations of the Frenchmen around me, no doubt grammatically perfect in French, sound ridiculous when translated. As an English speaker, that's how I heard them and that's how experienced the conversations, so remember at all times that this is just my version of events.

Bostonian proportions.

"*Wow, a huge traffic jam!*" I exclaimed gleefully in French, following my general rule that any time I knew the right vocabulary word, I would get my money's worth out of it.

"Uh, yes," Fermin responded in English, nonplussed. "It certainly is."

We spoke entirely in English on the way, as Fermin gave me a rundown of Savigny's organization. I would manage and play for the Elite team on Sundays, with two practices during the week, and help out with the second team's overlapping practices. The Elite team had its sights set on the European Championship in Prague in June, to which a French team could earn an invitation by winning either the midseason Challenge De France, or the French league championship. The Lions had won the Challenge the prior year, but took second in the league championship because they ran out of pitchers, prompting their search for a hard-throwing American with a Fu Manchu moustache.

Arriving in Savigny, Fermin pointed out my

apartment, and took me on a quick tour of the town. Perhaps oversensitive, I noticed that he pointed out several "haircutter shops," suggesting that my Mark Bellhorn look would not prove popular in France.

Fermin spoke intimidatingly perfect English, and from the moment we met, I had a good feeling about him. Friendly and considerate, his every action conveyed a willingness to go out of his way to make me feel comfortable, like handing me a fitted Lions' baseball cap and warmup shirt right when we met, as a welcoming gift. I would wager that less than .00001% of the world gets to enjoy the experience of stepping off a plane and being handed the paraphernalia of the team for which they will play; if you get the opportunity, I highly, highly recommend it.

After my brief tour of the town, Fermin took me to the "terrain"- the home field. I had looked it up online before my departure, finding that the Lions played at the Terrain D'Honneur at the Parc Municipal des Sports Jean Moulin, Savigny-Sur-Orge's town sports facility, named after a member of the Resistance during WWII. I found the field surprisingly well-maintained, featuring an all-dirt infield that accommodated the club's mixed-gender softball team and it's shorter basepaths. The outfield grass was neatly trimmed, with dirt foul lines stretching all the way to the stone walls (shades of Pete Reiser) in left and right. As Fermin led me onto the field, he pointed out the official scorer's box on the left field line, and the expanse of grass between home plate and backstop. I had one very important question.

"*How's the mound?*"

More than any other part of the field, mounds exhibit the greatest variation from one park to another, particularly at baseball's lower levels. The best slope gently from a rubber enclosed in clay hard enough to provide leverage for the rear foot, but soft enough to yield to a pitcher's idiosyncratic grooming efforts. The worst are adamantine cliffs from which the front foot falls precipitously to a different spot on each pitch, or flattened, pockmarked craters from which the rubber sticks up like a tombstone.

The Lions' mound was neither. Its shape was adequate, and it provided sufficient support, largely due to its cement construction.

"Le ciment," Fermin said with a shrug.

One more time, just to avoid it being lost in translation; the mound was made of cement.

I can't be entirely sure, but I think I blacked out for a few seconds, because when I came to, Fermin was saying something about how one of the older players had volunteered to replace the cement with something more traditional, and how I could probably make it happen sooner if I helped. It was like asking if I would take a one-time injection of antibiotics to cure terminal eyelid herpes; I didn't care if it took a pickaxe, a wrecking ball, or a crate of dynamite, I vowed to fix that mound, regardless of what Wile E. Coyote-esque contraptions I might have to use.

I paced off the field to figure out its dimensions: 357 feet down the line in left, 300 in right (albeit with an enormous screen evoking memories of Ebbets Field), and a cavernous Polo Grounds-esque 457 feet to straightaway center, which also featured a light post in play approximately 380 feet from home plate: Savigny's homage to old Tiger Stadium.

Fermin brought me to my apartment near the autoroute and directly across the street from a restaurant advertising itself as Chinese/Japanese/Thai food: such versatility! With some difficulty, we lugged my enormous duffel bags up the stairs to the second floor, where we found Christophe waiting in the hallway.

I ignored the apartment's impressively small size – roughly that of an American sports utility vehicle – and turned to Christophe, hoping to make a good impression. Fermin and I had spoken English, but as I sat down to talk to Chris, he said "En Anglais ou en Francais?" I had spent less than three hours in France, and still had no idea as to the quality of its pitchers, but I didn't expect to see many more obviously hanging curveballs like that.

"*French of course, or I should say, your choice,*" I responded in French. An easy one, perhaps, but I leaned back in my chair, confident I had passed my first test.

Starting in French, he asked about my flight, how I found France so far, and more pointedly, how I liked the apartment. I had to restrain my natural enthusiasm for fear of arousing suspicion. I wanted to grab him by the lapels and shout "Are you kidding me? You're putting me up in this place to play baseball! This is the greatest apartment in the world!" Instead, I murmured something about how it was lovely and I was happy to be there.

"Well, you know," he responded apologetically in English, shrugging. "It's French baseball." He shrugged, handed me a case of baseballs, and told me to visit Monsieur Berger at the nearby Credit Mutuel bank before the 8:00 board of directors' meeting at a local gymnasium so that the team could deposit my first massive €300 paycheck. Still dragging from the jetlag, I wandered around the corner to the bank, barely stepping through the door before the desk clerk exclaimed "*Oh, Monsieur Berger, the foreigner has arrived!*" (It was not the first time I would hear such an exclamation in France, before even saying a word.) Monsieur Berger ushered me into his office, grinning nervously as he established the account. Unfortunately, he couldn't change my American bills into Euros, leaving me without any local currency with which to buy dinner. The nearby butcher's shop and café refused to accept credit cards, so I grew increasingly worried about my ability to feed myself until I suddenly remembered; I only ate half of my Renzo Special on the plane.

I suppose few of you have seen a grown man brought nearly to tears by the thought of a two-day old, half-eaten sandwich. I inhaled the Renzo, offering silent thanks to Becky an ocean away before setting out to find the address Fermin had given me for the board meeting. I wandered into the gym, where a group of very short people were playing a surprisingly intense game of basketball. Mustering my best French, I asked the tallest one where I could find the baseball meeting.

Tellingly, he had absolutely no idea what the hell I was talking about.

I stammered again that I was looking for the '*team of baseball*', and that there was a 'reunion' somewhere on the premises.

"Ah, oui," he replied, mostly in English. "Zey are proah-ba-baly downztairz."

Downstairs, down a dimly lit hallway, Fermin ushered me into a small conference room. One by one, the board members arrived: a broad-faced, cheerful, heavy-set man named Christian who was the team's president, a quiet older woman, and a serious-looking man named Philippe, who greeted me with a dispassionately curt 'bonjour' and limp handshake. Perhaps jet lag had left me feeling self-conscious, but I couldn't shake the feeling that he had expected someone more physically impressive. Meeting the team's equipment manager Remi provided some consolation. The friendly 20-something had been voted the top pitcher in France two years prior, before a shoulder injury sidelined his career; Remi's 5'10" frame suggested that finesse could succeed in France, even in the absence of overpowering stuff.

The meeting passed in a blur of rapid French and occasional glances in my direction; I understood barely a word. Months of listening to French conversational tapes failed to prepare me for the slang-ridden management-speak in that cramped conference room. Struggling through the heat and jet lag, I focused on avoiding an international incident by dozing off in my first meeting with my new employer. When the conversation periodically trailed off, I snapped to attention only to find an awkward silence with everyone staring at me expectantly. Thankfully, Fermin would repeat what had been said, tweaking it for simplicity and speaking slowly to accommodate my American ears. He was tossing me softballs, and more than once, I thought "I have to buy that guy a beer for helping me out" before wondering if that social convention existed in this strange land. A bottle of wine, perhaps?

I did manage to pick up my first understanding of the club sport structure prevalent in France and throughout Europe, which in a lot of ways makes far more sense than the awkward American mishmash of youth athletics that you pay to play, college athletics where you play for free, and professional sports franchises where you get paid ungodly amounts. The club structure consolidates all three, with clubs organized locally, often around shared ethnic and cultural backgrounds. Many of these clubs grew organically out of groups of neighbors, with names reflecting some facet of their origin story; clubs like Manchester United might have resulted from the mergers of multiple clubs, while the Sheffield Wednesday football club famously derived its name from the original members playing on that day of the week. In the case of French baseball, they mostly took on American names to reflect the sport's origin, like the Hawks, Lions, and Huskies.

Savigny was an 'omnisport' club, meaning that it fielded teams across sports, genders, and age groups, making it possible to grow up playing coed volleyball and boy's rugby (or any number of other sports) for the same club throughout one's childhood. This weaves the clubs into the fabric of their communities, as children on the youngest *Minime* teams dream of someday representing the club in international competition at its highest level, where the teams resemble American professional franchises. It would be like the New England Patriots also having a coed 'under 10' volleyball team, a girl's ice hockey team, and an amateur senior tennis team in addition to their professional American football squad. The Lions' club, for example, had five or six baseball teams ranging from the Minimes (under 8) to the Cadets (middle schoolers, mostly) to the elite and 'over 40' teams, a handful of mostly coed softball teams, and other sports like rugby and football (soccer) that used the same facilities and had the same funding sources, although it seemed only the baseball team used the Lions nickname.

About an hour into the meeting, the conversation turned to me, and a suddenly very serious Philippe addressed me directly. He explained – speaking slowly first in French and then in English – that they wanted me to implement a general strategy and regimen for both the elite and second teams. Pretty straightforward, I thought, but he clearly took it very seriously, even interrupting me at one point to clarify a critical point about how he wanted the second team to practice with the elite team.

The meeting finally broke up at around noon California time, and the president gave me a ride home, leaving me with a gift of used pots and pans for the apartment. I fell asleep immediately, awaking 14 hours later to the realization that I still lacked local currency. With the banks closed, I found the closest place that would feed me in exchange for a MasterCard. Let the record show that my first French meal consisted of duck curry with white rice from the Pan-Asian place across the street. My high school French teacher, Mr. Hobert, would be terribly ashamed, but I was starving and my options were limited. Interestingly enough, I found that they do not serve water or tea when you sit down for Chinese food in France. They do, however, serve wine, a rosé, if you can believe it. The assumption, apparently, is that you're thirsty and weary from the road, and you need a pink wine to revive you.

I strolled through the winding, crooked streets of Savigny to visit Remi, shouldering past old women balancing baguettes on their bicycles and teenagers with tight, torn jeans, spiked fauxhawks, and dispassionate 'who the fuck are you?' looks on their stereotypically French faces. Fermin had apologized for Savigny, calling it 'depressing,' but to me, its drab appearance exuded an old-world charm. No building stood more than three stories, making the town seem like something out of Epcot Center, speckled with patisseries, tiny fenced-in yards, and incomprehensible traffic instructions written on its narrow streets.

The team's best pitcher in 2002 and 2004, Remi took a year off for his studies and had struggled with shoulder problems ever since. He printed me a photo for my team-provided "Orange Card" (which would allow me to travel freely on the bus and trains) and proudly showed me his DVD collection, offering to lend me as many as I liked. I noticed that American films were released in France with completely different titles; *The Rookie*, for example, was released as *The Champion's Dream*, and I challenge American readers to guess which Diehard movies were translated as *58 Minutes to Live*, *Crystal Trap*, and *A Day In Hell*.

He brought me to his cellar, which looked like Buffalo Bill's hangout from *Silence of the Lambs*. Pulling box after box from a cavernous closet, he outfitted me with a pair of game pants, belt, pullover, turtleneck, and a sweatshirt. After chatting idly with Remi, I took the 45-minute train ride into Paris, emerging from the subway station at Notre Dame, where I set about finding internet access. Earlier that day, I had found an internet café near Remi's place, where the clerk told me that they did not provide, in proper French, 'WeeFee.' Now a slick international traveler in a cosmopolitan city, proud to have picked up the local slang, I asked a Parisian passerby where I could find "*a bar with wee-fee.*"

"*All alone in a bar?*" he asked, shocked.

I stuttered, confused. "*Uh, or in a café maybe?*"

He rolled his eyes, chuckling.

"*Oh... I understood you to say* 'huit filles' ("*eight girls,*" which the French say almost identically). L'internet*, that's easier...*"

Embarrassed, I tried to gain ground.

"*Forget the internet- where is this bar with eight girls again?*"

Arriving home in Savigny, I stopped at the Petit Casino (a popular French supermarket chain), for they accepted credit cards, making possible my first home-cooked French meal. A few hours later, I had collected a few 'notes to self' regarding my culinary performance, or as it came to be known, 'The Incident':

1) It was courageous trying to piece together dinner from the limited ingredients available. It was less courageous to run in fear from the fresh meats they displayed. After all, when will I try horse sausage again?

2) My obstinate insistence that 'All French bread is good' proved as relevant as past maxims 'The Red Sox always fall apart when it counts' and 'I can tell when a craps table is about to turn cold.' The lack of fresh bread at that hour was not surprising, but the knockoff wonder bread cardboard I purchased remains so to this day.

3) Fried potatoes are delicious, and my ancestors' ability to make them under far harsher conditions provides inspiration. However, I will remember in the future that they aren't nearly as good when prepared without salt.

4) Or pepper.

5) Olive oil, for that matter.

6) An oven mitt might have been a good idea, too.

7) Perhaps less a culinary critique and more of a technological one, but plugging in an adapter to recharge my computer could have waited until after the potatoes were off the stove. They certainly would have fared better without the ensuing blue spark, loud popping noise, and sudden, enveloping darkness that caused me to flail wildly, knocking my vitamins and computer off the table, and fall, as the French say, "ass-over-tea-kettle."

8) My recovery from the sudden darkness was impressive. Who knew the illuminative powers of the iPod?

9) While I hope never to repeat the calamity, the evening was not a total loss. The meal was crisp but edible, and I made significant contributions to science by disproving the null hypothesis "If I cook something long enough, it will not turn black." I munched the potatoes in pitch blackness, illuminated only by my iPod and cell phone, and prepared for the next day's second team scrimmage.

CHAPTER 7: THAT'S BASEBALL

My iPod – even typing it feels quaint and anachronistic – woke me up early on Sunday to the strains of Ice Cube's *Check Yo Self*. The second team's manager, Yann, drove us thirty minutes to discover that our opponents scratched the game on account of its still-frozen field. The more I saw of French baseball, the more it reminded me of adult league ball back home.

On the way home, Yann and I discussed my strategic plan to emulate the 1985 Cardinals: run early and run often. At this level, fielding was the weakest part of the game, so we would exploit that weakness by running aggressively, putting pressure on the defense to field the ball cleanly and make accurate throws. Unless a Lion ran like he had a piano on his back (an expression that translated surprisingly well into French), I would send him. Suddenly, Yann turned to me, speaking candidly of the internal conflicts on the team.

"*There is a, I do not know, separation between the players of the two teams.*"

"*Really?*" I asked cautiously.

"*Really. The players on the N1A team...*" He paused, shaking his head and looking out the window. N1A meant 'Nationale Un', the first level below Elite, after which was Nationale Deux (N1B) and then Régionale, a level that everyone talked about as if its quality resembled that of a decent little league. "*They feel like the elite players mock them, and do not care about the second team. The Lions have always been like that; the players do not respect people they think they are better than.*" Suddenly he turned to me. "*They will follow you... but first you must show that you are stronger, better than they are.*"

The language barrier made it difficult, but I tried to

make my feelings on the matter emphatically clear. Elite team or no, this was French baseball, not MLB, and as far as I was concerned, nobody should big-league anybody.

"That's... the shit of the bull," I said. *"Listen, I do not know if I can..."* I struggled with the translation in my head. *"...change things, but I will do everything I can to ensure that we play as one team."*

Yann nodded and our conversation turned back to strategy. Perhaps not surprisingly, the French share the Canadians' irrational love of the bunt. I told Yann that bunting usually meant giving up a precious out, and so I would almost never call a bunt before the 8th inning unless I thought the batter could beat it out for a hit or was a sure out if allowed to swing away. We had gotten along swimmingly to that point, but for a moment, Yann reacted as if I had suggested singing *Das Deutschlandlied* before every game. Apparently, sabermetrics had yet to arrive in the land of baguettes and berets.

I changed the subject, telling Yann about the electrical difficulties I had caused by fumbling dinner the previous night. He enlisted the help of Jose, a Lion on the over 40 team with a reputation as a handyman. He found the blown fuse and MacGyver'd a temporary, innovative, and *highly* dangerous fix by completing the circuit with a carefully shaped strand of aluminum foil. We spent the afternoon drinking coffee in Jose's kitchen, assessing the validity of French stereotypes. The coffee was better, the pace of life more relaxed, but the French were definitely not rude. Aside from Philippe's hard-edged skepticism, everyone in the club had demonstrated incredible kindness and generosity. In the weeks before my first game with the Lions, people only vaguely affiliated with the team had lent me a bicycle, a microwave, their electrical expertise, a cell phone, a refrigerator, and a television/DVD player. At one point, Yann even left work early to come lend me some emergency euros when the grocery store declined my foreign credit card.

Fermin, Jose, and Yann all suggested that my reception had more to do with the game. "*That's baseball*," they all said, shrugging as if that's simply what baseball players do for one another. I found it oddly heartwarming to discover a deep spiritual kinship in a country theoretically abstracted from the game's origins and customs; I had never seen this degree of altruism among ballplayers. I saw a beautiful irony in the fact that somehow, traveling 6,000 miles had brought me into a group with no connection to baseball's origins but a truer sense of what the game meant than people who grew up playing it every day. French baseballers exhibited the passion of the converted.

The next day, wandering around Paris trying to find a café with eight hot chicks, I received a call from an unknown number.

"Allo? *Asldfjasdlwer Americain? It's Evan*?"

"*Ah, hello! Yes! It's Evan! Who is it?*"

"*I have* Rzadsilf*!* Popozao rutwayeh! (30 seconds of unintelligible rapid-fire French)"

"I'm sorry, I didn't understand."

"(another 30 seconds of staccato French, of which I understood "*your house*" and "*Henri Dunant*", the street of my apartment.)"

"*Oh, sorry...* (looking around as if for help from someone on the Rue de Bellechasse, finding none forthcoming.) *I'm not at home right now, I'm in Paris.*"

"Ok, Twizamp, *see you tomorrow.*"

"*Uh, ok...* (long delay, confusion, then acquiescence) *What time?*"

"*Between nine and noon.*"

"*Great! See you then.*"

It was the first time since the board meeting that I felt genuinely lost during a conversation. Who was that? Why were they at my apartment on a Sunday morning? I could only smile at the absurdity of things and go on my merry way. 'Someone's coming tomorrow morning. I have no idea who or what for, but... great!'

The buzzer rang the next morning, and I rushed downstairs to determine the mystery man's identity. Outside, I met a Moroccan youth asking me to sign for a package from San Francisco. Becky had slyly gotten my address and shipped me a few CD's, photos, and American candy a few days before my departure, so that they would arrive before homesickness set in. In my tiny apartment, I looked out upon the parking structure, eating a green apple Airhead and wishing she was there with me.

Over the next few days, I acclimated to the local culture. I noticed fewer berets than expected, but I estimated that one-in-five people carried baguettes, which compared favorably with the one-in-eight ratio generally seen in San Francisco's Noe Valley. I also started smoking – heavily – and got up to about a pack a day. It was all secondhand, mind you, but I definitely preferred bars where customers smoked menthols, because my resultant phlegm tasted so minty.

Trips into Paris provided my primary exposure to such smoke-filled environments, in the cafés and bars providing free internet access. It's tempting to say that *everybody* smoked, but it was closer to half. The French appeared to have something figured out. They had a beer or a glass of wine at almost every meal, smoked with enthusiasm, and yet managed to live longer than Americans of both genders. Part of me wondered if it was the bread.

The French cursed more frequently than Americans, but the curses were less vulgar. People thought nothing of dropping a "merde" ("*shit*") into conversations, but I never heard – or at least, understood – any truly profane curses, the likes of which come in handy on a baseball diamond. Mildly disappointed, I prepared myself for my first practice with the "elite" team on Tuesday.

While waiting at the bus stop to get to the 'terrain', a pretty young girl sauntered up and stood uncommonly close to me. I glanced over under the pretense of checking to see whether the bus was coming, guessing that she was about 20 years old. After a few minutes, she broke the awkward silence by asking if the bus went to the athletic center. As I was listening to motivational music on my iPod, the interaction started with the awkward tango of removing earphones and disconnecting listening devices.

I confirmed that it did, or at least, I hoped it did, and we both got off at the stop for Parc Municipal des Sports Jean Moulin. She followed me, suddenly grabbing my arm to ask if we were still heading towards the athletic complex. Dressed in full Lions regalia and carrying a baseball bat, I thought the answer fairly obvious, and nodded with a cocked eyebrow. She said that she was going to watch a friend play tennis before delivering some rapid-fire French gibberish, and I had to apologize for not speaking French very well.

"*It's cut*e," she said.

"*Excuse me?*"

"*The American accent,*" she continued. "*It's cute.*"

"*Oh, uh...*" I blushed. Look, I never pretended to be smooth, especially while being hit on while having a girlfriend. *"I wish that everyone else thought so, but –"*

"*No, really. Girls especially, we love the American accent.*"

It's tempting to paint a wildly inaccurate picture of myself as a suave, debonair international traveler, a power-hitting James Bond figure who takes such compliments in stride. Sadly, honesty compels me to tell the crimson-faced truth, with its stammered "*Uh, thank you, that's very kind...*" and awkward glances at the ground. Finally, we came to the closest corner of the stadium, with the gate in sight, when she exclaimed "*Oh, we've arrived.*" I told her that she would only have to walk another hundred yards to the main entrance, but she simply declared that it would be "*no problem*" and proceeded to scramble up and over the fence, dropping softly on the grass behind it.

"*Maybe I'll come and watch you play baseball later!*" she added before jogging off.

The French were friendly after all.

I walked into the cozy locker room at Jean Moulin feigning confidence and trying to look the part in a Nike baseball getup. One by one, the Lions arrived, demonstrating an unvarying introduction ritual even as the 8:30 start time loomed. Each ballplayer entered the room with a loudly declarative "BONJOUR," and circled the room one at a time, shaking hands with every player in the room, regardless of what stage of undress each player might happen to be in. Each one seemed to size me up during our handshake. *Is he any good? Will he give me playing time?*

At 8:30, I banged my water bottle on the wall to get

the players' attention. Stepping up on the bench, I began my carefully rehearsed introduction speech.

"Hello, my friends. I am Evan, the new coach of the elite team. I was born in Boston before I moved to San Francisco, so if you like the baseball club of New York Yankees, simply do not tell me, I don't want to know. As you can tell, I do not speak French very well, so, please, do not hesitate to correct me when I make a mistake. It is important to remember that I am a stupid yank, (a few laughs), *therefore please, do not be insulted when I say something stupid. (*a few chuckles and sidelong glances, trying to determine if knew what I had said*) I know this is already a very good team, so I want to put the emphasis on playing smarter, always knowing what one will do before the ball arrives. I want us to play aggressively...* (I braced myself for the award translation of this American joke...) *Therefore, even if they measure your time to first with a sand dial, I will make you steal."* I had obviously overestimated my language proficiency. Awkwardness permeated the locker room, and I looked around at a roomful of Frenchmen staring at me expectantly, quizzical looks

on their faces. *"I mean that we are going to run."* Chuckles, one possibly sarcastic cheer. *"A lot."*

Shrugging it off, I led the team out to the practice field to perform the dynamic warm-up routine I learned at Velocity, which replaced the static stretches we were all taught in elementary school gym class with active movements to stretch and warm up muscles. My naïveté in assuming that the team would appreciate a baseball-specific, injury prevention-focused regimen from the world's most advanced trainers quickly became apparent. According to Fermin, the team had traditionally just played soccer, done a quick long toss, and gotten started. The experts at Velocity, having trained hundreds of professional athletes, had come up with something a bit more sophisticated. Little did I know that the team's resistance to the dynamic warm-up would become the first obstacle to my credibility as the Lions' new coach. Ironically, it was probably the most valuable thing I brought to the table; no matter how well I pitched, I was never one of the top 10,000 pitchers in the world, whereas the warm-up routine was the brainchild of the top 100 baseball conditioning coaches alive.

Practice trudged on at a snail's pace, due partially to the problems I faced in translating complicated concepts into French. Days earlier, I had spent hours scouring the roster, determining the exact sequence in which players would transition from the group to group, but now in the moment, there was a lot of sitting around and waiting. I scurried from drill to drill, trying to explain each group's assignment. More disconcerting was the fact that a lot of players – mostly on the elite team – were half-assing it, offsetting the enthusiasm from others eager to try the American's new drills. Further delayed by players showing up late, we didn't get through the positional drills nearly as quickly as I hoped, cutting into our combined batting practice time. No matter, I thought; having seen the drills, we'd get through them more quickly next time.

After practice, I pulled the team together, and in as serious a 'coach' voice as I could muster, said that our initial struggles were understandable during the year's first practice, but that we would have to move faster. I hopped on the bus home, where the public service announcements on bus's interior walls distracted me from the team's glacial pace and low energy. Most were fairly straightforward tips on public transport etiquette, like "*If an elder needs a seat, give them yours!*" and "*If your telephone rings, speak softly- it concerns only you!*" However, many made me smile, like the one with a picture of a small dog tied up tight in a backpack: "*A domestic animal? Yes, if it is small and in a sack!*"

CHAPTER 8: HOTEL AUSTERLITZ

Fermin picked me up on Friday afternoon to give me a quick tour of Paris, grab dinner, and show me a few watering holes free from tourist traffic. (Savigny was 30 minutes outside the city limits, so I was strictly *pont-et-tunnel* material.) The back of Fermin's moped made for a comfortable ride, until we encountered a hailstorm of an intensity rarely seen outside of Hitchcock films. It came out of nowhere, and at first, I thought we were taking on howitzer fire.

We drove along the Seine to the Bastille and veered west along the Rue de Rivoli, Fermin pointing out points of interest. Paris has impressive, historic buildings like San Francisco has sushi restaurants and gay bars: too many to keep track of, even for locals. Having passed dozens of local attractions, I asked Fermin about one particularly imposing gothic stone building with Corinthian columns. "*Oh, hey... I don't know, man,*" the Parisian responded, stumped. *"Maybe another opera? Let's go eat.*"

We grabbed pizza near the Bastille, as Fermin regaled me with tales of his semester at a junior college in California. "These girls- all they wanted to hear was a little bit of French, and then they would do *anything!"* he exclaimed with a charming sense of wide-eyed innocence that belied the stereotype of the Frenchman-as-swashbuckling-international-lothario. We met his girlfriend and her friends at a bar, finding a French karaoke party in full swing. It was like a slightly less intoxicated American karaoke, but with a forty-Marlboro-minimum and a DJ's godlike control over the crowd. Periodically, he simply declared that he felt bored, and that the crowd should make some noise for his amusement, as a disco ball dropped from the ceiling and fog machine further clouded the already smoke-filled room. (They must train Marines for oxygen deprivation similarly, except the drill sergeants considerately play French pop music at slightly less ear-splitting volumes.)

The crowd surprised me, eschewing a 'too cool for school' attitude and instead going suddenly and inexplicably BONKERS. All around me, the French stood and danced wildly on the chairs and tables, writhing in spasms of pure euphoria. The change was so immediate, so inexplicably *drastic,* that I felt like maybe I had missed something, as if the DJ had just announced that everyone in attendance would receive three complementary cartons of Lucky Strikes.

My RER (Réseau Express Régional, or Regional Express Network) train left just after midnight, so I said my goodbyes and caught the nearest subway & connections to Paris Austerlitz, arriving a few minutes before the 12:12am to Savigny. I passed the time watching a drunken elderly Frenchman denigrate one of the subway workers for not being a French citizen; having left my iPod at home, it was the best entertainment available. After several minutes in the increasingly cold station, I began to long for the comfort of home. My hands went into my pockets for warmth, only to realize that I had left my keys in the jacket that Fermin had loaned me for our moped ride.

As the French would say, *merde.*

I would have just called Fermin, but the team had

given me a cell phone with just 5 prepaid minutes on it, which had expired. Naturally, I hadn't yet figured out how to recharge it. I had plenty of change for a payphone, but France's technological advancement dictated that none of its payphones accepted coins, only French telephone cards, which, of course, I lacked. I didn't even know Fermin's phone number for a collect call – did they have collect calls in France? – so my only chance to avoid a homeless, frozen night in a foreign country was to head back to St. Paul and hope that they hadn't left. I retraced my subway travels, changed at Bastille, and luckily, found Fermin and his friends where I left them, in the throes of another orgiastic DJ-ordained dance explosion. I retrieved my keys and said my second goodbye of the evening, took yet another trip on the 1 and 5 trains, and arrived once more back at Paris Austerlitz at about 10 minutes to 1.

As my commuter pass slid through the turnstile, I had a moment of doubt. On Monday, I had taken a 2:00 am train home, and certainly trains would run at least as late on Friday. Right? The turnstiles turned seamlessly, I stepped onto the same platform I had occupied a half hour earlier and found that Austerlitz was a ghost town. The screens that typically displayed the next train and its destination were all blank, and the only sign of life was a crew of Algerians cleaning the tracks. Why the last train would leave an hour earlier on Friday night than on Monday night, I will never know, but I discerned that the next train to Savigny would come four hours later, at 4:58 AM. With the prospect of a homeless Parisian night looming, a few carefully chosen expletives helped me come to grips with my unattractive options: a four-hour hang out in a now bone-chilling station until the pre-dawn train, a search for a hotel in Paris, or a cab home to Savigny. I doubted the success of the second option, as Paris hotels typically didn't pay clerks to hang around in the lobby waiting for late-night stragglers, and with only 30 euros in my pocket, a cab was beyond my means. Just five minutes after my second arrival at Austerlitz, I decided that any alternative was preferable to freezing on that platform, and headed to the exits in search of an ATM or hotel.

In changing from the 5 train to the RER station, I had

taken the internal changeover, which did not require me to leave the building. When I tried to exit to the street, I found every exit sealed off with iron roll gates.

Every.

Single.

One.

Austerlitz is a large station, with over a dozen exits. My anxiety mounted as I found each locked up tight as a drum. I waved through a chicken-wire gate to one of the Algerians, frantically shouting "*Sir! I am trapped in here and cannot escape! Sir, the doors are locked and I am not able to leave! Help me!*"

Good news, bad news. The good: for the first time in my life, I successfully conjugated the French verb "to escape." The bad: judging by his reaction, the janitor did not consider my predicament worthy of emergency aid, glancing away after brief eye contact and moving to another part of the room where I could no longer bother him.

I turned back and stared down the length of the empty station, coming to the cold realization that my decision had been made for me; I was staying the night at Hotel Austerlitz. I immediately recalled the scene from *The Warriors* where they scrap with the Punks – the striped-shirt gang on roller skates – in the bathroom of Union Square station. I made a mental note to lie in ambush in the toilet stalls if the Jones Street Boys or Van Cortland Rangers decided to make a move on me. The rest of my night went something like this:

1:17: 10 minutes down, four hours to go. I need to go to the bathroom.

1:31: As my efforts to fall asleep fail miserably, I realize that French rail system employees leave the intercom music on – at an unbearably loud volume – even after the station closes. A perky DJ voice tells me that I better like the hits of the 80s, 90s, and today, because I'll be listening to them for another four hours.

1:40: I've always loved David Bowie's *Let's Dance,* but I have a hard time imagining a situation more incongruous with its festive spirit than the one in which I currently find myself.

1:42: I love *Let's Dance*. I have it on my iPod. I know in my bones that I will never, ever listen to it again. Not voluntarily, anyway.

1:51: It's *Thriller* time.

1:59: Vincent Price's maniacal cackles at the end of *Thriller* echo creepily through the abandoned train station. My body starts to shiver, for no mere mortal can resist… I'm too tired and forlorn to complete the joke. I wonder briefly if Vincent Price is dead, and if so, when he passed. I decide he is, and guess 1998.[4]

2:11: I hate to sound like a critic, but if the French transit system were the Muppet Show, I would be one of the old dudes in the balcony singing 'Why do we always come here? I guess we'll never know…'

2:20: I hit rock bottom and begin to dig as Creed's *(Can You Take Me) Higher* assaults my eardrums. I begin sobbing openly. I am in the 8th circle of hell, and only Scott Stapp's solo work stands between me and number nine.

2:12: Once again, good news and bad news. The good

---

[4] Editor's Note: 1993.

news is that I drifted off to sleep for a moment, and hearing *Higher* was merely a bad dream, although my tears were very real. The bad news is that *Higher* was some sort of subconscious Faustian bargain in exchange for an imaginary passage of time. It is actually only 2:12 AM. I curse and spit on the train tracks, imagining they are Scott Stapp.

2:49: Things I wish I had with me right now: an acetylene torch, a functional cell phone, one of those handcars Bugs Bunny rides where you can pump up and down to move down the railroad track, Becky, the hollowed-out body of a recently-killed animal to keep warm Luke Skywalker-style, and a tumbler of scotch, more or less in that order.

3:14: Note to self: Next time you plan on getting stuck in a freezing, open-air train station in Paris at 3:00 AM, leave the boot cut jeans at home.

4:07 AM: I notice they've turned on the lights in the train next to me. I declare a moral victory.

4:08: The train is heated. It takes me roughly three-one-hundredths of a second to scoot in there and doze off.

4:58: The day is mine! The train to Savigny rolls in, and I'm on it like a hobo on a ham sandwich.

5:18: I awake with a start to the sound of the train doors opening, looking around frantically as I determine that we are at the Savigny-Sur-Orge station. I explode out of my chair like Lawrence Taylor beating a left tackle, for fear of missing my stop and further extending my public transit misadventures. Exhausted, I stagger home and fall asleep before my head hits the pillow.

What did we learn, children?

1) The Paris-Austerlitz station sometimes cancels all its trains without explanation, and when it does so, it is typically very, very cold; and

2) Never, ever forget your keys when planning a trip on an unpredictable French metro system.

CHAPTER 9: YOU COME AT THE KING, YOU BEST NOT MISS

After an uneventful Saturday (days tend to be uneventful when you go to bed at 6:00 and sleep past noon), I awoke on Sunday excited to be alive, to play some baseball in the Lions' intrasquad scrimmage and show the team what I could do. Though the weather report read 'two below zero,' I read it as 'Good God, you actually want us to play baseball in this weather?' I left my apartment wearing my lucky Belmont Hill football t-shirt, two long-sleeve t-shirts, my Lions' jersey, and my enormous Belmont Hill hooded sweatshirt, and still felt tempted to turn around and call it a day.

Despite the cold, I led the team through the same warmup with less resistance, although I attributed this less to my charismatic leadership and more to the paralyzing cold numbing any emotion, including insubordination. I gave an interview to a local television news program, my first as a pro ballplayer. I asked for a few takes to get my spoken French right, but they promised that the first take was perfect; all across the Paris metropolitan area that evening, I imagined Frenchmen tuning in to laugh uproariously at the dumb Yank trying to explain how "*only walks and errors have the ability to vanquish us, and if we will have the ability to avoid them, one hopes that we will have the ability to win the championship of France.*" Like Yogi Berra, but in heavily-accented French.

Bureaucratic snafus loomed ominously as the game started. The French Baseball Federation (which I came to call the 'Tres Lettres' after the mocking Mexican cartel nickname for the DEA) planned to use our scrimmage as the final exam for its official scorer's certification class. The exam proctor demanded that we make exactly one mid-at-bat pitching change during the first seven innings to challenge the students, and I made my first faux pas of the day by suggesting that we have free substitutions so I could observe every ballplayer.

"*You must obey standard baseball substitution rules for seven innings,*" he responded angrily.

"*Uh...*" I didn't know what to say. *"Well, I'll try to do that, but I need to observe 30 players, so-"*

"*No. You must.*" I started thinking of ways to persuade him before noticing that Christian, the Lions' president, stood among those frantically reviewing notes for the exam. Best to make nice with the guy who signs the checks, I thought.

"*Uh, OK.*" For the first time in France, I found myself having to hold my tongue. In the US, I'd have told them to take a long walk off a short pier – I had ballplayers to evaluate – but the club president's involvement encouraged uncharacteristic self-restraint.

Unfortunately, other land mines presented themselves. Yann and I decided to switch the batteries, so that the elite hitters would face elite pitchers, and the second team hitters would face second team pitching. This created a nightmarish substitution situation for the scorers, as Brieuc, for example, abandoned his right field position for the home team and immediately began pitching for the visitors. I tried explaining to the scorers that they should pretend two players with the same name played for each team, but it was hopeless, creating a near riot on the sidelines just as I was trying to earn credibility as a strategist. Enraged, the students taking the test seemed one substitution away from lobbing rotten tomatoes at me, as if I had banned smoking, berets, and cheese: oops.

After a few innings, we acquiesced and ended the exchange of pitchers between the elite and second teams, to make things easier on the scorers. (Obviously, this tilted the game heavily in favor of the now united elite team.) Busy managing substitutions, I didn't have a chance to play until the eighth, when I began warming up in the bullpen alongside Pierrick.

Pierrick was the catcher on the French national team, the closer and consensus best player on the Lions. He had a smooth swing, a cannon for an arm, and the calm demeanor of a veteran. I stepped in to catch him for a few warm-up tosses, appreciating that he threw harder than anyone else on the team, probably in the low 80s in freezing cold weather, when everybody loses a little bit of zip on the fastball.

I was ice cold when I stepped to the plate with two outs in Pierrick's first inning on the mound, with the same cleat-tap/cleat-tap/plate-tap/practice-swing warm-up routine I've used for as long as I can remember. I feigned a calm demeanor, trying to downplay the matchup's significance, even as I noticed the dugouts quieting and Lions veterans watching intently to see what I could do against the captain.

Pierrick started me with two fastballs, both low. Ahead 2-0, I figured I could safely expect another fastball, so I was sitting dead red, looking for something I could drive. I stepped out for a second to collect myself and recognize the fielders' positioning: deep to left and center, normal depth in right, with the corner infielders pulled up for the bunt.

Pierrick third offering gave me just what I was looking for, a fastball belt high. In the cold, the shock of bat-on-ball impact surged through my forearms straight to my spine as the ball rocketed into left field. Off the bat, I thought the leftfielder might track it down, but the ball kept rising, sailing over his outstretched arms as I cruised in for a stand-up double. As I removed my batting gloves at second, trying to avoid eye contact with Pierrick so as not to show him up, Yann came sprinting over from his second base position to swat me on the ass.

"*Now they will follow you!!!*" he muttered excitedly, careful to keep the volume down and hide his ear-to-ear grin from the elite players.

Not since my crackerjack off Langone had hitting a laser beam felt this good. I had used the last bat I made before leaving home, right after one of the scorekeeping students opined that it was too small, and would break if it hit live pitching. (Name of the Bat? *Canes Martis Elabare*- 'Let Slip the Dogs of War.' I got your broken bat right here, *mon ami.*)

Pierrick struck out the next hitter to end the inning, and I ran into the dugout to a smattering of high fives. Burly third baseman Vincent joked in English "Hey man, you passed!" while the other veterans razzed Pierrick for giving up a bomb. I didn't have a lot of time to enjoy it, as I immediately entered the game as a pitcher. I didn't have my best stuff, and survived only because I was facing the weaker second team hitters. With one out, Pierrick came to the plate and ran the count to 3-2 before I remembered Fermin's comment that French pitchers tended to throw curveballs only when ahead in the count. The Yellow Hammer I threw surprised him, and Pierrick rolled it over into a weak groundball to second, although flashy second baseman Yann Dalzoto[5] booted it for an error. I escaped the inning with a groundball double play, and then struck out the side in my second inning. All in all, a good stat line – 2IP, 0H, 4K, 0BB – but one that hid some mediocre pitching that benefitted from questionable strike zone discipline from the second team hitters.

I left the field relieved just to be employed, given my inadvertent antagonizing of the Tres Lettres, happily

[5] I have intentionally left out most people's last names, but 'Yann Dalzoto' was just a really fun name to say. Good ballplayer, too. Obviously, he's a different Yann than the one who coached the second team.

convinced of two things: 1) I could still mash belt-high fastballs in any hemisphere; and 2) even in freezing French weather, there was still nothing better than an ice-cold beer after baseball.

CHAPTER 10: THE MINI-MES

After a frustratingly slow Tuesday practice, Wednesday found me rejoicing in the French baseball schedule, which required only that I attend biweekly softball practice on Mondays, elite practices on Tuesdays and Thursdays, Minimes (players under 10) on Wednesdays, Cadets (11-14 or so) on Fridays, and doubleheaders with the first team on Sundays.

I loved the Minimes (literally, '*the minimums*', although my friends back home reading about my exploits on the www.havebatwilltravel.com blog called them the Mini-Me's) at first sight. Maybe it was the accent, their ill-fitting uniforms, or the innocent, unbridled joy they brought to the game; either way, the combination produced breathtaking, paralyzing cuteness. Should the Spanish ever come storming across the Pyrenees in an unanticipated invasion, France's best defense would involve sending the Cute Brigade, a crack team of French seven-year-olds trained in the art of haplessly trying to put on a catcher's mask three sizes too large for their head, clumsily succeeding only in obscuring their vision. The effect would render anyone in the vicinity defenseless, preserving the nation's safety.

As proof of their intolerable cuteness, I advance the following (translated) exchange, which took place when young Rafael stepped to the plate and Tom ("Tum" to the natives) encouraged him during our scrimmage, only to encounter resistance from Francois in right field.

Tom: "*Hit well, Rafael!*"

Francois: "*No, Rafael, hit softly!*"

Tom: "*Hit like a lion! Hard!*"

Francois: "*No! Like a mouse!*"

That was what passed for trash-talking among

French adolescents; the American sandlot equivalent would contain at least six f-bombs. If the 2006 Savigny Minimes were the Murderer's Row of cuteness – and I believe they were – then Tom was their Ruth, Francois their Gehrig. But if I look back on my first days in Savigny, I recall how Jose's son stood alone. He was to cute French children what Mike Tyson was to hostile, antisocial boxers: the *ne plus ultra*, the iconic standard that defines the genre. Sloppily missing the toast with his knife and smearing Nutella on his cheek was his devastating right hook.

The day's other highlight occurred during batting practice, as I showed Rafael how to turn on inside fastballs. The other kids chatted animatedly, about what I couldn't tell, but I could see that it involved liberal use of the 'air bat' (Ted Williams' version of air guitar, gesticulating and miming a swing with an imaginary baseball bat.) When I finished my explanation, I turned to the nearby group and asked what was going on. One brave kid stepped forward, looking up at me with enormous blue eyes.

"*It seems that you had the hit of the match on*

Sunday!'

In awkwardly stammered French, I gave my best "three clichés" interview from *Bull Durham*. "*Uh, well, you know, just, uh... got a good pitch to hit, y'know, and... stuck the bat out... uh, good things happen if you get good pitches to hit... uh, just trying to help the team win.*"

What a doofus.

CHAPTER 11: BAD MOON RISING

"*That's all?*" Fabien asked as I tossed my cleats into the back of his car.

"Oui," I replied. With a wife and two kids, Fabien had purchased the French version of the station wagon, which despite its implication of roominess had just two doors and the approximate width of a pack of Dunhills. Politesse dictated that I afford Guillaume – the team's oldest player at 42 and a former starter on the French national team – the respect of the front seat, so I shook his hand with the requisite 'bonjour' as he held the shotgun seat forward so I could squeeze myself into the back.

"*How do you feel?*" My new teammates asked, pulling

onto the autoroute toward the preseason tournament that would mark my first competition against other French teams. I had heard such questions since my arrival in France. "*How does the American feel? Does his arm feel strong? Can he pitch a complete game yet?*" (The answers were 'fine, mostly, and no f'ing way, not yet at least.') When I heard those conversations swirling around me in the dugouts during practice, I understood their implications, but pretended not to hear or understand. I could either play or I couldn't, I reasoned, no need to try to play politics about it.

"*Are you ready?*" they continued.

"*I hope so!*" I said, laughing. Apparently satisfied, Fabien drove on toward Montigny, pontificating on how Paris produced better bread than any other region – the air, he opined – and on France's chances in the upcoming World Cup.

The intrasquad scrimmage had put me at ease with respect to France's level of baseball. The Lion's best player was Pierrick, voted the third-best pitcher in France the previous year, and I crushed his best fastball over the leftfielder's head. When I pitched to him, I induced him to ground weakly to second, so I figured I could handle anything the French threw at me. After years of wondering if I was good enough, I had peeled back the curtain, seen the wizard, and found him less intimidating than imagined.

The Montigny Cougars played against Savigny's second team in the N1A division, and we would face them and Savigny's hated rival Rouen. The team's official scorer informed me with great pride that Montigny's artificial turf field was the finest in France, and with only Savigny's cement mound as a reference, I was inclined to agree. Dirt cutouts at each base dotted the artificial turf, and raised stands seated nearly 500 spectators with an electronic scoreboard. It had the feel of a college stadium back home, and I felt reassured by the overall level of organization. Frankly, it was reassuring just to see bases ninety feet apart from each other.

I stubbornly took the team through the dynamic warm-up, encountering lingering resistance. In our first game against the hosts, I started Gaetan, Savigny's other big off-season acquisition from La Guerche de

Bretagne, and batted myself eighth. In the on-deck circle, I reminded myself not to do anything stupid, just keep my hands inside the ball and get a pitch to drive. I came up with a man on third and one out, feeling immediately conflicted. The pitcher seemed eminently hittable, and I wanted nothing more than to hit the damn ball to Belgium in my first official at-bat as a Lion… but I had just spent two full weeks preaching the importance of situational baseball, and this situation called for me to hit the ball on the ground to the right side in order to score the runner from third.

Conflicted, I swung through a 2-1 curveball and lost my grip on the bat, sending it flying over the third base coach's head. The crowd of a few hundred tutted at the expensive American import looking like a jackass. Brains won out over testosterone, and I humbly slapped a 2-2 fastball on the ground to the second baseman for an RBI in my first Savigny at-bat. Whatever the Lions wanted from their American import – run production or hilarious bloopers – I provided it. In the third, I slapped a soft liner into right to score two, and we ran away with the win 10-0. I was 1-for-2 with three RBIs…

not bad for the first half of the day's doubleheader, I thought.

Suddenly, hordes of invading Rouen players – silent, heads down, all business – came swarming through the first base gate for their choreographed warm-up routine, missing only the Imperial March from *Star Wars.* They had earned their reputation as the Yankees of France by poaching talented players from other teams, and played solid fundamental baseball without any goofing around. They even wore white uniforms with pinstripes, adding to the 'Evil Empire' effect.

I took my position in the third base coach's box to begin the second act of the doubleheader, and we immediately jumped on their lefty pitcher. Backup catcher Dus ("Doos") crushed a ball down the leftfield line, and Vincent came steaming around second base huffing and puffing. As the leftfielder struggled to corral the ball in the corner, I gambled and sent Vincent home. He was a great guy – very funny, a tough out, and a good third baseman – but he was not blessed with lightning speed, and as he turned the corner around third, he seemed to downshift from 'very slow' to 'almost going backwards.' Nevertheless, he slid in just under the tag for our first run, and Dus scored on a booted ground ball to make the score 2-0.

Guillaume started and worked through four innings before I took the mound to start the fifth, feeling good despite a hasty warm-up and the cold. My plan began with a fastball, up and in: buzz the tower a little bit. I reared back and let one go with everything I had… and left it out over the plate. Dus's glove, originally positioned inside, drifted right, inches and inches away, to catch a ball that never arrived. The leadoff hitter slapped a groundball back up the middle and after just one pitch I found myself going from the stretch with a runner on first.

This was the point at which the American was supposed to bear down and strike out the side, make a statement to the assembled crowd by dominating the next three hitters. Unfortunately, that's precisely what I did not do. I walked the next guy, and after a stolen base, I had runners on first and third with nobody out.

I then witnessed the French's infatuation with the bunt. They love it. They can't get enough of it. I knew the French adored small ball, but I could never have imagined that they would bunt in the fifth inning against a pitcher clearly struggling to find the plate. Vincent fielded the bunt easily at third, looked the runner back... and airmailed his throw into right field, scoring a run and leaving me with runners on second and third, still nobody out. Again they bunted, a lousy one right back at me, which I fielded cleanly and shoveled to Dus for an easy out at home. Now, granted, Rouen had gotten bailed out by Vince's error on the first bunt, but I hadn't retired a hitter yet. I cannot *fathom* the rationale behind handing free outs to a pitcher struggling like that.

Rouen's generosity calmed me down a bit, and I ran the next guy to 0-2 before dropping a particularly nasty Yellow Hammer for a called third strike. I tried to do the same thing to the next guy on 1-2, but I gripped the ball a little too hard and released the dreaded 59-footer, which bounced in front of the plate and kicked up high off Dus's shoulder pad to the backstop, scoring the runner from third with ease. I threw a soft curve on 2-2, flinching when I saw that I had left the eminently hittable offering up in the zone, but Brieuc rushed in to snare the soft line drive in right, and we escaped an only moderately disastrous fifth inning.

It was not how I had hoped to begin my French pitching career: 1 Inning Pitched, 1 Hit, 2 Runs, 1 Earned Run, 1 Walk, 1 Hit By Pitch, 1 Wild Pitch, 1 Strikeout. However, it was positively Koufaxian compared to the next inning, a comedy reel of pitching bloopers, blunders, and generally ill-advised decisions. In an official game, I might have yanked myself out after one inning, recognizing that I just didn't have my best stuff. In my first performance against elite competition, though, I wanted a strong second inning to show the guys that it had been an aberration. I had one problem.

I.

Could.

Not.

Throw.

A.

Strike.

I couldn't find the strike zone with a compass and a road map. Every fastball and slider was up around the eyes. The umpire's strike zone wasn't generous, but it was fair, and I was not making it tough on him with pitches on the corners; when I missed, I missed wide. It wasn't the mound, which was significantly more comfortable than the concrete monstrosity in Savigny. It was just me, and I sucked. I walked the first two guys on 11 pitches, then missed a perfect opportunity to get out of it by bungling a double play, getting just one out at second. After a seeing-eye groundball up the middle and a well-hit line drive to right, I was in a real jam. Recovering briefly to strike out the next guy on a slider in for the second out, I gave up another ground ball base hit just out of Vince's reach.

With a 1-2 count on the next hitter, Dus called for the Yellow Hammer. The batter stuck his elbow out over the strike zone for a cheap hit-by-pitch. I recognized this particular #76 as the same one I had rung up with a Hammer in the first inning, so I was doubly irritated that he had pulled such a bush league maneuver to avoid a second backwards K. Christophe called time, visited me on the mound, and asked how I was feeling. Having already thrown over 50 pitches, I was tired, and we agreed that I would only face one more hitter. Four errant fastballs later, I stormed off the mound with the sacks juiced and four runs already in, struggling to recall the last time I pitched so poorly.

Fortunately, Pierrick came in to clean up my garbage and escaped without further damage, as I summoned all of the willpower in my body to resist one of those bat-breaking, water cooler-tossing dugout tantrums that always make SportsCenter. We tacked on a few extra for a final score of 12-8, winning despite my meltdown. After a performance that crappy, I preferred to get out of Dodge faster than Brutus leaving the Senate steps, but my teammates wanted to watch another Rouen pitcher in their second game against Montigny, so I stood against the railing for an inning or two, silently reliving each slider that didn't slide, each fastball that I left up. At one point Pierrick called over laughing "Evan, ça va ('*everything ok*')?" I nodded but made no effort to conceal my disgust at my performance, staring stonily out at the field as Rouen dominated the Cougars.

Demoralized, I tried to focus on the day's few positives. There weren't many... but at least I hadn't gotten shelled. Against the defending champions of France, I had only allowed a few seeing eye ground balls, I reassured myself. If they had taken my best fastball and turned it around 450 feet to straightaway center, I would have to start questioning whether I belonged. That hadn't happened; when I made good pitches, I got guys out. I just didn't make enough good pitches: a problem of execution, not ability. I also felt reassured that my teammates hadn't turned on me, as I expected some teams might. Everyone was joking around, trying to lift my spirits. Marc gave me a high-five, reassuring me, "*Eh, it's the first game, no big deal.*"

CHAPTER 12: THE FINEST SCHOOLS

I awoke Monday morning – the first day of spring – to find the sun pushing through the shades in my shoebox apartment, signaling a new day, one in which I had yet to give up five runs in less than two innings. After a long run, I caught a train into Paris to clear my head at a blues jam near the Porte de Clignancourt and blow a few tunes on harmonica with the house band at what had to be the most American bar in Paris. I heard more English than French, and the experience perfectly replicated the blues jams back home, right down to the drunk who kept trying to jump on stage uninvited.

After a listless, rain-drenched practice on Tuesday, I took Fabien up on his offer to visit INSEP, the Institut

National du Sport et de l'Education Physique, where he and Guillaume worked for the French Baseball Federation. Fabien coached the Espoirs ('Team Hope') consisting of the country's best players under 21, which somehow featured a few Lions who were 23. I was tempted to ask why there were 23-year-olds on the so-called 'under 21' team, but I already knew the response would be "*It's complicated, Evan. France is complicated.*" By the beginning of my third week in France, Fermin had voiced that refrain no fewer than 50 times.

As we wound through the suburbs of Paris, Fabien explained that INSEP served as the national sporting institute for nurturing French athletes in Olympic sports, essentially replicating the collegiate system in the United States. It was a captivating, if unintentionally amusing discourse, as the head coach of the nation's youth team delivered it while chain-smoking, lighting each cigarette off the butt end of the previous one.

"*What happens next year,*" I asked naïvely, "*when baseball is no longer an Olympic sport?*" In a somewhat misguided burst of anti-American sentiment, a recent vote at the IOC had ruled that baseball would be phased out of the Olympics by 2008. (Even recognizing my own biases as an American and a ballplayer, it seemed silly to me, regardless of one's opinions of America, to punish countries like Japan and Cuba disproportionately – they rely on baseball for medals far more than the U.S. does – by banning an increasingly global sport played by roughly a thousand times as many people as other Olympic sports like 10m Air Rifle and Skeleton. Apparently, if you invade a few countries against world opinion, you lose your national pastime as an Olympic sport. Them's the rules.

"*Well, we don't know yet,*" Fabien said, measuring his words carefully behind a flash of irritation. "*But it looks like the baseball program will move to Toulouse.*" It was sort of like asking a typewriter manufacturer what he thought of the new Apple personal computers in the late '70s.

"*Okay... So, how big is INSEP?*" I asked, eager to change the subject after my faux pas.

INSEP's 74-acre campus sits on the outskirts of Paris,

some 30 minutes from Savigny. Starting at age 16 – or even younger in the case of early-development sports like gymnastics – the best athletes from all over France move to the facility to train twice daily. At INSEP, the Lions had three of the best middle infielders in the country in Romain, Yann, and Florian, the country's starting catcher in Pierrick, and pitchers Brieuc and Gaetan.

Savigny's older players like Vincent, Jérôme, and Christophe had all trained at INSEP before moving on to graduate studies or full-time employment. Of all the Lions, only Modeste, Serge, and Sebastien had never played at INSEP, although resident prankster Marc had reportedly been asked to leave for his ceaseless antics and dubious work ethic. Looking back across my decidedly unimpressive career, the only national body to express interest in me was not the USOC but the IRS. I wondered whether the nation's best ballplayers would listen to a guy who, at their age, hadn't even won 'best in the Metro West region of Boston with a funny Irish name beginning with the letter M.' (Congratulations to the Atlanta Braves' Kevin McGlinchy!)[6]

One assistant coach stood out to me as he worked with the catchers. He caught for Senart, a Paris-area Savigny rival loaded with mercenaries, and had played on the Cuban National Team as recently as 2002, where he caught guys like <cough> Jose Contreras <cough> while I was <cough> teaching middle school math and science. That humbling moment aside, I took solace in watching France's best ballplayers. From the moment I first told friends I wanted to play baseball in Europe, their most common question was "Well, how good are they?" INSEP had 20 good athletes, ballplayers capable of looking great on any given play. That's baseball; anyone can look great (or terrible) on occasion, but the true measure of a ballplayer is consistency. Looking out across the INSEP field, I saw flubbed grounders, missed cutoff men, popped-up bunts, and pitchers who couldn't find the strike zone. Major leaguers are more machine than human, snatching every bad hop with the predictability of a Swiss watch. With each misread fly ball, however, I saw the Espoirs for what it was: a

---

[6] https://www.baseball-reference.com/players/m/mcglike01.shtml

bunch of very good ballplayers, some better than me, who nonetheless made a whole lot of mistakes. Rather than disgust or contempt, I felt a sense of comfort and belonging. My people! It had taken the crossing of an ocean to find the highest level at which I could play – and, more importantly, get paid some trifling sum – without feeling outclassed.

I hopped a ride with Pierrick back to Savigny, watching with bemusement as a car full of French national team players began singing along in thick accents with a hot 'new' 50 Cent track released six months previously in the U.S. Their inability to pronounce the chorus notwithstanding, their enthusiasm for the 'gangsta' lifestyle was impressive, even leaning out the window to proclaim it to other cars as we careened through traffic. It was the first of many times that I would encounter the paradox of France's noble resolve to protect its identity from American cultural imperialism and its adoration of all things American.

At the request of the elite team players (and against the wishes of the board), I had moved practice up an hour and separated the N1A and elite team practices. I had copied practice plans from the USF coaches, who held the distinct advantage of knowing that every player would attend every practice for fear of losing their scholarships. Coaching the Lions afforded me no such luxuries, so I separated the less-committed N1A team from the more serious elite team. Sadly, our first practice without the second team showed no improvement. Drills still lagged, and players moved as if waist-deep in molasses. Just three days before opening day, we had our worst practice to date: a zipless, half-speed affair that lacked the urgency I wanted before Sunday's opener at La Guerche.

I pulled the team together to give them my second inspirational speech of the year. "*In the States, we have a saying that practice should be work, and the games should be play. That means we should work so hard during practice that the games are fun by comparison.*"

Translation is more art than science. Scanning the blank stares around me, I found my audience hopelessly lost, but plowed ahead.

"*On Thursdays before games, I want more intensity,*

so that we enter Sunday's games relaxed."

My motivational speech was not working. Hyperactive Romain was so confused that he couldn't help but stare, mouth agape, while the more focused players like Sebastien and Vincent just squinted. Cutting my prepared speech short, I got to the punch line I had practiced in my apartment.

"*Listen, I just want us to be relaxed on Sundays, because, as we say in the States... 'I don't care who wins, as long as it's us.'*" Certainly, such a cleverly phrased joke would win over the crowd.

Their eyes glazed over. I pulled the team into a huddle, had everyone put a fist in the pot, and we shouted "Allez les Lions" ("*Go Lions*") en masse.

Despite another lackluster practice, I left the field energized. With opening day just two days away, I wanted to show the La Guerche Frenchies (as I imagined it, every team was called the Frenchies until proven otherwise[7]) how baseball was played back in the U-S-of-A. On the train back from Paris the next day, I

[7] As it turned out, almost all the mascots are English words.

received a call from Philippe, the very serious Savigny board member. He casually asked me to meet him for a beer at the train station, but I perceived an underlying purposefulness in his voice. Chalking it up as mere nervousness about the dawning of a new season – or possible backlash against my decision to separate the teams' practices – I agreed.

"*How do you find the team?*" he began, staring intently at me.

"*It's good. It's strong defensively, especially in the infield. There's a good team spirit, and I think we're coming together.*"

"*Who are you going to start in the first game?*"

"*I've decided to go with Gaetan. I asked him if he would prefer not to start against his former teammates, and he said that he was excited for the challenge.*" I sipped my beer, realizing that I'd pay $20 for an ice-cold Anchor Steam instead of the watery 1664 swill that was France's top seller.

"*And you, will you be pitching this weekend?*" In retrospect, it was the other shoe dropping.

"I'm not sure. My arm is still a little sore from Montigny, because 60 pitches is more than I usually throw as a closer, but we'll see. If it's necessary, I'll throw, but I'm told that La Guerche is a weaker team, and so I may be able to rest my arm for next week."

"*Yes, of course.*" For the first time, he looked away. Throughout the conversation, he had never diverted his steely gaze, as if constantly measuring, evaluating, looking for weakness. It made me slightly ill-at-ease, but I had felt slightly ill-at-ease through most conversations thus far in France, frequently struggling to keep up with the language.

He went on to reiterate how the team needed someone to "pull" them, as he put it, to unite them and put them over the top, which clearly meant over Rouen. He asked about practices, weighing in on the topic of splitting the first and second team workouts.

"*Ideally, I think they should practice together,*" he continued. *"It shows the second team how much they must improve to play on the first team, and it builds the pipeline of talent we talked about, where you could bring a player up to the first team for a weekend when you needed him.*"

This was an awkward point. The communal practice philosophy had been Philippe's brainchild, and I faced the unenviable task of voicing the elite players' rebellion against it. I explained delicately that players on both teams had resisted, adding that Fermin and I had settled on a compromise where we would practice together once a month: a valiant effort, but not one Philippe wanted to hear. Fortunately, he changed the topic.

"*I am sorry about your girlfriend's travel plans,*" he said, shrugging insincerely. "*We thought that on this first road trip, you should stay with the other players and not be separated from them... to establish the team's spirit.*"

Earlier in the week, Fermin had mentioned the board's decision that Becky couldn't travel to La Guerche with us. It seemed a little silly, but I acquiesced as a gesture of being a good soldier. Breaking the news to a girlfriend intent on flying 6,000 miles to watch me play baseball, however, I discovered that she didn't share that same attitude of tolerance and acceptance.

After a nasty spat, Becky insisted that I front the change fee to reschedule her flight to arrive on Sunday, and I would meet her in Paris as soon as the team returned from La Guerche. In the interests of domestic tranquility, I agreed.

"*No problem, Philippe. My girlfriend understands, of course.*" She didn't, but I resolved to deal with one problem at a time.

CHAPTER 13: OUT IN THE COUNTRY

I met up with Brieuc, Vincent, and Sebastien at the field the next day. The second team didn't play that weekend, so I also invited second-teamers Yvan and Gael to come face the La Guerche Hawks with us, hoping that seeing the elite level would inspire them. Long-time friends, they left a third-division team together to move up to Savigny's N1A team, and seemed happy to be along for the ride.

We hopped in Yvan's unusually large car, the size of a small minivan and thus enormous by French standards. As we rode west through the pastures of Bretagne, racking up some 40€ ($56) in tolls along the way, my new teammates quizzed me on all things

American. I asked about the recent student rioting around the Sorbonne – did it have anything to do with the riots south of Paris in November?

"*Oh, no, not at all,*" they explained. "*That was completely different. That was in the south, in the ghettoes.*"

"*Oh. Why did they riot?*"

"*Uh... racism, I guess,*" they responded. "*And economic reasons. They're upset there aren't any jobs.*"

"*And what about the students at the Sorbonne?*"

"*Totally different. The students are demonstrating because of a new employment act that the prime minister proposed. It allows companies to fire someone for any reason within two years of hiring them.*"

Fermin's explanation on my ride from the airport had familiarized me with the issues. From my American viewpoint, the French economic system seemed predicated on a societal preference for certainty over opportunity; that is, the French preferred a heavily-regulated economy with massive social safety nets, worker-friendly labor policies, and high tax rates in order to make getting poor – or for that matter, getting rich – nearly impossible.

"*What's the problem?*" I asked. *"That's how it is in the U.S. You could work for a place for 30 years, then get fired with two weeks' notice."*

You would think I had suggested drinking coffee with dessert, instead of after: a truly barbaric proposition to the French.

"*It's not like that here. Once you're hired, you're hired for life, and the students want that same protection in their first job.*"

Gael interrupted. "*But the problem is that all the older people have jobs and it's impossible to fire them no matter how stupid they are. Businesses are stuck with workers who take months off, lying that they're sick, and so companies can't afford to hire new workers. That's the* <u>*real*</u> *problem.*" A foreman at a landscaping business, he exhibited a distinctly more pro-management attitude toward labor relations than Vince, a physical therapy student, and Yvan, a student with more radical leanings.

"*So the students are rioting because they're upset that there aren't any jobs?*"

"*Demonstrating,*" Vincent corrected me. "*But yes, pretty much.*" Same difference, I thought.

Upon arriving at the Formule 1 Hotel in nearby Chantepie, the team settled on a chain restaurant called the Buffalo Grill, which caters to the French stereotype of American cuisine. Navigating the aisles festooned with dime store Indians and waiters wearing 10-gallon hats, I imagined that I felt the way an Australian must feel at Outback Steakhouse. As we tucked into our Steaks de Cowboy and Entrecotes (ribeyes) de Texas, the conversation turned to America. All eyes rotated my way as Marc asked me the question I had dreaded since my arrival.

"*What do you think of George Bush,*" he asked, cocking his eyebrow cartoonishly. "*He's a real asshole, non?*"

The table laughed. Treading lightly over ground I had already covered in the car ride, I reiterated that I was not a Bush supporter, but that unlike many critics, I didn't think he was genuinely evil. I gave him the benefit of the doubt that he actually believed his decisions were good for the country, even if his administration's incompetence made those decisions backfire.

That seemed to satisfy the table, and conversation moved on to girls, music, and an upcoming party in the Latin Quarter. As half the table lit up cigarettes, someone at the end hailed a friend leaving the restaurant. Two stylishly dressed twentysomethings ambled over to our table and began shaking hands. Vincent leaned over and whispered in my ear:

"*The one on the left is Antoni Piquet.*"

"*The pitcher for La Guerche?*"

He nodded, and I frowned inwardly. Piquet was a starter for the national team. Before facing a strong pitcher, I preferred to build him up in my mind until his purported dominance reached the point of absurdity, so I could silently ridicule him. It helped me cut them down to size and loosen myself up. After all, when I finally stepped into the batters' box, how could I possibly be embarrassed if I failed to get a hit off the great Antoni Piquet, the baddest pitchmaker this side of the Atlantic Ocean?

Meeting him in person meant I had to put a smiling, cheery face to the name, and couldn't feign surprise the next day when he stood any less than 6'5", 250 pounds. I shook his hand, introducing myself politely, trying to avoid sizing him up.

"*Who's the other guy?*" I said, turning back to Vince.

"*That's Serge. He's the umpire.*" Noticing my raised eyebrow, he added, "*They're friends.*"

La Guerche is out in the sticks, so Sunday morning found me admiring the beautiful, rolling green hills of northwest France, wondering if a more unlikely location for a baseball field existed in the world. Heavy rains the night before left the field lush and vibrant, and I was eager to knock heads with Piquet.

I DH'ed myself, batting seventh, and faced him with a man on first in the second inning. On his second pitch, he buzzed a fastball up and in, and I ducked back out of the way at the last second, his brushback pitch nearly grazing my chin stubble as it whistled by. I didn't think much of it at the time – at that level, pitchers often missed the plate by wide margins – but in hindsight, I think it might have been a 'Welcome to France' message, to show the American that Piquet wouldn't be intimidated. I worked the count for a walk, then stole second, and eventually scored on a ground ball to the shortstop. In my second at-bat, Piquet busted me inside with another fastball, and I shattered my bat – a fast-tapered ash model that I had labeled *Finis Coronat Opus* ('the finish crowns the work') – trying to turn on it, producing only a weak groundout. My third at-bat was even more frustrating. Piquet ran me to 1-2 on successive curveballs. I guessed correctly that he would come back with another inside fastball, and thought I had gotten the barrel of the bat around in time, but found myself holding another toothpick, as fragments of *Res Ipsa Loquitur* ('the thing speaks for itself') showered across the field. Piquet easily fielded my soft pop up.

Everyone in the dugout cracked jokes about me breaking two bats in a game. Wood bat makers in

America charge exorbitant shipping costs to France, so everyone there uses unbreakable composite bats to avoid frequent costly replacements. I had opened myself up to mockery by making my own bats to use in France, but I knew that my insistence on chasing inside fastballs meant that these busted sticks were the fault of Evan Meagher, the hitter and not Evan Meagher, the bat maker. I was 0-2 with a walk on the day, and while I wanted to give the N1A guys some at-bats, I didn't want people talking about how the American had gone hitless. I declared to the bench that I would bat once more before subbing out, with *Ad Astra Per Aspera* ('to the stars through adversity'), the one bat remaining from the three I had brought to La Guerche. Fragments of the other two stuck out from the top of the dugout garbage can like tombstones.

"*There is an expression in France, Evan,*" Marc began gleefully. "*Never two without three!*"

The rest of the bench laughed, and I grinned to hide my irritation. In my fourth at-bat, I slapped a soft groundball to the shortstop, exploding out of the batter's box with that silent panicked optimism: *maybe*

I can beat the throw to first. Still in great shape from my Velocity training, I glided across the bag two steps ahead of the throw. Let the record show that my first official hit as a Lion was a little dinker of an infield hit off the Great Piquet... but it's a laser beam line drive to center in the scorebook.

After announcing to the scorer that Marc would replace me as DH, I got my first heckling from a French fan, who chided me in accented English "*I think that's a good idea. I don't know if you showed up out of shape, or what, but...*"

Visions of Ron Artest going into the stands flashed before my eyes, but I simply gave him a look as if to ask 'you're not seriously trash-talking me during a French baseball game, are you?' He became a lot friendlier in between games, when Gaetan introduced him as the Hawks' former coach.

My stat line – 1-for-3 with a walk, two stolen bases, and a run scored – looked good on paper, but I lamented breaking two bats. They were good soldiers and deserved better. In one sense, it was the optics that bothered me; a broken bat grounder doesn't hurt the team any more than a popup, but the literal destruction of the hitting instrument has greater visual salience with observers, suggesting the hitter got overpowered. After my shellacking at Montigny, I was sensitive to such appearances. More poignantly, I felt a sense of loss when I dumped the bats in the trash bin. They were totems of months of sacrifice and training in San Francisco, deposits I had made into a bank account whose balance represented my confidence that I could succeed in French baseball. Putting them in the trash felt like an unexpected withdrawal, a fraying of the threads connecting me to home. I had to tip my cap to Piquet, a French national team pitcher who threw very well in a 5-0 loss. He had a heavy fastball and a decent curve to go with his best pitch, a late-breaking slider that reminded me of a guy I faced in San Francisco.

La Guerche was a mid-level team without a second ace to match Piquet, so I started our subs in the second game, reasoning that guys who drove four hours and stayed overnight should get to play. Our starter Guillaume Gisbert (not the older Guillaume who coached at INSEP) ran into trouble after we staked him to an early three-run lead, and I faced my first managerial quandary in the fourth, when Romain's second error loaded the bases with two outs. The next batter crushed a hanging curveball into the gap in left, and we were suddenly down 5-3. With Guillaume's pitch count rising, I considered bringing myself in, but with my elbow still feeling tender, I preferred to save myself as a last resort. Fortunately, Guillaume got out of it with a popup, and we went on to win 11-6.

The game had its moments; in the seventh, I inserted Gael at catcher and Yvan in left to get them some playing time. In his first elite at-bat, Yvan looked terrible on a first pitch curveball, waving at it helplessly and eliciting a round of jeers from the bench. He recovered to foul off a few pitches before lining out on a well-hit ball to the center fielder. As he jogged back to the dugout, the bench greeted him with a round of applause and laughter. Gael followed, and though he struck out swinging, he too returned to a chorus of applause from the veterans, who cheerfully hazed the rookies.

I considered it a success. We had not played our best,

but we won both games despite three errors from Romain at short. Personally, I regretted how my overeagerness to do damage at the plate had led me to reach for some pitches out of the strike zone, but I had gotten my first official hit as a Lion out of the way. As a manager, I felt comfortable, got everyone into the game, and had enough pitchers left at the end in case things had gotten hairy. Ultimately, though, I knew that the Lions hadn't brought me to France to go 1-for-4 and play a few innings in right.

After an interminable wait for the official scorer's sheets – I had been instructed by Fermin that under no circumstances could I leave without them – I walked stiffly to the shower, only to find that everyone had left except for Sebastien's tiny Renault. Unfortunately, four of us still needed a ride home, and all the other Lions had left us with the equipment bags. As Sebastien cursed this '*typical Lions shit,*' we dialed Yvan, Vincent, and Gael in the hopes of getting them to return to help out. Twenty minutes later, we finally got through to them and arranged to meet them on the autoroute, where we waited another 45 minutes. They pulled into the rest stop howling at the sight of Sebastien's tiny car overloaded with three of the team's heaviest players (plus poor Brieuc) and all of the equipment piled literally to the ceiling on our laps.

CHAPTER 14: NOT TONY GWYNN

Becky and I spent two romantic days in Paris before returning to Savigny, where we settled into a wonderfully indulgent lifestyle. Waking up around 10, we would wander about town collecting dinner ingredients, stopping first at the butcher for a conversation typical of my early days in France, covering six crucial issues:

No, you're right, I am not from France;

From the United States, actually, not England;

San Francisco, although I was born in Boston;

No, just learned French in high school;

Absolutely, I adore France;

You're too kind, but with this accent, I know that I spoke French "*like a true American*," which never failed to elicit a smile and a compliment.

Formalities dispensed with, we became fast friends, and our conversations over the daily purchase of "*pork chest*" and "*between the ribs of beef*" (literal translations for pork belly and ribeyes) ranged from British soccer hooliganism to the geopolitics of Mad Cow Disease. Unsurprisingly, he believed that American and British beef producers had manufactured the crisis to profit from consumers avoiding European beef. Our bags full of the butcher's finest, we moved on to one of two bakeries, each literally within a stone's throw – even with an injury-prone throwing arm – of each other. Sometimes their cheese enticed us; if not, we'd move on to the local fromagerie or '*cheese store*.' Having satisfied the three critical elements of a French dinner – meat, cheese, and bread – we returned to my apartment, laughing at our good fortune.

We spent Wednesday with the Minimes. Becky observed from the sidelines, as the children gawked at only the second Asian person they had ever seen; their own rightfielder, Pierre, had been adopted from an orphanage in Beijing. Becky was adopted by an Italian family in Rhode Island after being born in Seoul, and her offhand joke that she had 'married into the Mob' in response to my inquiry about her Italian surname not matching her (breathtaking) appearance when we met at a wedding had delayed my pursuit of her by approximately eleven seconds. Between Becky's strong identification with Italian-American culture and Pierre's prototypically French face, they both served as strong 'nurture' data points in the 'nature vs. nurture' debate.

For Thursday's practice, I created a sophisticated plan addressing two weaknesses that surfaced against La Guerche: hitting the curveball and turning the double play. To my incalculable frustration, the players met it with a level of enthusiasm I might associate with the imposition of a 75-hour workweek. Lethargy reigned despite my exhortations, and with 15 minutes left in practice, I realized we were missing two players. I asked where they were, and received only a shrug and murmur that "*they left.*" I ended practice early, explaining to the remaining players that practice had been unacceptable, and that we would need greater intensity despite playing one of the league's weaker teams that weekend.

I pulled Fabien aside and asked him what the hell had gone wrong.

"*Uh...*" he began, looking off in the distance pensively. "*The players... they are used to more. More grounders, more swings, more...'volume.' I think that's it.*"

He didn't make eye contact, and he chose his words deliberately.

"*I don't understand. I designed that practice to get everyone a lot of 'volume,' but everyone was moving at half speed. What's going on?*" While far from perfect, the practice plan should have gotten every player at least 75 swings in the cage.

"*I don't know.*" He responded wistfully, his ensuing silence damning. I knew the truth: the practice plans were sound, but the execution was terrible.

They had stopped listening to me.

In the locker room, a surprisingly upset Vincent confronted me, angry that the practice had dragged, and he had only taken a handful of swings during a practice that he squeezed in between physical therapy classes. On the defensive, I insisted that the practice plan called for him getting a lot more swings in, but the team's lethargy – combined with his showing up 30 minutes late – had made it impossible. A half-dozen Lions started speaking very passionately in rapid-fire French, not all of which I understood. Dus at one point said something, and the team quieted; he repeated it in English.

"*What I mean to say is, you are a good player, but you are not Tony Gwynn. You are not coming out of the Major Leagues.*"

I had understood only about 80 percent of the words spoken, so the pointed remark came without context. I resisted the urge to joke that both Gwynn and I talked funny; we had that in common at least. The conversation ended when I declared that we had to be better, myself included, and that our Tuesday practice plan would be designed to keep everyone moving at breakneck speed. I passed Fermin on the way home, and his face betrayed real concern even as he assured me that the situation was salvageable. For the first time, I started to worry about my credibility with the team.

The next afternoon, I stopped by Remi's house to pick up a spare Lions' t-shirt for Becky to wear during Sunday's game against the Bois-Guillaume Woodchucks, a bottom-tier team from Normandy in the elite division. French baseball works on a promotion/relegation structure, just like the European soccer leagues. The Woodchucks had won the N1A championship two years prior, earning promotion to the elite division, where they promptly lost a handful of their best players to retirement or poaching by other teams like Rouen, and had played the role of league doormat ever since. Descending into the nineteenth-century basement that served as the Lions' equipment storage, he asked me what happened on Thursday.

"*Fabien told me that players were upset that they weren't getting enough swings, but...*" I trailed off. "*I'm willing to change things, but it's tough to figure out what to change. What do you think?*" I tripped over the words, struggling to express abstract concepts in French. Remi, on the other hand, was always eager to try out his English, and responded in equally broken phrases.

"I seenk zat, zee playerz? Zey like more to do zere stretcheeng all togezer. Eet ees not a cloob, military, yes?"

I nodded to indicate yes, ours was not a military-style club like Rouen.

"Zome playerz take more time to do zeir stretching, otherz not zo long, if zey come from INSEP... zey prefer stretching togezer, in a circle, and... bavarder? Chat? Zat ees eet?"

"Yes, that's it," I replied. (They preferred to chat in a circle while stretching.)

"But I do not zeenk eet ees a probleme with you. Zey like you. I zeenk zat you joost need zome – " he searched for the words in English " – leetle adjoostments."

I thanked Remi for his honesty, and biked up the hill for the Cadets' practice at the Moulin Vert, still soaked from the week's rain. Of my 28 days in France, it had rained roughly 20, and I pointed this out to the cadets as they trickled in for practice, exclaiming "*You know what? In pictures of France, all one sees is the Eiffel Tower, the sun shining down on the Seine...*"

Fermin called that night as we headed out to dinner, sounding agitated and even more stressed out than usual. He had just left a Lions' board meeting, and had to cancel the next day's lunch we had planned with our girlfriends. Instead, he and Philippe wanted to meet me at the brasserie across from my apartment.

"Fermin," I said, "You've got to level with me here. This sounds like I'm walking into a meeting with guns drawn. What the hell is going on?"

"It's not good, Evan, but... I'd rather talk to you in person."

CHAPTER 15: WHEN THE WHIP COMES DOWN

I didn't sleep a wink that night. I just stared at the ceiling, hoping that the discussion was merely a preventative effort to address the problems at practice.

I had never been fired. Even through some dark days as a teacher, I managed to avoid the axe, despite being generally lousy at the profession. Despite a few close calls, no organization had ever decided, after hiring me, that they would be better off without me.

I showed up a few minutes early to find Philippe sipping an espresso. He glanced around for Fermin, but the awkward tension grew so great that he began without him.

"As you know, we had a meeting of the board of

directors last night, and we came to a decision that you may find... disagreeable." He spoke slowly in French so that I would understand, never once blinking or breaking his stare, even to look down at his espresso. "*As you know, there have been some problems at practice, so we have made the difficult decision to end the partnership between you and the club. I am sorry, and while I am sure you are disappointed, it was the decision we had to make in the best interests of the club.*"

It was at this decidedly inconvenient juncture that the waiter asked if I wanted anything from the bar. I briefly contemplated how to translate 'give me that bottle on the top shelf, and put the whole thing on this guy's tab even though I'm only going to need the jagged top half of it,' but instead I gave him a curt "non, merci."

Fermin arrived, pulling up a chair with a silent nod. Philippe continued, giving the official reason as my failure to unite the team as a coach. Players liked me as a person, but had complained about inefficient practices and expressed unhappiness with the team's direction. I lacked experience with exit interviews, but it occurred to me that every once in a while, through all the spin control and double talk, someone says something – intentionally or otherwise – that cuts to the heart of the matter.

"*I think it would have been ok, you know, if you weren't as good a coach but were playing, you were pitching, but...*" Philippe's voice trailed off. *"You're not. Your elbow –"*

"And that's baseball," Fermin interrupted in English. "There's nothing you can do about that." Even in the most wretched of moments, I appreciated Fermin's effort to make me feel better.

Fermin was playing good cop here; Philippe, as I had strangely anticipated in that first jetlagged meeting just three weeks prior, played hatchet man. The sudden silence stopped my reminiscing, and I realized it was my turn to say something. I looked them both in the eyes and cleared my throat.

"*Well, I think it's a mistake, and a bad decision,*" I began in measured French. "*I think it's a mistake to fire someone so quickly; I just found out there was a problem at practices on Thursday, and I haven't even had an opportunity to make adjustments or defend myself. I think it's a mistake to fire someone who has won the only four games he coached. I think it's a mistake to fire someone who made such a commitment to you."*

My voice had begun to rise, and I fought to keep it under control.

"*I packed my life up, moved everything I owned into storage, and flew 6,000 miles, and here you are, dismissing me without even letting me defend myself. It doesn't look good to turn your back on a person who's made that kind of commitment to the club. And I think it's a mistake to pass judgment on a ballplayer's ability after one or two games. Our shortstop struck out four times on Sunday and made three errors, and I still think he's the second-best ballplayer we have after Pierrick.*" I was referring to Romain; for some reason, I seemed to hold him in higher esteem than the other coaches.

I looked at Philippe and then Fermin. Philippe blinked once and sipped his espresso: cold, emotionless, almost reptilian. This was a *fait accompli.* Despite the advance notice from Fermin's phone call, it felt like a surreal, almost out-of-body experience. I was getting canned.

At the end of any relationship, there are two ways out. You can get all the venom out there on the page, throw every verbal javelin. Overturn the table, scream that you've been wronged, wrap it all up in f-bombs and middle fingers; sometimes, maybe, it's for the best. According to Hemingway – who knew a thing or two about the French – it always ends badly, otherwise it wouldn't end. Sometimes it's best to get the raw emotions out there, burning and bleeding, so you can get closure, instead of letting them churn inside you in a mental vat of "esprit de l'escalier."[8] I've taken that route on occasion. Never a graceful dancer – or for that matter, shortstop – I wasn't afraid of ungraceful exits, never shied away from confrontation.

For some reason, I chose the more dignified approach in that Savigny bar. I continued, now much more slowly, my emotions under control, in English.

---

[8] A coincidentally French expression that translates as "staircase wit": all those things you think of on your way up the stairs, wishing you had been calm enough to think of them in the heat of the moment.

"I think it's a mistake, because I know that I can compete at this level. I know I haven't played my best baseball in a Lions' uniform yet, and I know I can help this team win more games than it would without me."

Now was the time to unleash the tirade, burn the bridge, get my money's worth with a bombardment the likes of which hadn't been seen in Europe since Dresden.

I didn't.

"But if that's the board's decision, I understand it, and I will respect it. I don't agree with it, but I will respect it. I just want to say this: I've never half-assed anything on a baseball field in my life. Whatever I've had, I gave it, and I did that here. I didn't half-ass any the games, and I sure as hell didn't half-ass any of the practices."

Philippe indicated that he hadn't understood the last phrase, so I looked to Fermin for translation.

"*He said that he didn't do anything halfway.*"

Philippe nodded, and I continued. "I've given the Lions absolutely everything I had, and if that wasn't enough, well, that's your decision, not mine. So, tell me this: is today my last day as a Lion? Am I gonna play in tomorrow's games?"

Fermin and Philippe exchanged a brief, awkward glance, and Philippe responded in French.

"*We've left it up to you to decide, out of respect to...*"

If I had received the news via email, giving me time to craft my response, I might have given more thought to the awkwardness of playing with a team that didn't want me, said 'screw it,' and made the perfectly reasonable decision to spend the next two days in Paris with my girlfriend, trying to forget about it all. I'm glad that didn't happen. For once in my life, I'm glad I shot my mouth off before thinking.

"YOU'RE GODDAMN RIGHT I'M GOING TO PLAY IN THAT GAME."

They said that Christophe would coach the team, and I should inform him of my decision to play so he could plan accordingly. The shock began to wear off as I shook their hands and apologized for not being the player they wanted me to be, struggling to maintain an attitude of pride and dignity that belied my bewilderment. I walked the half-block to my apartment in a daze and found Becky waiting.

"Well, kiddo... They fired me."

She didn't say anything. She just gave me a hug.

Four weeks in France had taught me a lot. That Saturday, I learned that having to tell my girlfriend, who had flown 6,000 miles to see me play baseball, that I had been fired ranked below all other experiences in the world except telling her over the phone. I realized how much Becky meant to me as she comforted me in my reaction to the most disappointing news I had heard in 10 years, which to be fair, indicates a pretty charmed decade.

I left Christophe a voicemail to let him know that I was going to play, and that my arm felt strong enough to throw a few innings. We headed into Paris and tried to enjoy the day, visiting the Eiffel Tower and then the oldest restaurant in Paris, La Petite Chaise. I had a martini, and we toasted to the Savigny-Sur-Orge Lions, to my firing, and to the future of my baseball career, whatever it might bring. We caught a cab to the Etoile, and walked down the Champs-Élysées, taking in the sights and sounds of the world's most famous byway. But then, a funny thing happened on the way to the Arc de Triomphe.

Christophe's name had flashed on my cell phone at the Eiffel Tower, but my phone crashed and lost power when I tried to answer. I rebooted the phone and tried him several times at dinner, again during the cab ride, and then while we were on the Champs-Élysées, only getting through once for a brief second. He left a message, but I lost power again while trying to check voicemail. I assumed the worst; he had polled the other players and they preferred that I not play.

As we strolled past the Arc de Triomphe, awash in lights, Christophe finally got through, and my phone's feeble energy systems held up.

"You're going to start tomorrow, Evan," Christophe began in his always-close-to-fluent English. "You know, uh, as a peacher."

"Sounds good, Christophe."

"It is, you know, all I can do for you," he said, earnest and unapologetic. "It's your game, so you go as many innings as you can, and you finish."

He paused.

"So uh, bring your best stuff."

"Thanks, Christophe. I will."

Standing on the Champs-Élysées on a Saturday night, with thousands of tourists and club-goers streaming past me, I felt a moment of singular clarity. Yes, I would start tomorrow. My first start since high school.

From a game management perspective, it made perfect sense; starting me on the mound would get me out of there the quickest, minimizing the awkwardness. I chose to focus instead on the neat symmetry of the thing. Maybe it was the dramatic setting, my emotional state from getting fired, or just the wine from dinner, but I was struck with a new sense of purpose. I'll start, all right. I'll start, and I'll throw everything I've got, because this is it. The end of the road.

I'll start tomorrow's game and go as far as my right

arm, my wits, and my determination will carry me, and as always, I'll push it further than I have any right to. Even without a tender elbow, two innings had been my maximum in San Francisco, so I figured it would be a short appearance. Maybe three innings. Whatever; I would go out on my own terms.

CHAPTER 16: THEY SAY GOODBYE, I SAY NO-NO

I walked into the locker room as if I didn't know any better, as though I was still the coach. I gave every player the standard 'Bonjour,' eye contact, and firm handshake. I tried to keep my head up, proud and regal (or so I imagined) through an interminably awkward silence. The *players* had fired me, and now I had to sit and watch as they filed in and offered lukewarm greetings and goodbyes. Finally, Philippe, Fermin, and Christophe arrived, closing the door behind them.

Philippe gave the expected party line. *Because of difficulties, we have decided to replace the current coach. We gave him the option and Evan has decided to play today, so this will be his last day as a Lion. While we're sorry that it didn't work out, I'd like to take this opportunity to thank Evan for his contributions...* you've heard it all before. Fermin spoke briefly about the near-term logistics in my absence; Christophe would coach the team until they could recruit another player/coach from the United States or Canada.

I looked around at the clubhouse. There were 11 players, just half of the team. In retrospect, unsurprising; no one wants to watch a funeral.

Christian, the team president, spoke next and revealed some discord in the executive ranks. "*You've thrown away a perfectly good manager,*" he lamented in a direct criticism of the players. "*And after one month! Who will come here now, after we've fired someone after just a month?!?*" Christian had always been more management than baseball – he was never out there shagging flies or taking BP – so the half of the team that was present didn't seem to take his criticism seriously. Maybe it felt to them more like an HR problem than about my quality as a ballplayer, and they had made their decision and wanted the whole wretched mess to be over with. After all, I had already been fired, but as he held the assembled players to account, I still appreciate his kindness to this day.

"*There is an old saying in the United States,*" I began in French, and a few players chuckled, accustomed both to my awkward translations and to me beginning sentences this way when I tried to explain abstract baseball concepts, like '.300 hitters hit .300 off of mistakes' and 'get ahead and expand the zone.' "*The saying is, 'The manager's toughest job is not deciding whether to bunt with the score tied in extra innings. It's telling a ballplayer that he's through, done, finished.' Maybe I'm that old ballplayer that needs to take a hint. I don't agree with the decision – I feel like I've still got a few bullets left in this arm – but the board has made its decision, and even if I don't agree with it, I understand it, and I will respect it. What I do know is this: I've never done anything halfway on a baseball field, and that extends to everything I've done as a Lion. You've decided that I'm not good enough to be here. I disagree. But it's your decision to make, and I want you to know that it's not because I didn't try hard enough. In the end, I'm just sorry I wasn't the player you wanted. No hard feelings."*

Most of the Lions just stared at the ground.

"*Listen. I wish you guys nothing but the best, and I hope you go on and win the championship of France, and I'm sorry I won't be a part of that. But in the meantime...* Ce n'est pas grave (*It's no big deal.*)"

A few uncomfortable handshakes and pats on the back later, I jogged out from the locker room, ready to face the Woodchucks in my last game in France. As a point of pride (and from my continued belief that the best baseball trainers in America know what they're doing, regardless of what the INSEP kids thought), I sprinted out to left field to perform the now controversial dynamic warm-up from Andrew at Velocity Sports.

I was all alone, no Lion within 100 feet of me. My soon-to-be-former teammates gazed on with some curiosity from an unusually overpopulated dugout. We always had more players at home games than away games, but it seemed like every Lion had come out of the woodwork to see whether the fired American was really going to go through with it.

I took my time getting loose, then called Pierrick over to the bullpen to start throwing, when I realized that something was terribly wrong.

It was raining.

Hard.

The familiar pregame adrenaline kicked in, kickstarting an urge to show the Lions what they were giving up. I was ready to rock & roll. Instead, I found myself sitting in the corner of a dugout filled with Frenchmen who no longer desired my services as their coach, waiting for the rain to stop.

"I can't believe it, kiddo," I laughed cynically to Becky. "My last chance to play, and this is what I get. A damn rainout."

It made for the perfect epilogue to my French baseball career: a huge buildup, then massive disappointment. For the next hour, I sat in gloomy silence in the dugout, watching raindrops pelt the all-dirt infield and that goddamned concrete mound.

'Someone else can fix that nightmare,' I thought. Guillaume The Younger, the crafty lefthanded pitcher, walked up at one point, put his arm around me, and surprised me with an unanticipated apology.

"*It just seemed kind of cold to me.*"

"*Thanks, Guillaume,*" I said, noting the sincerity in his eyes. "*It's a cold world. You've got to supply your own heat.*"

He nodded sagely, and we went back to waiting for the skies to clear, knowing that we were approaching the point where it wouldn't matter anyway. Even if the rain stopped, the field would be too soaked for play.

Just before noon, the clouds parted suddenly and majestically: nothing but blue skies. To my surprise and delight, the scorer waved us onto the field; we would play after all. I warmed up for the second time, hoping that I still had enough bullets left to last me three good innings.

Nervous, tired, but nonetheless thrilled to stand on a mound as a professional ballplayer, I stared in at the first batter, a crouching little guy, no more than 5'5".

Pierrick called for a fastball in and I silently thanked the suddenly dry heavens as it found its way for a strike. The batter fouled off a slider, and I faced my first two-strike count of the day before making him look silly with a snappy Yellow Hammer. My first official strikeout as a professional. Maybe my last.

The next hitter took two called strike fastballs and a Hammer at the knees, returning to the dugout without ever lifting the bat off his shoulder. With two up and two down by the strikeout, I was starting to feel myself, but I walked the next two guys on nine pitches. The memory of my debacle in Montigny, lurking in my subconscious since my dismissal on Friday, came roaring back. I tried to stuff the memory away, ignoring the uneasy 'here we go again' feeling.

I need not have worried. One fastball later, the #5 hitter grounded softly to Vincent at third to end the inning.

I struggled like that for the rest of the game. My sliders hung consistently, I had trouble keeping the Yellow Hammer out of the dirt, and I had such difficultly locating the fastball that I joked to Pierrick that any time he wanted a fastball outside, he should just signal for one inside, assuming that I would keep missing badly. It was just one of those days when I didn't have my best stuff, and had to gut it out inning to inning, trying to get by.

It was also a no-hitter.

While I slogged it out on the mound, the Savigny hitters crushed the few strikes they saw from Bois-Guillaume's beleaguered pitching staff. We won by slaughter rule, 20-0 after five innings. The Woodchucks had only won three games the year prior, so they didn't have a great offensive reputation, but a no-hitter is a no-hitter, regardless of the asterisks attached.

I struck out nine, allowed only those two first-inning walks, and only had one ball hit out of the infield (a popup to shallow center). When I ended the game by striking out their burly third baseman, I ran off the field to Becky's embrace.

"I'm so proud of you, baby," she said with a kiss. "I love you."

I shook everyone's hand in the post-game circle, where Christophe thanked me to a smattering of polite applause. I repeated my locker room sentiments, wished everyone luck, and then Fabien pulled me aside to introduce me to Bois-Guillaume's coach.

In the second inning, Fabien had mentioned that Bois-Guillaume might be looking for another ballplayer, so I knew in the back of my mind that my final appearance as a Lion might double as an audition for the Woodchucks. With the season already started, I considered it a longshot, but just in case, I gave Seb, the B-G coach my phone number and email, and told him to call me if they needed another arm. As we walked back to the Savigny dugout, I realized I didn't want another fiasco like the one I had just endured.

"*Hey,*" I said, stopping to look Fabien in the eyes. "*Be honest with them about me. I am what I am.*"

"*I will, of course,*" he replied. "*I think you can help them. You would be their best player, you could lead them...*" His voice trailed off, as I reflected on how I failed to do either in Savigny.

I said my last goodbyes, the awkwardness diluted by the natural glow of victory, and Becky and I walked home, stopping on the way to verify that ice cold beer – even French swill from sushi restaurants in Savigny-Sur-Orge – after a victory on the baseball field tastes better than anything else in the world. I showered at my apartment, wondering how much longer I would call the shoebox at 31 Avenue Henri Dunant home. Exhausted but strangely at peace, we took the train into Paris for our last night together before Becky's flight home, to eat at Hemingway hangout Brasserie Lipp, drink champagne, and toast to Savigny, to asterisked no-hitters, and to my brief but illustrious career as a professional baseball player.

CHAPTER 17: COME BACK BRIGHTER

I called my parents on Monday. I think that's one of the rules of parenting: if your son moves to France to play baseball, gets fired, and calls to vent about it, you have to take the call, even at six in the morning. My parents were right about one thing: 24 hours always helps. (So does throwing a no-hitter.) They pointed out that all I ever wanted to do was say that I got paid to play baseball, and I had: my lifetime earnings from baseball would forever be non-zero.

Knowing most teams had their rosters set, I considered declaring victory and resigning myself to bumming around Europe until I sat for the Chartered Financial Analyst Level III exam in Paris in early June.

My parents reminded me that I had named the blog about my journeys *Have Bat, Will Travel*, not *Have Bat, Will Travel Once, And If Anything Goes Wrong, Will Run Home Crying to Mommy.* (Fortunately, www.hbwtoaiagwwrhctm.com was taken.) The hard part was over; I was in France, and I had proven I could play at the country's highest level of baseball. More importantly, if I were going to listen to someone who told me I wasn't good enough at baseball, it probably would have been one of the first 10,417 times I heard it, not the Lions, who merely happened to be the 10,418th. Resolving to soldier on, I looked on the lighter side of things. Getting fired is no laughing matter... except in this case, where it was goddamned hilarious. I had just been fired by a French baseball team. By any objective measure, that was funny. I mean, do you have any idea how *hard* it is to get fired in France?

Particularly given the recent riots – ahem, *demonstrations* – over the controversial employment termination bill, you had to give the Lions credit. The French were great at bread, cheese, and cute children, but 'hurrying' was not their forte... and yet within 24 hours of one lousy pitching performance and one bad practice, the board of directors had convened and dropped me like third-period algebra. Had the French acted so quickly and decisively at Waterloo, they would be singing *La Marseillaise* in Berlin today.

Subsequent conversations with Fermin and Christian made it clear that the coaching situation had been a proxy for my play. For all the lip service about slow practices, they fired me because they didn't think I was good enough or healthy enough. Savigny had lost the championship to Rouen the year before because they ran out of pitchers, prompting their first ever search for a foreigner to put them over the top – '*pull the team,*' as Philippe said. They wanted the French equivalent of Pedro Martinez circa July 1999, and instead got David McCarthy[9] circa August 2004: a smart, hardworking, aging ballplayer with a little pop

[9] I agonized over this comparison for hours. Who's the right comparison? I thought of John Tudor, a surly type who just kind of gutted through games with weak stuff but got results, and Rickey Henderson circa 2003, an aging guy getting by on speed and attitude alone, but figured that his pedigree would be too much of a distraction. I settled on McCarthy because of the Stanford connection as much as for his ability to both pitch and play a position, although it's imperfect, both because I lack his defensive prowess and because my career never exhibited the promise that McCarthy's did as a first-round pick out of Stanford. It's perhaps telling that in the midst of a career crisis, it was matters like these that I spent the most time thinking about.

and a decent glove, who could throw a few innings on the side. Can you blame them for their disappointment? Make all the cracks you want about how much talent 300€ a month buys you, but the fact remains that they expected me to come in and *dominate*, and that's not what happened.

After dropping Becky off at the airport, I headed to Eglise de Paintain just outside Paris. Perhaps out of a sense of obligation, Fermin had invited me for lunch at his apartment after the Bois-Guillaume game. I wasn't sure he believed me when I assured him that there were no hard feelings – '*pas de malaise*,' as he had helped me translate.

"So, what are you going to do now?" he asked me as we lounged in his living room.

"I'm waiting to hear back from a few teams. Fabien said maybe the Woodchucks would be interested, and I met a guy from the second division team in Paris..." My voice trailed off. I didn't know what I would do if neither panned out. "And if not, I'll hit the road, I guess, try to find a team in another country."

Fermin stared in disbelief. "Really?"

I didn't know what to say. Yes, really. Apparently, he thought I would leave town? He couldn't believe I would stick it out and try to keep playing. I just moved 6,000 miles to chase a dream, and he expected me to turn tail and run?

"Wow. You are a little bit crazy," he said, smiling.

I smiled back. "I guess so."

"You know, that was a really American thing to do. Playing on Sunday, I mean."

"Yeah?" I replied.

"Oh, definitely. Any French player would have just said 'Fuck it,' you know, 'I don't want to play with these fucking guys anyway.' I don't think anyone expected you to show up."

I laughed, both at his depiction of what a French player would do, and at the way he said "fucking guys" in his 'stuck-up French person' mimicry. In my month in France, no one had given Americans a greater compliment. Forget storming the beach at D-Day or propping up wine prices; showing enough obstinacy to play in a baseball game for pride alone had earned the highest French endorsement of American character.

For the next few days, my cell phone's silence proved deafening. Each morning I went for a run before taking the train to Paris to check my email. The team had offered a severance package exorbitant by American standards but draconian by French, allowing me to stay in the apartment until they found someone new. I had no desire to make an awkward situation worse by hanging around a town that didn't want me, so I gave myself two weeks – until April 20th – to leave the apartment.

The problem was my elbow. Ever since that twinge on the second-to-last pitch against the Woodchucks, it had throbbed anytime I moved it. During my celebrations with Becky in Paris that afternoon, I had worn a bulky arm-and-shoulder-icing wrap underneath my button-down shirt, cutting a Quasimodo-like figure as we walked through the Latin Quarter. Daily icings did little to mitigate the pain, and I grew genuinely worried about my ability to pitch in the unlikely event that a tryout materialized.

As uncertainty turned to despair, I realized how pathetic I would look in the eyes of everyone who had supported and rooted for me, offering encouragement on my blog. I had quit a good job, and for what? One month in France? Two pitching performances, one a real stinker? Some dream of playing professional baseball this turned out to be. I tried rationalizing it with the notion that there was nobility in the striving even if it ended in failure, but I couldn't displace the gnawing fear that I would look back years later and regret such a self-indulgent, unrealistic stunt.

Then my cell phone rang.

"Allo?"

"Hey, Evan, it's Fermin!" Fermin always exuded cheeriness on the phone. "Uh, is now a bad time?"

"No, no, of course not," I said, clearing my throat.

"I've got some good news. I talked to Seb at Bois-Guillaume... They want you to come play for the Woodchucks."

CHAPTER 18: THIS MUST BE THE PLACE

Baseball's a funny game. The line drives are caught, and the squibbers go for hits. Hit a ball 400 feet in Seattle and it's an out; hit a ball 300 feet in Boston[10] and it's a home run. Still, there's a certain transparency to it all; the game is hard, but not terribly complicated. If you keep your head down and do your job, the bounces will even out in the end, and people will recognize your success or failure for what it is. You can't hide. So if you ever find yourself pitching your last game for a team that has already fired you, against a team that might potentially hire you, I recommend throwing a no-hitter.

---

[10] Fine, 302 down the line in right, and you have to put a lot of English on it.

Suddenly, there were arrangements to make and paperwork to fill out to hasten my legal transfer to the Woodchucks in time for Sunday's games. I focused primarily on figuring out where the hell I was going, having never heard of Bois-Guillaume until a week earlier. Immediately after our lunch, Fermin had called Sebastien Grimaud of the Woodchucks to see if they had any interest in a washed-up ballplayer with a gruesome moustache. Evidently, they were; Seb even apologized that he hadn't called, because he hadn't found an apartment that could accommodate me, my girlfriend, and their soon-to-arrive Australian pitcher. Having met Becky on Sunday in Savigny, he assumed that she had moved to France with me. After Fermin assured him that I was traveling alone and Becky had returned to the US, they verbally agreed that Bois-Guillaume would purchase my contract from Savigny, making me a Woodchuck and allowing me to claim that I had been the center of a blockbuster trade in which the Woodchucks acquired RHP/IF Evan Meagher for cash and his dwindling inventory of homemade bats. For the record, Bois-Guillaume acquired me from Savigny for the player registration fee, which was approximately the price of a tank of gas. Gas is *very* expensive in France, though, so the Woodchucks may have overpaid.

Fermin walked me through the particulars, making me promise repeatedly that yes, I would remember to buy my ticket to Rouen from Gare St. Lazare for Saturday at noon. He grew frustrated, asking if I was paying attention, but in my defense, it's hard to pay attention while jumping up and down, silently mouthing the words 'Holy Shit!,' and giggling uncontrollably. Seb called me soon after, and I formally accepted his offer to join the Woodchucks.

"That's great, buddy!" he said in English with a curiously weak accent. He sounded more like a Malibu surfer boy than a Norman, although I realized I had no idea what Normans sounded like. I complimented him on his spoken English, and he responded with pride that he had spent a semester studying and playing baseball at the College of Marin, just across the bridge from my old place in San Francisco. "We're, like… really looking forward to having you!" Thus concluded the most turbulent, bizarre, surreal week of my life. I would go from Savigny to Bois-Guillaume: from a title contender to the league's doormat. It was like being traded – if that's what you call getting acquired for the price of a really good bottle of wine – from the Boston Red Sox to the Kansas City Royals.[11] I would trade the Lions' blue and white for the Woodchucks' silver and black, and Savigny's 40-minute train ride to Paris for Bois-Guillaume's 10-minute drive to Rouen, the largest city in distant, rural Normandy.

I felt genuinely excited about sharing an apartment with the as-yet-unnamed Australian. My Savigny apartment had gotten lonely, and besides, I had never met an Australian I didn't like. Hell, I hadn't met anyone that met an Australian that *they* didn't like.

From that moment – that silly, glorious, life-altering phone call that joins the Langone dinger and the double on the Monarchs as one of the turning points in my baseball career – I had less than 48 hours left in Savigny. I regret that I never got to bid farewell to my butcher, who graciously welcomed this Yank to town, or to the Minimes, or to Yann and Jose, whose

[11] This comparison was far more apt when I wrote it in 2006 than today, with the Red Sox mired in last place.

kindness on that first day in France has stayed with me through the years. Perhaps in another lifetime.

Fermin picked me up on Saturday morning and helped me downstairs with my enormous duffel bags. We drove to Gare St. Lazare, talking about life, baseball, and life some more. No resentment, no apologies, and no bitterness, just a couple of friends shooting the breeze. When we arrived at the station, I felt a pang of sadness that Fermin couldn't join me for the next leg of the adventure, and not solely because he would have been a great help schlepping my bags up the escalator; honestly, what had I packed for, the Crusades? I would miss him, and I hoped that we would keep in touch.

At the top of the escalator, I waved goodbye to Fermin as he pulled away in his girlfriend's car, which had bookended my tenure as a Lion. After a minor confrontation with the conductor – which began with him declaring that under absolutely no circumstances could he allow my bags on board, and concluded with him shaking his head in frustration and waving me along after I offered to buy a second ticket – I boarded the train and settled into my seat. Incidentally, if you ever want to irritate some French people, try bringing three massive duffle bags, plus a backpack and garment bag, onto a high-speed train. They would have preferred I simply release a pillowcase full of crickets.

I said my silent goodbyes to Paris as the train pulled away. The cityscape soon gave way to the rolling hills of Normandy, and I felt an enthusiasm and wonder faintly reminiscent of my transatlantic flight to Charles de Gaulle. Savigny hadn't worked out; so be it. I was on my way to new adventures, no doubt every bit as fanciful. Bois-Guillaume adventures, I thought to myself. *Woodchuck* adventures.

Too excited to sleep, I booted up my computer to see who we would face in my first game as a Woodchuck, only to see… Rouen, whose savage ass-kicking probably sealed my fate in Savigny. Onwards and upwards, I thought. What… I expected it to be easy?

When the train pulled into the Rouen station, I dragged my luggage upstairs and met Sylvain, the president of the club and the part-time player I had struck out to end the no-hitter in Savigny.

"Bonjour, Eh-vahn!" he began with what I came to recognize as a thick Norman accent[12]. "*It's super that you have come to Bois-Guillaume! Welcome! We need a strong pitcher like you, with your curving ball that is... bizarre!!!*" With this he raised his open hand in a big loop, starting at his waist and climbing to his shoulders before dropping sharply down back to waist-level, as if describing a cartoonishly pregnant belly in front of him. I could only assume he meant the Yellow Hammer I threw him. Big and barrel-chested with an ear-to-ear grin, he reminded me of the Obelix character from the Asterix comic book series we read in Mr. Hobert's French class. He pumped my hand enthusiastically. I liked him immediately.

Once we lugged my baggage out to the main road, we found a skinny 20-year-old double-parked and blocking the one-way alley that, judging by the line of cars backed up behind him, accounted for half of the egress from Rouen's only train station. Apparently, Normandy had not embraced the concept of the parking lot. Sylvain transferred my duffel bag to the back seat and

---

[12] It was subtle, but Normans spoke slower than the Parisians, and have a throatier pronunciation as they drag out syllables.

introduced me to Clement, Bois-Guillaume's Fermin equivalent who fit nearly every common American stereotype of the French, minus the arrogance: handsome, a little shifty, somewhat effete, and flirtatious enough that you would never trust him alone with your girlfriend. A student at the Sorbonne, his degree in Sports Management had an internship requirement that he would complete with the Woodchucks. Dropping Sylvain off with another spirited handshake, Clement and I drove into downtown Rouen to eat, finding the team's sponsor – the Tex-Mex-themed 'Rest'O'Rock' restaurant – closed.

Instead, we wolfed down steak frites at a brasserie next to Rouen's Old-Market Square, site of Joan of Arc's immolation. (Later, Sylvain would jokingly point out how well the flowers grew underneath the memorial cross.) Between mouthfuls underneath the prototypically Norman crooked wooden beams, Clement explained the Woodchucks' situation. It stood in stark contrast to the Lions, who felt the team could coach itself, and merely needed someone to fill out the lineup card and pitch seven shutout innings every weekend to carry them to a championship.

Like most European sports leagues, French baseball operated on a 'one up, one down' relegation system. The last place team of the elite division suffered demotion to the N1A division, while the N1A champion earned the right to ascend to elite. Bois-Guillaume had shocked everyone by winning the 2004 N1A championship, earning promotion to the elite ranks. At the higher level of competition, they had a predictably tough 2005 season, entering the final weekend in seventh place, one game ahead of last-place Paris Université Club, or 'PUC,' pronounced somewhere between 'pook' and 'puke.' The Paris-based club – which, counterintuitively, had no affiliation with any university – had fallen on hard times following the defection of their best players, Fermin among them, to Savigny.[13] Clement explained with glee that the Woodchucks had played PUC in that final climactic

[13] While Savigny players had implied to me that such talent poaching was the province of arch-rival Rouen, I began to recognize a pattern in which the ability of French players to change clubs on a whim inevitably resulted in the concentration of the best players on the best teams, making it nearly impossible for a struggling club to rise from the bottom and compete. In direct contrast with French economic policy, French baseball was rigged to make the rich richer and the poor poorer.

weekend, and after dropping the first match to draw even, eked out a dramatic victory to stay out of the cellar and send PUC to relegation.

"*So PUC is now in the second division?*" I asked, "*The N1A?*"

"*No. Not exactly,*" Clement grimaced. He flashed a wan smile, mustering the tact to tiptoe around the implication. "*PUC has always been very well connected, very popular... until recently. It is the only club in Paris, so it would be a grave embarrassment for the Federation to have them in the second division.*"

"*And so...?*"

"*So the Federation expanded the league to nine teams just to keep PUC in elite. Saint-Lô ascended from N1A, and PUC stayed anyway.*"

Clement's diplomatic veneer did little to hide his irritation. Clearly, the Federation would have extended no such clemency to Bois-Guillaume. The rest of the league considered the Woodchucks outsiders, underpowered party crashers in an elite division that hadn't expected them – more established clubs like

Cherbourg or Montigny were expected to ascend that year – and yet hadn't quite figured out how to oust them. Whistling past the graveyard, Clement explained that Eric, the French-Canadian president who led the team into the elite division, had relinquished the presidency a year ago, sparking a series of leadership changes that accelerated with some unnamed scandals that brought the club to its knees in 2005.

The team's morale suffered – a "*negative ambience*," translated literally – and in the offseason, several young, talented players left for teams like Rouen and Toulouse, dismayed with the infighting, the team's poor record, and the aura of embarrassment. Given such an ignominious backdrop, the team had simple objectives for 2006; win enough games to remain in the elite division, improve on last year's noxious team atmosphere, and develop enough young talent to become competitive down the road. They wanted me and Matt (the Australian) to coach jointly and stay just competitive enough to survive. In effect, the Lions wanted me to be the second coming of Nolan Ryan, while Bois-Guillaume just wanted me to be Crash Davis from *Bull Durham.* Anyone who has paid attention so far – or God forbid, actually seen me play – can easily identify the role for which I was better suited.

We backed carefully out of Clement's miniscule parking space and mounted the hill to Bois-Guillaume. I sat in the dugout and soaked in my new environs, the damp Normandy air soothing me as we watched the Bois-Guillaume softball team's victory over Le Club Andelysien de Baseball & Softball (CABS). (When it comes to jokes that only a Red Sox fan could find funny, the pitcher's #25 above the "CABS" logo on the back of a jersey surely tops the list).[14] After the game, we drove the 43 kilometers to Neufchâtel and my new, club-provided apartment.

We rode in silence down the Normandy autoroute as the shadows grew long. I wanted to exude friendliness and enthusiasm, but the day of travel, lugging those duffel bags around, and speaking so much French left me exhausted.

"*This is Neufchâtel?*" I asked when we finally pulled

---

[14] During the bad old days of the 1980s under General Manager Lou Gorman, the Red Sox clubhouse was so toxic it was described as "25 guys taking 25 cabs."

off the highway.

"*No, not yet,*" Clement responded. "*We're going to Eric's, to meet some other Woodchucks.*"

Great, I thought. Another awkward first meeting en masse. After miles of rolling hills, we entered a small, isolated complex of two-story houses separated by hedges and wire fences. I noticed the children's toys and playground swing in Eric's backyard, which reminded me of why he had relinquished the presidency.

"Salut Les Boys!" a voice shouted from the front door. I had heard that accent before, but couldn't quite place it. Slowly, it dawned on me: the thick nasal patois, the mixed Franglais... It was the Quebecois accent I learned on a middle school French trip to Montreal. I knew at once that it had to be Eric.

The second Clement said we would visit Eric, my guard had gone up. Our conversation at lunch had made clear that though he had officially ceased to serve as the club's president, Eric still wielded a great deal of influence around the club. The last guy I met fitting that description at a French baseball club had fired me, so I felt understandably cautious. Approaching the silhouetted figure, my eyes adjusted to the dim light until I could make out a slender man in his mid-30s, grinning jovially, with salt-and-pepper hair and a few days' stubble.

"Eh, Bonjour!" he shouted, pumping my hand in a vise-like grip, clasping his left hand over onto my forearm to make me feel welcome or prevent my escape. "*It is you, yes, Eh-von?*"

At that moment, even with the harsh sting of Savigny's unexpected rejection fresh in my mind, I knew that this Eric cat was alright. His eyes jumped out at you: wide with amazement, like a child overjoyed that his best friend had come over to play.

"Ah, oui. Eh-reek?" I responded, using the French pronunciation of 'Eric'.

"Bienvenue! Hey, I speaka, a little in-GLISH? Come on, Seb and Sylvain sont la-dedans, entrez, entrez!" Gesticulating wildly, he patted me on the back and greeted Clement, speaking rapidly blended English and French and ushering us into the living room, where we found Seb, Sylvain, and Eric's beautiful wife Virginie. (I later found out that in his youth, Eric served in the Canadian military, and to celebrate his honorable discharge, set out on a trip around the world. He intended to visit 50 countries, starting in France and continuing east, but only made as far as Normandy before meeting Virginie, falling in love, and settling down.) I felt my guard slipping as Virginie's hug and Seb, Sylvain, and Eric's warm smiles put me at ease despite myself.

"Une Bee-enh?" Eric asked, not waiting for a response before filling the frosted glass he had thrust into my hand from a liter of beer. I like these guys already, I thought. I would later find out that despite a litany of nagging injuries, Eric still pitched occasionally, caught, and filled in as shortstop or centerfielder on the elite team. He had relinquished his role as president before the prior season, but could not bring himself to leave the game, even with two young children whose cuteness rivaled the Minimes. Before it was even half-empty, Eric filled my glass again with beer: German, as it turned out, showing that Eric shared a taste for quality beer that couldn't be satisfied by the local swill like 1664, or as I called it, French Rolling Rock. We toasted to the season, and Eric complemented me on the game I pitched against them, calling my curve '*terrible*,' which translates best to 'nasty.' I agreed, as it's a fine line; some days it's *terrible*, and some days it's just plain terrible. Eric then grabbed a pen, and with Seb's help, started sketching out the list of players who would be there the next day.

"*We have Seb*," Eric began, pointing towards a grinning Seb. "*He plays shortstop. Also catcher. Matt-you*[15]*, the Australian, he won't arrive until Wednesday, but he plays third and pitches. For pitchers, we have...*" Uh oh, I thought. We don't have a lot of pitchers.

"*Quentin,*" Seb volunteered. "*The young one, from INSEP. He can also play infield.*"

"He's a good kid," Eric continued without missing a beat. "*Very good spirit. There's also Matt-tyuh, also*

[15] As will soon become clear, we had two Matts: Matthew, the Australian, which the natives pronounced as "Matt-you" in a nod to English pronunciation, and Mathieu, the young INSEP player, which followed the more typical French pronunciation of "Matt-tyuh," rhyming with "duh."

from INSEP."

Virginie made no effort to conceal a frown upon hearing the name. Sylvain looked away.

"*He's a good catcher,"* Eric blurted out. "*And I can play anywhere."*

"Anywhere?"

"All nine positions!"

"Oh la la!" Seb interrupted, gently mocking Eric's claims. "*First base?* This guy*..."*

"*You remember, last year, I played three innings against PUC!"* Eric responded, with mock outrage. "*No errors!"*

"Oh la la..." Seb and Sylvain murmured, with a dismissive intonation I recognized as the Norman equivalent of busting a guy's balls. It started at a low pitch before falling off entirely, conveying mocking disbelief.

"*There's also Vince, a good pitcher, a lefty."*

"He plays first, too?" I asked. Lefties are traditionally stuck with first base or the outfield, because it takes too

long to field ground balls at the other infield positions and turn to throw to first: a legacy of the game having been designed by righthanded people.

"Bien sur! *And Pierre, outfield or second base. Of course Aldo, left field, very intense, bats leadoff. Maybe Stephan will come, he plays catcher... Maybe Seb Grou or Eric Fournier?"*

"Not at elite, but maybe, if we need them." Seb interjected.

"*And Rafael, the Venezuelan.*"

"*Wow, another foreigner?"* I asked. Maybe this team had a little more talent than they showed at Savigny. Eric chuckled.

"*Not like you think... he's not here for baseball like you. On Sunday, he tried to do the bunt...*" The others giggled as Eric pantomimed squaring around to lay down a bunt, then recoiling as if punched in the face. "*Oh, the ball ricocheted right up and hit him in the eye, gave him an eye of butter black, a... how does one say,* bleck eye?"

I nodded, grinning ruefully. That list had only seven

or eight ballplayers.

"*And you, Sylvain? Where do you play?*"

"Uh..." He seemed uncomfortable with the question, but leaned in earnestly, eager to provide an answer. "*Uh... anywhere, uh... I don't play usually on the elite team, but can play third. I am not afraid of getting hit by the ball.*"

At 250 pounds, you shouldn't be, I thought. The ball should be more afraid of getting hit by you.

We chatted and sipped our beers. They seemed genuinely happy to have me there, welcoming me with open arms. If that sounds familiar, it's probably because I felt precisely the same way upon arriving in Savigny, and I flinched, wondering if my lingering elbow soreness could lead to similar rejection from the Woodchucks.

I understood roughly half of the rapid French exchanged between these close friends, a massive improvement from my first meeting with the Savigny board. Finally, Clement and I left to get a good night's sleep before the next day's games against Rouen. As we left, Virginie grabbed my arm and pulled me in close, locking eyes.

"*Win or lose*," she said in slow, deliberate French, "*Just improve the team ambience. Last year wasn't fun, and for the first time, I didn't want to go watch the games. I preferred to stay home.*" Her eyes attested to real anguish. "*Just make sure it's fun*."

CHAPTER 19: THE EMPIRE STRIKES BACK

Clement's persistent knocking awoke me from a deep slumber. I made coffee from the instant packs Virginie packed for us (she seemed genuinely embarrassed to give instant coffee to an *Americain*), and we drove the 45 minutes back to Bois-Guillaume from Neufchâtel. I tried to memorize the directions along the way, for the 49km (30 miles) on Normandy autoroute A-28 would soon become my daily commute.

I arrived to find the Rouen team already at Bois-Guillaume's humble field, looking every bit the Prussian invasion. Perhaps it was their military precision, or the shortstop with the blue eyes and blond hair, or their American ballplayer – from the University of San Francisco, no less – that had to excuse himself to stay on their tightly regimented schedule after I introduced myself as a friend of Troy's. The Huskies brought 18 ballplayers up the hill from Rouen, while we had only nine: welcome to the second division, I thought. With my elbow still sore, I played myself in left field, avoiding humiliation except in the fourth inning, when Rouen's catcher hit a towering fly ball to left center that seemed to hang up forever. I drifted, drifted, drifted, back and to my left, and caught up to it around the warning track. At the last instant, I snagged it in my glove while falling, diving, stumbling... mostly, I-don't-know-what-the-hell-I'm-doing-in-the-outfield-ing. Halfway through it, my failure to communicate that I had it resulted in a minor collision with Aldo, who had moved over to center to accommodate me. I had hoped to make a more graceful first impression.

I didn't know it at the time, but Aldo would become one of my best friends, and by far the most unforgettable character I met in France. Short and wiry, with a receding hairline that showed his 34 years of age, his intense solitary pre-game warmups revealed his burning passion for the game. I'm tempted to say that Aldo had a little bit of Napoleon in him, but in truth, I think Napoleon had a little Aldo. In nearly 20 years of organized baseball, I had never met anyone who wanted to win more than I did; Aldo was the first. He approached the game with a single-minded fury, a relentless determination to win at all costs, but he also displayed a level of respect for the game's institutions and etiquette that would be remarkable even in the U.S., never mind in a land where baseball ranked behind badminton in popularity.

An unrepentant bachelor and mama's boy, Aldo had turned his apartment into a shrine for his two loves: baseball and fantasy. Room-sized posters for the Lord of the Rings and Spiderman movies covered his bedroom walls. He had drawn slightly risqué sketches of female anime characters and hung them in his hallway, which always made me feel a little awkward when his mother came over from the apartment building next door to do his laundry and tidy his apartment. His living room featured miniature figurines from famous ballplayers throughout history, and his closet held caps from at least half of the teams in Major League Baseball. Months later, as I sat watching a Red Sox game on his internet connection at two in the morning – his job providing security to a large tech conglomerate allowed him to keep strange hours – I asked him how he had cultivated a passion for an American game for which most Frenchmen couldn't care less.

"*It's a mystery,*" he mused after a moment of reflection, his eyes glowing with wonder. "*A match came on TV, I think it was the Cubs... I watched it and I loved it, but... I just knew what was going on without anyone telling me the rules. Somehow, I knew them already. Then I found the Woodchucks and played as a* Minime. *I just showed up and started playing. I just knew how to play, just like that.*"

Aldo had been the Woodchucks' Cal Ripken: over 25 years with the same club. He had helped drive their improbable ascent from N1A to elite, and spoke with disgust of how players on that N1A championship team had voted to move into elite without fully considering the sacrifices it would require. Many had been All-Stars at the lower level, but struggled against the stronger elite division competition, and lacking Aldo's all-consuming devotion to the game, their commitment to the team waned accordingly. Throughout the summer, I saw his frustration at how far the team had fallen, and how its 'all-for-one' spirit had gone by the wayside.

In BG's all-wood dugouts, dotted here and there with youthful graffiti, I told Aldo the famous Yo La Tengo story[16] as I apologized for our collision. The dugout atmosphere needed some levity, as our young INSEP catcher Matthieu seethed with embarrassment, offering excuses for his booted ground ball an inning prior. "*You see,*" he said as one of the two American infielders from USF mishandled a ground ball. "*Even the American made an error!*"

My misadventure in left would not prove the final collision of the day, as I took an 0-2 curveball off the left bicep for my first French HBP in my second at-bat. Two batters later, I found myself at third when Seb

[16] Playing centerfield for the infamous 1962 Mets, Richie Ashburn suffered through a series of collisions with Venezuelan shortstop Elio Chacon, because the Spanish-speaking Chacon failed to understand Ashburn's screams of "I got it!" Ashburn learned to yell, "Yo la tengo!", Spanish for "I've got it." A few games later, Ashburn shouted "Yo la tengo!" running after a popup and saw that Chacon backed off, only to get run over by left fielder Frank Thomas, who spoke not a word of Spanish.

dinked a flare into left field. Retreating back to the base, I tagged up, even though Seb's pop fly was shallow. As soon as the ball hit the leftfielder's glove, I sprinted home, surprised to see the ball arrive a half-step before I got there.

One of my first questions to Fermin upon arriving in France concerned the legality of crashing the catcher. Adult leagues in the U.S. had the 'we have work on Monday' rule preventing collisions at the plate. It had made my week to hear that in France, I could knock the catcher flat. Unfortunately, I had started my slide without anticipating a play at the plate, so I could only give the catcher half a shoulder, like a fullback trying merely to slow down a blitzing linebacker with a chip block, instead of the bone-crushing, Ronnie Lott-style pancaking I would have preferred. Still, it proved sufficient, knocking the catcher on his back and squirting the ball loose as the Woodchuck crowd (all 20 of them) roared in appreciation. The takeaway was clear; anyone who stood up the crosstown bullies from Rouen, even in some small way, was welcome in Bois-Guillaume.

We played them tight until the fifth, when it quickly went from 11-7 to the final score of 25-9. Vince – the young lefty with the cockeyed hat that I recognized from the Savigny game – threw reasonably well, but left some fastballs up in the zone, and Rouen's bats warmed up in a hurry. They ripped three home runs in two innings, one a monumental blast to left that still hasn't landed.

We dropped the second game as well, hanging in for a few innings at 7-3 before it got out of hand. Two vaguely competitive games were as much of a success as we could have hoped for. Apparently, France's online baseball message boards had exploded after the dual 20-0 blankings of Bois-Guillaume by Savigny, the first of which had been my no-hitter. Some posters had questioned whether Bois-Guillaume really belonged in the elite division, while others criticized Savigny's foot-on-the-gas, base-stealing and hit-and-running in game two in order to reach the 20-run mercy rule cushion as quickly as possible. Despite Rouen's vastly superior talent, the Woodchucks put up enough of a fight to boost morale going into games that we had a more realistic chance of winning.

I was just happy to start hitting. Lost in the drama surrounding my departure from Savigny was an annoyingly ill-timed slump; I had started the season an unimpressive 1-for-7. Against Rouen, I lined a 2-1 fastball into left in my first at-bat, and then went down in the zone to pick an 0-2 curveball off of my shoe tops and smash a sinking liner past a diving shortstop, a good piece of bad-ball hitting that earned a look of wide-eyed appreciation from Eric in the first base coach's box.

"*I've always hit the curveball well,*" I said with a satisfied wink, finally starting to feel like the ballplayer I knew I could be.[17]

I finished 3-for-7 with a HBP, two runs, a stolen base, and an RBI. It wasn't dominant, but it led the Woodchucks in hits. It seemed to me that three hits every weekend would be the minimum necessary to keep my job, at least until I could earn some of my

---

[17] The pitcher throwing that curveball was named Joris Bert, a former Woodchuck poached by the Huskies. The following spring, he would be drafted 596th overall by the Los Angeles Dodgers, making him the first French MLB Draft pick. He lasted two seasons in the Gulf Coast League, hitting .240 before returning to France.

paycheck on the mound. Judging by the number of times I had to explain my forearm pain to every *Thomas*, *Richard*, and *Henri* in the dugout or on the picnic bench that housed our limited fanbase, the team was definitely disappointed that I couldn't pitch yet. While I outwardly expressed hope that I would pitch the coming weekend in Montpellier, my anxiety grew with every painful forearm twinge. Not pitching would make it harder for BG to justify keeping me on the payroll, but I also didn't want to come back too early and jeopardize my ability to take the mound in September, with the Woodchucks' demotion on the line.

I spent Sunday night doing my part to fight global warming by attaching half the ice in Normandy to my left wrist, right knee, and throwing elbow. Like many Americans, I relaxed with a little Sunday Night Baseball with Joe Morgan… with the exception that I watched a game between the Giants and Dodgers from 1992, on a VHS tape borrowed from the random assortment of decades-old games that constituted the Woodchucks' Baseball Library. Joe Morgan explained that the keys to the game for the Giants were keeping Brett Butler off the basepaths and getting to Orel Hershiser early, before segueing into a commercial for the ill-fated Olympics Triplecast. I noticed a young kid named Royce Clayton starting for the Giants, but he was hitting .186, and it didn't look like he would last very long in the Bigs. As I said, baseball's a funny game: Clayton would recover from that slump and go on to record 1,904 hits and make one All-Star game in a 17-year MLB career.

CHAPTER 20: OUT HERE IN THE FIELDS

On Monday, Sylvain, Seb, and Eric took me to the local supermarket, upholding the team's tradition of buying foreign players their first groceries to stock the fridge. As we stalked the aisles, loading up on cheap carbohydrates, Eric and Sylvain told me about Matt, the Australian who would arrive on Wednesday.

"*He's a very strong pitcher and third baseman,*" began Eric. "*You will like him, he is a...* bon vivant." He chuckled, rolling his eyes, as I looked at Sylvain for clarification.

"*He played for us last year with a friend of his, Ben, another Australian,*" Sylvain added. He stared down at his shopping cart, as if to escape Eric's influential gaze. I had already ascertained the power dynamic between them. After Eric's resignation and the leadership carousel during the disastrous 2005 season, Sylvain took over as president despite his youth and limited playing role as an emergency reserve on the elite team. As his shopping cart slowed to a halt near the curiously non-refrigerated boxes of milk popular in France, I could tell he wanted to speak his mind despite Eric's efforts to put a positive spin on things.

"*It was shit*," he finally exclaimed, ignoring Eric's glare. "*They complained a lot, smoked hashish, caused all sorts of problems. Matthew cost us 500 euros worth of phone calls home to Australia on the clubhouse phone, and denied it! Then they got drunk and drove the car around in circles on the soccer field. It was an embarrassment! The other one, Ben, he tried to hit on the young girls of the club!*"

"*Really?*" I blurted out, laughing at this unknown Australian's pure gall.

"*It's not funny!*" Sylvan shouted, throwing up his hands.

"Uh, of course not. It's not funny at all," I agreed, noting how the Australians' mischief remained something of a sore spot.

"We didn't want any more foreign players because of them, but Matt emailed us in March. He apologized for last year, and he said he wanted to come back, that he was very motivated this year. We didn't want him, but we needed a pitcher!" He spoke the last few words in mock falsetto, making the universal sign language gesture for 'not my idea' by cocking his head to one side and rolling his eyes with a shrug and a hand flourish.

"You'll like him," Eric interrupted, casting a sidelong glance at Sylvain. *"Here, have you had this? It's very, very good."*

He handed me a tin of pickled mackerel.

When I first met Matt on the corner of Rue de Joyeuse and Rue Coignebert, we shook hands. I didn't know it at the time, but we would never shake hands again. Clement had driven six hours roundtrip to De Gaulle

Airport to get him home in time for lunch with the Woodchucks' brain trust, but I detected no hint of gratitude from the burly newcomer. I introduced myself, chalking up his limp handshake and quick glance away from me to his fatigue from two long flights with a layover in Dubai. I got my first taste of Matt's volatile temper after that evening's practice, as the slim turnout prompted a stream of invective from the Australian, who cursed out the team for most of the ride to Seb's apartment in downtown Rouen. I drove; though 24 years of age, Matt did not possess a driver's license.

We dined at the apartment Seb shared with his girlfriend Zoe, where she made a delicious cheese-and-potato casserole he called *tartiflettes.* I recognized Zoe immediately as a pistol, noting her sassy attitude and the way she rolled her eyes every time Matt spoke. There was a history here.

Matt and I spent the next few days feeling each other out. I could tell he had a big chip on his shoulder, and his mercurial mood swings made for an unpredictable home environment. Sometimes he was chatty, as on his first day, when he asked me whether I supported President Bush. Other times, he would merely grunt in my direction, fixated on the television, which puzzled me, as France had but five or six channels, all showing profoundly bizarre French talk shows. I had trouble following along with them, so I asked Matt what was going on.

"Oh, fuck if I know, mate. I don't speak a fuckin' word of French."

"That sucks, man," I blurted out, trying to comprehend how a guy could spend seven months in a country and not pick up even a smattering of its syntactically and grammatically identical language.

"Couldn't be fucked, mate," he said, shaking his head and looking out the window. "Just couldn't be fucked."

Our isolation in the distant town of Neufchâtel-en-Bray didn't help. Famous for its eponymous soft cheese – whose reputation Kraft had unfortunately corrupted in America by using it to label its bland, low-fat cream cheese product – Neufchâtel was a good 45 minutes from Rouen. Before Matt's email in March, the Woodchucks hadn't planned to employ foreigners, so they were still scrambling for housing arrangements when Matt (and later, I) entered the picture. Luckily, one of Aldo's cousins was moving out of his apartment in Neufchâtel, leaving it empty for the summer. He donated it to the club free of charge, but its remote location proved suboptimal from the perspective of a horny-but-antisocial 24-year-old Australian.

"Unnnnnnnnnnnnnnnnnnnnnnnnnnh!" he groaned one morning, lying on the mattress we had set up in the spare room. "I can't fuckin' believe we're all the way fuckin' out here!"

I stared out the window at the idyllic cow-covered Neufchâtel hillside. Matt had a point.

"You want to go into town?" I said, hoping to change his mood.

"Nah, it's a fuckin' hour drive! Why waste the petrol?"

"No, I meant here, Neufchâtel. We could just walk downtown, see what there is to see." I didn't relish the awkward task of trying to cheer up someone who had no interest in cooperating. “We could grab lunch from one of those patisseries.”

“Man, those little shops are way too fuckin' expensive!” he shot back accusatorily, as if laying the blame for Normandy's (frankly, pretty low) cost of living squarely at my feet. “Besides, what the hell am I gonna do? I can't talk to these people.”

Such were our interactions. After a while, I stopped suggesting alternatives, knowing that they would meet with the same relentless negativity. If Matt wanted to go to Rouen, I drove, happy for an opportunity to check email, and otherwise, I was content to stay home and study for my upcoming CFA exam.

On Saturday, we met Eric, Seb, and Sylvain at Woodchucks world headquarters to grab the team's equipment before driving down the winding hill to the Rouen train station. The team piled onto the two-hour train to Paris, switching to the 14 line on the Paris metro at the St. Lazare and riding to Gare de Lyon, where we caught another train to Montpellier. If you ever want to get funny looks, bring a French baseball team through the Paris metro with sacks of bats, balls, and helmets.

Our late arrival forced me to break a rule I held ever since discovering In 'N' Out Burger: never, ever eat at McDonald's, or 'MacDo's,' as they called it Frogside. Fermin had insisted that it was better – or at least different – in France. It is not. Eating MacDonald's in France is like ordering Bud Light at Octoberfest: ill-advised and unnecessary given the vastly superior options available.

One Big Mac & fries later – ballgame or no, I refused to pay 6€ for a salad from Micky D's – we racked out at Montpelier's Formule 1 ('Formula 1') Hotel, the same chain of French budget hotels the Lions visited in La Guerche. Eric described the Formule 1 as an institution in French baseball, as its remote locations and cheap rates allowed teams to travel to away games without breaking the bank. Think 'EconoLodge,' but smaller, cheaper, and more... French. A ballclub can cram three players into a room about the size of a pitcher's mound, using a double bed and a lofted bunkbed. The woefully inadequate number of communal toilets and showers often leads to queues of strangers in the hallways during morning rush hour, waiting in their towels and bathrobes. These small shower cubbies have an auto-clean function that scrubs the recently abandoned vessel with boiling water, noxious gas, and spinning blades after every occupant leaves. I may have made that part up, but I still got nervous after a few minutes in one, worrying that the auto-clean might start with me still inside.

Formule 1 provides a free breakfast, or as the French seem to think of it, the least important meal of the day. French cuisine is of course amazing, but it lacked a counterpart to the grand American breakfasts of eggs, home fries, and bacon. Instead, the F1 hooked guests up with bread, butter, and coffee: the daily rations at the Chateau D'If during the Monte Cristo days. Like the bathrooms, this meal is communal, meaning that a French baseball team troops down to the lobby to eat this bread-and-butter feast with the same stunned travelers it just met outside the showers.

Every field in France had its quirks, but the home of

the Montpellier Barracudas exemplified French baseball in all of its overenthusiastic, ill-advised glory. The ballfield – a term I use loosely – looked like the grounds crew had used an aerial shot of a ballpark as a template but had received the photonegative, with the colors reversed. It featured an all-dirt outfield and an artificial turf infield. Most strikingly, the artificial turf – about six inches thick, with a sturdy black rubber base underneath the familiar green surface – simply sat atop the infield dirt. The grounds crew hadn't bothered to dig down six inches and excavate the dirt so the turf could sit level with the dirt basepaths. Instead, there was a half-foot lip all around the infield, wreaking havoc on infielders. Balls might unexpectedly ricochet up to a fielder's neck, as he tried to avoid spraining his ankle running from turf to dirt. Hitters were not immune from the danger: with a six-inch wall a few feet in front of home plate, hard ground balls could hit the lip and rebound back at the hitter's face for an embarrassing and painful foul ball. The outfield wasn't much better. Depending on the compactness of the dirt, a groundball could squirt all the way to the wall or hit a sandy patch and stop before an outfielder could scoop it up. Wrigley Field it was not.

Matt's bristling body language during the long trip south put me on edge for the game's lineup decision. Hoping to get him on my side, I cut my own warm-up short – not a problem given the searing elbow pain I felt with every throw – to grab the lineup card and sidle up to Matt on the bench.

"What do you think, hombre?" I said, blowing a bubble and trying to affect an insouciant cool that belied my growing apprehension about how Matt would act as a teammate and fellow coach. His withering stare suggested we had a bumpy road ahead.

"I was thinking Aldo first, Matthieu second, then you hitting third. Sound good?" I soldiered on with the same faux cheery confidence.

"Yeah, whatever."

Perhaps this would be easier than I thought. I could deal with apathy.

"Cool. Eric told me you played third, so I was going to..."

"Nah, I'm not playing fuckin' third this year." He spat

a stream of tobacco juice from the leftover Skoal I lent him, found some caught in his teeth, and started picking at the obstructing tobacco shreds with his index finger.

Silence. I waited for an explanation why he refused to play the position that would maximize his value. None came.

“Alright, man,” I began, trying to hide my exasperation. “Just tell me where you want to play.”

“Don’t give a fuck, mate.” A long pause ensued, as I contemplated sticking him at catcher just to see his reaction. “Center.”

I penciled Matt into centerfield, and myself at second base, batting fifth. Despite icing it all week, my elbow exploded in agony on my first warmup throw, constraining me to dart-style throws for the rest of the game to minimize pain. I can’t lie: it was pretty ugly.

We started Vince again, and for the first time I could watch him closely from the infield. His two-seam fastball ran away from right-handers, but he relied on a big, sweeping curveball as his out pitch. He struggled with his control, walking the first two hitters before giving up consecutive fly balls that Aldo misread, turning outs into doubles and leading to four runs in the first inning. I settled in for a long day. The Barracudas were their own worst enemy, though, running into two double plays and losing two runners to Vince's devious pickoff move.

"*Nice job, buddy!*" I exclaimed in the dugout to Vince. "*Those runners didn't know what hit them!*"

"Bah, oui..." Vince responded with a self-deprecating smirk and a gesture at his chest, as if to say 'obviously, why would you expect anything less from a pitcher of my stature?' Bah – sometimes sounding more like 'pah' to my American ears, as if the speaker had started making the 'B' or 'P' sound but gave up halfway through – was one of those weird little French interjections whose meaning varied based on context. Here, it translated loosely as 'come ON guys... it's ME we're talking about,' like ironically flipping one's hair or brushing imaginary dirt off one's shoulder in mocking self-congratulation.

With that kind of attitude, Vince and I were going to

be good friends.

Meanwhile, we scratched out only three hits, but parlayed them into five runs – with me scoring two of them – through six, finding ourselves down 6-5. At the end of the seventh, jogging back to the dugout, I caught Matt as we approached the bench. Upset at having popped out with two men on to end a rally in the top half, I wanted to change things up and try to get something out of the offensive black hole the bottom of our lineup had been all day.

"Hey, man, hold up," I muttered quietly, tapping Matt on the shoulder. "I'm thinking bunt-and-run if we get a guy on and get ahead in the count. Whatta ya say?"

I hadn't pegged Matt as a guy who loved to chew on questions of strategy, but it seemed courteous to discuss it, even if my imagined scenario was so unlikely that only 'France Invades Belgium En Route to Berlin' might raise more eyebrows. Still, I never anticipated the look of revulsion on Matt's face.

"Fuck me, mate, I don't give a shit."

Our conversation had taken us to the third base

coach's box, where I stood for a second, staring vacantly at Matt's retreating figure. I glanced around at the Woodchucks hustling back to the dugout, hoping none had heard Matt's disinclination even to *pretend* to care about the game's outcome. Fortunately, I found no one listening, and spat in disgust before turning to stare out at centerfield. To look on the bright side, Matt's hostile apathy meant that I could call for a bunt whenever I damn well felt like it.

After a leadoff walk, I called for the hit-and-run, which paid off with an infield hit. We loaded the bases on another walk, bringing Pierre to the plate. One of the youngest Woodchucks, Pierre stuck out like a sore thumb on the team's roster. He was roughly the same age Quentin and Matthieu, but had little in common otherwise. The latter two lived at INSEP, three hours from Bois-Guillaume, and played on the Woodchucks only temporarily as 'mutés,' players lent from INSEP to elite teams to spur their growth as ballplayers. Pierre lived at home with his family, whose involvement in the Bois-Guillaume club merited a soap opera.

He and his brother Yves grew up playing with the

Woodchucks' youth teams, while their uncle Jean-Luc coached the N1A team under Eric's presidency. Over time, friction had grown between Jean-Luc and Eric, and last year's scandals – one of which involved Jean-Luc's daughter Laura accusing Matthew of walking in on her naked, a charge that both Matt and Jean-Luc denied – compelled him to leave Bois-Guillaume to coach an N1A team three hours away in Cherbourg. Pierre remained at Bois-Guillaume, though whether out of loyalty to the club, discomfort with his uncle's heavy-handed managerial style (he reportedly had signs for 15 different bunt variations, a level of complexity far exceeding the team's talent), or mere inertia, I never knew. I was just 10 days into my time at Bois-Guillaume, and knew none of this backstory. I recognized Pierre as by far the most studious, cerebral Woodchuck, but my impression of him centered around two things: his voice, and his swing.

Pierre spoke two octaves higher than any male his age, in a falsetto whisper resembling thin ice in the Alps: impossibly high and ready to crack at any second. Though I eventually came to look past his caterwauling and appreciate the caring, thoughtful individual behind it, my first exposure to his Owen Meany-esque screech had me looking around at my teammates, certain they had conspired to play a joke on the American.

Unfortunately, his swing made his voice sound like Barry White by comparison. Pierre swung a baseball bat like a man on a surfboard trying to hit a moth with a balloon animal. As Pierre stepped to the plate with the bases loaded and nobody out, 0-for-2 on the day with two ugly strikeouts, it occurred to me that perhaps a bunt made sense.

When the count went to 1-1, I had to take the bat out of his hands. I flashed the bunt sign, and he nodded; never a good move if you have any interest in disguising your intentions. He stepped in, squared far too early, and reached out of the strike zone, popping the bunt foul. At 1-2, I resisted the temptation to call for another bunt, and let him swing away, regretting it immediately when he started his wristy, moth-swatter's hack a full second late on an inside fastball.

With only one out, we still had an opportunity to put some runs on the board. I gave leadoff man Aldo the bunt sign on 2-1, and he also fouled it off before striking out, chasing a fastball up out of the zone. He slammed the bat on the ground and stalked back to the dugout, fuming.

Matthieu tapped weakly to second to end the threat. Shaking my head, I grabbed my glove and trotted out to second base, only to watch a clearly tiring Vince give up two more runs; lacking bullpen depth, we had no choice but to stretch Vince as far as he could go. We threatened again in the ninth, forcing Montpellier to bring in their hard-throwing submarine closer to finish us off, sort of a French Dan Quisenberry ("Le Q"). With two outs and the bases juiced, Pierre surprised everyone by hitting a high chopper just out of the pitcher's reach, and for an instant I thought he might beat it out. The shortstop made a genuinely impressive play, charging in and throwing a dart on the run to get Pierre by two steps: game over.

In the second game, I got my first look at Matt, who threw five solid innings, giving up two runs. He had a powerful fastball that ran into the mid-80s, and mixed in a baffling splitter that knuckled wildly on its way to the plate. We trailed 3-2 in the seventh, when I lofted a soft, sinking liner into left and took second as the ball squirted off the left fielder's glove. We tied it on a sac fly to center, and I stole third on the next pitch before scoring on a wild pitch to give us an unexpected 4-3 lead.

At the end of the inning, Eric motioned me towards the end of the dugout, speaking hesitant, broken English. "You think that Matt... He could..." He glanced around quickly.

"Francais*, Eric,* Francais*, go ahead.*"

"*Do you think that Matt could come in to close the game? Just one inning, maybe?*" he continued in French. "*It would be incredible to win this match.*"

"*I'll ask, Eric... I don't know.*"

Bracing myself, I walked over and tapped Matt on the shoulder.

"Hey man," I began. "This would be a huge win if we can pull it off. No one expected us to hang with these guys. You got another inning in you? I know you already threw 90 pitches, but we're running out of arms, and it would break these guys' backs if they saw our big Australian hoss coming back into the game."

I looked over at the Barracuda bench, clearly invigorated by Matt's absence. Turning back to Matt, I saw only a supercilious stare and an apathetic shrug.

"I'm just saying, man... your health is more important than any one game, but Eric wanted to know if you had it in you. Otherwise we've got to run Eric or Seb out there... who knows how that'll go."

Matt shook his head and looked away, discharging a long stream of tobacco juice.

"Ah, mate, what the fuck?" He spat again. "What, they think I'm some rubber arm?"

He turned to stare at the hillside. He was making up his mind, and to this partial observer, it didn't look good for the Woodchuck nine that day.

"Nah," he continued. "I'm not doin' it. Fuck that."

I looked down at my shoes, trying to hide my disappointment. "Okay, man," I said, starting to nod slowly. "Okay. That's fine. Hey, great job earlier." I patted him again on the shoulder, and jogged back to

Eric, noticing the entire bench staring at us as Quentin popped out. Plunking myself down next to Eric, I stared out at the field and shook my head. "*He says he's finished.*"

Eric's shoulders slumped, and we both knew it was over. "*I am sorry. I tried to convince him.*"

Though unquestionably the inferior team, we had pushed the Barracudas right to the brink and nearly taken game one, forcing them to use their closer to finish us off with the tying run on second. In game two, we suddenly found ourselves up a run with nine outs to go, clinging desperately to a fragile lead and hoping the wheels would stay on the bus long enough for us to sneak out of town with a stolen win.

As so often happens against a superior team, the wheels did not stay on the bus.

They fell off the bus.

They rolled down the street.

They ricocheted off an onrushing 16-wheeler.

They bounced over the cliff, plummeting out of sight before emitting one last soft {poof!} and an accompanying Wile E. Coyote-esque puff of smoke upon impacting the canyon floor below. Four hits, four errors, three hit batsmen, and three walks later, we found ourselves on the wrong end of a 10-4 loss that had seemed so promising just two innings earlier.

We showered in silence and drove back to Montpellier in the Barracuda's minibus, making our train just in time.

It was small consolation that no one expected us even to play the first-place Barracudas close. Had we not wasted so many opportunities in the first game and played better defense in the second, we could have pulled out both despite the vast talent discrepancy. Frustratingly, it would have helped had we had another arm in the bullpen, I don't know, maybe a hard-throwing American just dumb enough to think he could have made a difference if his elbow didn't scream in protest every time he tried to throw. While I had certainly shown my capacity to get lit up by the better teams in France, I knew that if I had been at 100%, we would have had a shot at that second game.

So ended the Woodchucks' brief and unexpected

appearance in third place. On Thursday night, the Tres Lettres had confirmed the rumor that Savigny's treasurer – Philippe, the same guy that had given me the pink slip – had been tardy in mailing the check for four players' licenses to the Federation. That meant they had all played illegally in my four games with the Lions, all wins against La Guerche and Bois-Guillaume that would become forfeit losses, dropping Savigny from 4-0 to 0-4. Meanwhile, another Parisian team called Senart had used too many foreigners; only two can play at the same time, and the coach had foolishly gambled that a third foreigner's recent marriage to a French woman would naturalize him in time so as not to count against the two-foreigner limit. Savigny therefore retroactively forfeited their first four games 9-0, and Senart forfeited its two opening day wins against Bois-Guillaume. The Woodchucks had benefited doubly, turning four losses (two of them 20-0 drubbings by the Lions) into four wins and finding themselves 4-2 going into Montpellier.

It also closed the door on the Ev Meagher era in Savigny. Instead of 4-0, the team's record under my stewardship will forever stand an ugly 0-4; no wonder they fired me! Moreover, the Federation's decision wiped my pitching appearance against Bois-Guillaume from the books, making me the answer to a pretty good French baseball trivia question: name the only pitcher to throw a no-hitter and lose.

CHAPTER 21: ROCKET 88

We got back to the Rouen train station late that night. Matt and I hopped into our club-provided car for the long drive back to Neufchâtel. My recent relocation had introduced many new characters into my life, but I held closest to my heart my new automobile, christened Le Woodsmobile. It was new to me, anyway, as it appeared to have bounced around Normandy since the Reagan administration.

Officially a 1986 Renault Spring 5, Le Woodsmobile's idiosyncrasies (like the huge faded woodchuck logo with the shit-eating grin on the hood) begat its true charm. For example, the heat defiantly refused to turn off, and many team members thought that contributed to its gas mileage, which resembled an SUV towing a speedboat with the anchor down. It struggled mightily up hills, and I risked both my life and my rotator cuff when attempting to turn a steering wheel seemingly equipped with power anti-steering. The radio had but one functioning speaker, located just above the right rear wheel, and the driver's seat had long remained locked at an angle of recline that Superfly might have chosen had he deigned to cruise downtown Bois-Guillaume looking for talent. In short, Le Woodsmobile was a ray of sunshine on even the cloudiest of days, one that never failed to make me smile every time I saw it and wince when I had to drive it.

Unlike the urban sprawl of most U.S. cities, Rouen ends the moment one leaves downtown, and the autoroute to Neufchâtel quickly becomes an idyllic panorama of horses, hills, and haystacks. On the average morning drive into B-G, I saw more cows than cars, the big beasts grazing happily between overgrown German bunkers on land valued some 60 years earlier at hundreds of human lives per square mile. Matt and I spent a good part of that summer driving around

Normandy in a car roughly the size of an American refrigerator. I shouldn't overstate Le Woodsmobile's importance, but I soon separated my life into two parts: the part in which I drove the Woodsmobile, and the part in which I did not, which I forgave only because it led to the former.

The shortage of French radio stations added to the absurdity of our commute to Bois-Guillaume; there were exactly two. One was called Skyrock, and seemed, from what I could discern of the breakneck, slang-heavy French that dominated its airwaves, something akin to a top 40 station back home, taken to the extreme by playing only a handful of songs ad infinitum.

The other station didn't come in very well.

Stuck with Skyrock, we heard the same four songs, over and over and over again, all summer long. I will never forget them; I never *could* forget them, burned as there are into my memory from literally hundreds of listenings.

Jeune Demoiselle by Diam's

S.O.S. (Rescue Me) by Rihanna

Enfants de la Lune ('Children of the Moon') by Ana Torroja & Psy 4 de la Rime

Snitch by Obie Trice, featuring Akon[18]

By mid-May, the steady diet of the same crappy hip-hop songs had me ready to drive the Woodsmobile off a cliff. Fortunately, Wednesday practices kept me sane, after which the usual suspects of Eric, Seb, Sylvain, and Aldo would invite Matt and me for a kebab and a beer. Kebabs are the French equivalent of burrito joints; ubiquitous, cheap greasy spoons offering delicious comfort food with high cholesterol content. The kebabs were run by immigrant Greeks, Turks, and Arabs who had brought their native cuisine to France. During these weekly kebab trips, I came to love an Arabic treat called 'basbousa,' a cake of honey suspended in semolina, baked in a sheet and sliced into squares. (It's popular throughout the Middle East, and goes by other names like namoura, revani, and hareseh, depending on location.) The sugar content bordered on criminal,

---

[18] Through the wonders of technology, I created a playlist so you can get the full Woodsmobile experience: https://tinyurl.com/ybkl2zzm

and after one or two basbousas, I felt like I could walk out of the kebab shop and lift the Woodsmobile over my head.

We then proceeded to the Underground Pub, the only local establishment that carried Sylvain's favorite: Beamish Irish Stout. Sylvain had really grown on me. His shock at discovering that I only ate maybe 25 hamburgers a year cracked me up; he apparently assumed that Americans ate them twice daily. I found his toothy grin infectious, and his enthusiasm for Irish beer and Larry Bird familiar. One night, after a few post-practice beers, Sylvain led the charge to head downstairs to check out the Underground's karaoke scene.

I always prided myself on being a good teammate, which can mean a lot of things: giving a pep talk to a slumping hitter, staying late to practice bunting, or sacrificing yourself to move a runner over. As I learned that night, sometimes it means playing wingman throughout the wee, tiny hours of the morning in the nightclubs of Rouen while your Australian roommate chats up a pair of Mexican exchange students. They were studying business at the local French university, which seemed akin to taking courses in Feminist Studies at the Citadel.

Matt aggressively pursued one of the ladies as I nursed my beer. When he sweet-talked his – unfortunately, *our* – way into an invitation to return to their dorm, I put my foot down.

"No way I'm driving dude," I tried to reason with him. "We've had way too much to drink. Come on, let's just crash at Seb's place."

"Fine, fuck it man, I'll drive."

This proved to be a terrible idea. As we careened through the streets of Rouen with an unlicensed Aussie of questionable sobriety at the wheel, I made a silent checklist of who should receive what in the event of my passing. We whizzed past a music store, and I resolved that my sister should get my CD collection (it was 2006, after all); a near-collision with a newspaper kiosk reminded me to give my framed Boston Globe from the 2004 World Series to my father. Matt brushed a curb as he turned off the main road, and the girls in the back flinched.

"Hey- Australian!" Matt bellowed with a shrug. He had used it as a flirtatious excuse throughout the night, each time one of the girls reprimanded him for being too rude or too aggressive. With white knuckles and a sense of pure amazement, we arrived safely at the girls' dorm, having stalled only twice at the red lights at which Matt deigned to stop.

Matt's dogged pursuit of one girl left me alone in the cramped dorm room of the other, making small talk in an effort to deflect what was becoming increasingly clear as a make-out attempt. Commenting on the time, I offered to grab a few Z's on the floor, but she insisted that I take the bed while she inflated an air mattress. Exhausted beyond the point of chivalry, I agreed and quickly fell into a deep slumber.

That's *definitely a hand,* I thought to myself suddenly, my sleep interrupted by a rustling underneath my borrowed blanket. And yup; that is definitely my crotch.

"WHOA! Hey! Hold on there," I started, springing out

of the prone position to find my host positioned over me aggressively.

"What? What's wrong?" she slurred, confused.

"Look, I, uh..." I rolled my eyes. "Look, I just- I can't. I'm flattered, I just..."

"What? Is it true? Are you..." Her eyes opened wide, pupils the size of neurons. "...Gay?"

I flashed back to earlier in the evening. In wooing his preferred target, Matt had turned to my host and boozily exclaimed "Hey, don't worry about him- he's gay! Ha! Just kidding." He pointed to himself. "See? *Australian!*" Clearly, the comment had stuck with her.

"No, Jesus, I'm not–" my years of living in San Francisco kicked in – "look, there's nothing wrong with that, it's just..." I gave up, figuring that someone else could fight the gay rights battle with my new catholic friend. "Look, I have a girlfriend, and I just can't."

"You do?" she asked, unconvinced.

"Yes. Look- I'm sorry."

She paused, squinting as if to see past the façade and

identify my lifestyle of rainbow flags, Madonna dance parties, and sticking my head into the mouths of tigers.

"But... don't you think it is a sin to be gay?"

For the first time since meeting him, I laughed – albeit bitterly – at one of Matt's jokes. *Fucking Matt.*

"No. I don't. Good night."

A time-lapse video of that night would show a repeating cycle wherein I fled her awkward non-embrace to the air mattress, only to be awakened sometime later by her renewed and surprisingly determined effort to place a drunken kiss in the general vicinity of my lips. After parrying a few advances with my sleepy aikido, I would retreat to the high ground of the small mattress, and the cycle would repeat. As soon as the sun streamed through the blinds, I bolted out of bed, thanked Isabella for her hospitality, and hightailed it out of there, calling Matt's cell ten or twelve times until he finally answered and met me at the Woodsmobile.

"Fuckin' A, mate," he started. "That bird had plastic sheets on her *bed*. What's that about?"

I shrugged.

"You reckon she pisses herself?"

Exhausted but already focused on the doctor's appointment that Eric had arranged for me that afternoon, I simply couldn't muster the enthusiasm to pursue this great mystery.

"Who knows, man," I muttered. "Who knows."[19]

That Thursday, I met Eric at the doctor's office, my elbow still feeling like it had been stabbed with a rusty steak knife. Already fired once for pitching poorly, I winced at the prospect of being fired for not pitching at all. On the way, Matt's words over dinner two nights earlier echoed through my head.

"You better get that elbow in shape, mate," he spat. "Foreigners here... they want you to pitch or hit bombs. If you don't pitch..." He had studied my face, taking obvious pleasure in my discomfort.

---

[19] Several friends argued I should delete this section, but I didn't, because it happened. Moreover, it humanizes Matt. If it isn't clear by now to the reader, Matt was a very good ballplayer, a terrible roommate, and a vastly worse teammate. Literally none of the things Matt ever did felt relatable to me, except this one, where he was just a mid-20s single guy trying to 'move, shoot, and communicate' – as my Dad said from his Navy days – with the opposite sex. As completely shitty as he was to be around on a daily basis, Matt deserves to be humanized, at least on the rare occasions when he acted like a human being. This was one of those times.

The doctor ushered us in and complimented me on my French. He examined the elbow and took a few scans, declaring that the inflammation in my elbow had resulted from me favoring my surgically-repaired shoulder. Not serious, he determined; it simply needed anti-inflammatories, ice, and rest.

I prayed he was right.

CHAPTER 22: ENFANT TERRIBLE

Anger.

When I think of Matt, the first word that comes to mind is anger. He had torrents of anger churning inside of him, rivers of bile that spilled out on everyone in his immediate proximity. I never did figure out why; for whatever reason, Matt greeted the world with a sneer and an upturned lip, seeing people and things only as potential threats or potential targets. Even as I write this, my vexation having faded over the decade since my last contact with the man, I know it would be fundamentally dishonest of me to describe him – or at least, the 2006 version of him that I got to know – as anything less than a bitter, greedy, dishonest malcontent, an inferno of borderline sociopathic hostility whose concern for others ended at the tip of his nose and whose directionless rage knew no boundaries.

He was also, however, a great pitcher.

Especially in France.

Standing 6'1", 235 pounds, Matt had prototypical right-handed power pitcher physique and mechanics. He had nasty stuff and pinpoint control, and in a league full of less physically imposing Frenchmen, his contemptuous scowl made him every bit as intimidating on the mound as it made him insufferable off it.

Our roommate situation spiraled rapidly out of control. His resentment of everything and everyone wore on me, and his unique perspective on baseball baffles me to this day. Matt respected no ballplayer unless they were better than him. With such ballplayers in short supply in France, he was, to paraphrase Phillies GM Ed Wade's comments on Curt Schilling, a horse every seventh day, a horse's ass the other six.

With a hostile Australian as the only Anglophone in my life, I could not wait to welcome Alex and Jools to town. One of my closest friends in the world, Alex held a unique distinction as my only 'daughter,' having followed me in the lineage of the disgrace/honor that is the Stanford marching band's Tree mascot. She left London at 18 to play volleyball at Stanford before turning to less respectable pursuits like being the Tree, infecting everyone with her devil-may-care attitude, relentless pursuit of hijinks, and ability to drink massive quantities of lager. After graduation, she took a job teaching and coaching north of London, where she met and married Jools, a jovial Welshman that everyone liked immediately.

I picked them up at the Rouen train station so we could do what we do best: talk about how cool we once were over a few cold ones. I realized with a grin that my life had become so bizarre that drinking Normandy cider with two Brits at a sidewalk café in Rouen could make me feel *more* at home. I reveled in the opportunity to shoot the bull with a few friendly faces and relax, speaking comfortably in English with someone other than Matt, without fear of offending a French host with a misconjugated verb.

I had crossed an ocean, staked my job on my tenuous baseball skills, and taken life with an ill-tempered Aussie in stride, but friends like Alex and Jools kept me focused on the bigger picture. Sure, the ever-looming specter of getting fired again loomed large, but their words of support reminded me that I had the greatest friends in the world rooting for me, friends who would hang even my modest accomplishments on the moon. After all, as they pointed out, I had already succeeded; I had convinced not one but two teams to pay me to play baseball. "You'll always be able to tell your kids that, Evan!" Jools pointed out. "'Shaddup! Yer Dad was a professional baseball player. Eat your greens.'" For that, I will always be in their debt.

I bid them goodbye the next morning at their cheap downtown hotel, trying to conceal my disappointment at the prospect of returning to life without them. Matt picked me, hopping unceremoniously from the Woodsmobile's driver's seat so I could drive us back to

Neufchâtel, where we had promised to help Eric build his new house.

Eric had recently purchased a ramshackle turn-of-the-century brick house on a beautiful lot just outside town, and we eagerly accepted his offer to work renovating the place as a way to help out a teammate and earn a few extra Euros. It was a big project, to put it mildly. Built around the same time as Fenway Park, it consisted of crumbling brick walls and a dilapidated barn. We started by demolishing an upper floor with crow bars on a jobsite that would make OSHA blush, then smashed through a layer of tile and dug down ten inches to make room for the sub-floor heating coils popular in France. We faced our first setback when Matt threw his crowbar down and refused to continue.

"Look at this, mate, it's a fuckin' joke! I'm not gonna break my fuckin' back for this shit! I got 250 Australian from my mate back home for work like this! I'm not gonna slave away up here, we might fuckin' break an ankle!"

"How many Euros is 250 Australian?" I asked, trying to change the subject as I yanked away another hay-encrusted beam from the crumbling ceiling.

"Eh, it's like half, so what, hundred or so Euro." He rested his chin on the handle of his shovel, scowling.

"What the hell, man. Might as well take the extra paycheck where we can get it."

We broke for lunch and cold Heinekens, and I took solace in the fact that the backbreaking work hadn't aggravated my elbow. I connected my iPod to a mini-speaker, and we passed the day swinging shovels in Normandy, listening to the Meters and the Stones, feeling like the inmates re-tarring the roof at Shawshank. I soaked up the Normandy sun and looked forward to avenging my broken bats against the great Antoni Piquet.

That night, another Eric – Woodchucks backup Eric Fournier – invited us to his half-completed house near Forges-Les-Eux to watch the soccer match between Paris Saint-Germain and Olympique Marseille. A diehard southerner, Fournier rooted hard for Marseille as we watched on a tiny screen in his unfinished upstairs loft, accessible only by ascending a rickety ladder. As we watched Marseille defeat their rivals in the French equivalent of a midseason Red Sox-Yankees match, Matt demanded more and more wine, despite Fournier's pleas that he slow down, for fear of having a headache the next day against La Guerche.

"Nah, mate, I'll be fine," Matt insisted. "Pass the fucking wine, eh?"

CHAPTER 23: GOOD TIMES, BAD TIMES

Two baseball teams meet on a Normandy field for a doubleheader and do the exact same thing: win one, lose one. One is thrilled, the other furious. Guess which one I played for?

Against powerhouses like Savigny, La Guerche matched Piquet up against the weaker starter, hoping to steal a split. Against weaker teams like the Woodchucks, they did the opposite, throwing Piquet against our better starter, assuming they would win the other game. Meanwhile, Bois-Guillaume knew they could beat the Hawks with a few breaks, even against Piquet. A few bounces here or there, and who knows?

My excitement for the rematch made it hard to sleep

on Saturday night; even a call from Becky failed to calm me down. She had been a real trooper during the weeks since her departure, calling me religiously despite the time differential and my inability to call her on my team-provided cell phone. I always left my ringer on at night, never knowing when she might dial me up and introduce a little sunshine into the generally wretched home environment I shared with Matt.

That night, however, I wanted no sunshine; like the New England Patriots, I clung to any slight, real or imagined, to spur my motivation. Four weeks of hindsight had allowed me to convince myself that busting two bats and failing to pitch against La Guerche had contributed to my dismissal in Savigny. I wanted revenge.

After a scoreless top half of the first, I kicked the dirt in the back of the batter's box with my right foot to dig in and lead off against Piquet. The umpire cried 'play ball!' in a thick accent, and I barely blinked before finding myself behind Piquet 0-2. Furious, I battled him for eight or nine pitches, fouling off three breaking balls and fighting off a fastball down and in while taking a few balls away. I doubt that he recognized me as the American from Savigny whose bats he'd unceremoniously broken, but he saw me crowding the plate, and tried to bust me inside with a fastball on the hands once we reached a full count.

In my years as a San Francisco Red, I took pride in never avoiding a fastball inside enough to earn me a free pass to first base, so I often led the league in HBP. Piquet missed the zone by just three inches, but it was enough for me to take the heater off the bicep, jogging to first with the voices of Reds regulars Ben and Dallas shouting "DON'T RUB IT!" ringing in my ears. I stole second, but was stranded there. Jogging back to the dugout, I hoped that the Woodchucks' brain trust valued on-base-percentage as highly as their American counterparts like Billy Beane, made famous in Michael Lewis' *Moneyball.* Until my arm recovered and I could pitch again, sparking the offense from the leadoff spot was the only way I could earn my paycheck.

Things got interesting in the seventh, as I came to bat with no outs and two men on. Suddenly, the heavens opened, and the umpire signaled for a rain delay, but not before I noticed the third baseman playing me deep behind the bag. When play resumed 20 minutes later, I laid a perfect bunt down the third baseline, beating it to first without a throw for my second hit of the day.

Good pitchers reach back for something extra with runners on base, and I give Piquet credit; he did just that with the bases juiced. He struck out three Woodchucks looking to eliminate the threat, and that was all she wrote. La Guerche had capitalized on opportunities with runners on base, and our inability to return the favor proved the difference in the game. The seventh inning marked the second time in three games that we had loaded the bases with no outs and failed to score: 6 batters, 5 strikeouts, one groundout, zero runs. It's impossible to imagine worse situational hitting.

After the 6-1 loss, we gathered on the grass behind the third-base dugout, as Matt had declared before the game that every team always uses the third base dugout as its home dugout.

"Uh, no, Matt..." I had blurted out, already regretting contradicting him. "At Fenway, they don't. Or in Baltimore. Kansas City." He glared at me. "Seattle, too,

Saint Louis... Texas. Philly, I think." Matt's exasperated sneer made clear the worthlessness of the confrontation, so I threw up my hands, and we took the third-base dugout.

Between games back home in San Francisco, guys usually ate sandwiches or fruit. In France, ballplayers had full lunches prepared by their wives or girlfriends, including an éclair or chocolate croissant for dessert. Point, France. As we gathered for the second game, I reiterated my pep talk from that morning. "*We were in that game, we just didn't take advantage of opportunities. Game two will be different. Today, we play to win.*"

We started poorly, as young Matthieu from INSEP couldn't find the strike zone, walking three in the first. He almost wriggled out of the jam, but with the bases loaded, two outs, and a 3-2 count, the runners took off with his windup, spooking him, his pitch sailing to the backstop. The runner from third scored easily, but Matthieu's outburst of performative frustration – stomping his feet and turning away from home plate as if to show everyone in attendance how *unlike him* that was – distracted him just long enough to allow another runner to score all the way from second base on the wild pitch. It was embarrassing; La Guerche hustled while our guy dogged it. I never faulted a ballplayer for making a physical error, because you can't just will yourself to become more talented or more skilled in the moment... but errors of laziness or carelessness were literally the only things you *could* control.

Free passes plagued Matthieu again in the second, putting us down 5-0 with a potentially long day ahead of us. Recognizing the body language of a broken man, I put Matthieu on a short leash in the third. After two more four-pitch walks, Matthieu stabbed at the throw back from Seb, turning and shaking his head furiously as I noticed something I had not seen since Little League; Matthieu was starting to cry.

Lacking pitching depth – it was always a struggle to find 18 innings every weekend – it made sense to try to squeeze another inning out of him. A nasty little part of me wanted to let him twist in the wind not for tactical reasons, but to teach him a lesson. It hadn't taken long for me to recognize the divisive element that little

Matthieu brought to the club. Every weekend, upon arriving with Quentin from INSEP on a train ticket purchased by the club, he made it clear that he considered playing for Bois-Guillaume beneath him. He styled in the batter's box, preening like a young, French, white, 5-foot-6 Barry Bonds, twirling his bat with a hubris that belied his sub-.200 batting average and more than two strikeouts per game. Off the field, draped in the baggy jeans and flat-brimmed hats of the American rappers whose braggadocio he so desperately attempted to emulate, he mocked and condescended to the other young players like Vince and Pierre, in a clumsy effort to reinforce his superiority as one of the players chosen to represent France's under-18 squad. Suddenly, all that posturing, the pigeon-chested bullying and bristling arrogance, had been stripped away in front of everyone. For a second, I felt tempted to let the world see exactly where the Matthieu of his mind ended and the Matthieu of reality began.

And then, as he fought back tears and desperately tried to collect himself, I remembered that Matthieu was just a kid, and my mind flooded with visions of another kid fighting back tears after a hard-fought strikeout against the mythical Steve Langone. Matthieu was just 17 years old, his waterworks on the mound proclaiming it to all in attendance. Even if the best thing for the team might be to let the game humble him a little bit, so he would show his teammates some respect, maybe it was more important to do the best thing for the *kid,* no matter how repugnantly he sometimes carried himself. I decided to get him the hell out of there, bring in the similarly named Australian that he so looked up to, and end Matthieu's humiliation.

"Un moment!" I shouted to the umpire, calling time and jogging to the mound. Matthieu offered no resistance as I took the ball from his relieved hand and patted him on the ass. "*Good job. You did the best you could with what you've got. Replace Matt in centerfield.*"

Momentum in baseball is strange, unpredictable. It shifts so palpably that even the spectators who cannot understand the game – many of whom regularly attended Bois-Guillaume games – can feel it. I imagine that an alien could watch a first baseball game, never even attempt to understand its arcane rules, and nonetheless identify that critical moment where one team surrenders momentum and the other seizes it. Matt came in throwing *gas*, and like clockwork, the mood in both dugouts flipped. Suddenly, the game was not a question of how much the Hawks could pour it on, but whether they could hold an increasingly tenuous five-run lead. We cut the lead to one in the fifth when Aldo ripped a double to left center, scoring two and bailing me out from what I expected would be a scathing diatribe of criticism from Matt. (I had foolishly asked Stephan, a part-timer who hadn't played regularly since Bois-Guillaume's N1A days, to lay down a high-pressure squeeze bunt in a critical situation. It had backfired spectacularly.)

Later in the inning, the second base umpire suddenly stopped play and tossed Piquet out of the game from his shortstop position. Piquet had turned to Matt, who was standing on second base, and said "These fucking umpires suck, huh?," thinking he could get away with it because most umpires spoke only 'Baseball English.' Unfortunately for Piquet, this ump understood him perfectly, and after tolerating several complaints about balls and strikes from him in the first game, decided he had heard enough.

Even though Piquet had long since left the mound, his ejection reinvigorated the Woodchucks. The rally continued with Matt lumbering home on a passed ball to give us our first lead of the game, 6-5. I high-fived Aldo in the dugout, but I could see the storm clouds gathering. Unwilling to share in the euphoria, Matt sat sullenly at the end of the bench, 10 feet from the closest Woodchuck, wearing his trademark scowl.

"How you feeling, man?" I asked.

"I'm only gonna go one more," he replied, pushing out his lower lip and squinting.

So this is how it's going to be, I thought. *Matt wants everyone to know that he doesn't care, that if they want him to do the job they hired him for, they have to beg him.* I stared at Matt with a goofy, stunned grin. Struggling to find the words to convince Matt that the team needed him to gut it out for the sake of winning a game, I realized that Matt and I were about as far apart as two people could be. We both played baseball, but the similarities ended there. Matt played it a lot better, but he took no joy in it, and he would rather hit two home runs and lose than go hitless and win. He didn't give a rat's ass about the other guys on the bench, whose furtive sidelong glances revealed their curiosity as to the outcome of our conversation.

My fists clenched. I turned back to him, staring coldly. I didn't care that he represented everything that I thought was wrong with the team, with sports, with the world. He didn't care whether we won or lost? He was using the team? Fine, I thought, we'll use you right back. I swallowed hard, furious that though I would rather address him as a man, he had forced me to treat him like a petulant child.

"Hey, you've pitched great, man. Totally understand if you're ready to throw in the towel," I started sweetly. I felt like choking on the saccharine-tinged bullshit spewing forth from my own mouth. "How about this? You wanna start the seventh, see how it goes? It'll give Eric some time to warm up." Eric always battled when we needed him, but I knew, Matt knew, and the Hawks knew that pulling the Australian would let them right back in the game.

"Fine. Fuck mate, whatever."

"Great." I had never felt such revulsion, but I maintained my appreciative façade, trying desperately to call Matt's bluff. "Hey, I got you at 55 pitches through four, so we'll keep an eye on that." I pulled the number from somewhere between the base of my spine and my pelvis, and I had no intention of keeping an eye on anything other than the scoreboard.

I gazed out at the bench behind the backstop, where Aldo's mother sat in her usual seat, then glanced down at my elbow, cursing at its uselessness. None of this would be necessary if only I could throw a baseball the way I did in San Francisco. I could let the Australian sulk all he wanted, and take the mound myself; maybe we'd win and I'd be the hero, maybe we'd lose and I'd wear the goat horns, but at least I wouldn't be in this ridiculous position of placating the *enfant terrible*. In fact, if I pitched well enough, the little bastard might even show me and the team a little respect, and if not, I could tell him to go fuc-

I stopped, sighing. What was the use? For better or for worse, I was in Normandy with a bum elbow and my polar opposite for a teammate, and all I could do was make the best of it. Feeling suddenly very tired, I walked past the row of seated players, muttered to Eric to warm up, and tried to ignore the shocked look that crept across his face. I didn't want paranoia to spread through the team. It would be hard enough to cling to this one-run lead even if morale remained high.

For the last three innings, a feeling of ominous dread swept through the clubhouse any time we made the third out and had to take the field again, giving the Hawks a chance to tie it up. I looked across the diamond and counted just four fielders – Eric, Seb, Aldo, and me – who wanted the ball hit their way with the game on the line. Terror consumed the others, who clearly wanted nothing more than for the game to end without them being the one to screw it up. As he circled under a pop-up in the eighth, Matthieu trembled visibly, and when it finally settled uneasily into his glove for the second out, he raised it above his head triumphantly, as if holding the yellow jersey for the Tour de France.

I didn't dare speak to Matt, for fear that bringing up our conversation would remind him that he wanted to come out of the game. I instructed Eric to hustle to get out to centerfield at the start of each inning before Matt could think twice, making a return to the mound the default status quo for our moody Australian.

Miraculously, it worked. I have no idea why. Maybe his competitive instinct kicked in, or maybe he only said he was through to see if we'd beg him to continue. Doesn't matter. He kept walking out there and dealing, and his stuff, always good even on his worst days, was nasty.

Matt's velocity dipped in the ninth, and the Hawks mounted a rally, putting two on with one out. I cringed at second base as the visitors resumed their rhythmic Atlanta Braves-esque chant and pounded on the dugout walls, but Matt bore down and got the second out on Seb's nice backhand play in the hole. With our small fan section of one dozen (rounded up) cheering wildly, Matt blew away the last hitter with a fastball at the letters. I pumped my fist at the game-ending strikeout, and stopped to enjoy the looks on the faces of the other

Woodchucks. I hadn't seen smiles that big since my arrival in Bois-Guillaume.

We practically danced through the postgame handshake line, grinning stupidly at the split doubleheader. The Hawks made no effort to conceal their disgust at dropping a game to the lowly 'Chucks. I gathered the team together on the left field line, congratulating everyone on a hard-fought win. Just as I turned to give him the symbolic game ball – he hadn't won the game all by himself, but it was close – Matt interrupted me to give his own postgame speech.

"That was fuckin' shite." He began, as I recoiled with befuddlement that he could be so negative in the afterglow of our first win. "Fuckin' droppin' popups, boys, Matthieu not coverin' home, takin' third strikes, walkin' guys. I mean, I'm '*happy*', ok?" His pronunciation made his use of the word seem sarcastic. "I'm '*happy*'. That's just not how baseball is played, mates. Not fuckin' how baseball is played."

I took some solace from the fact that he had limited capacity to dampen the euphoric mood in Woodchuck nation, primarily because most of the Woodchucks couldn't understand a word he said. They could read his tone, though. They knew Matt's anger all too well, and immediately adopted their various coping mechanisms. Matthieu stared eagerly up at his role model, desperate to curry favor. Eric understood more English than most, and winced accordingly at every scathing criticism of a teammate, but even Matt's nonsensical anger couldn't wipe the grin off his face. Others just smiled obliviously. Pierre picked at stems of grass and Stephan smoked a cigarette, staring contentedly across the field.

"Okay, Matt, thanks," I said, returning the interruption. "*Great job, guys- Sylvain said we're all headed to the Resto Rock for dinner, so shower up!*"

We poured into the kitschy, self-proclaimed "*Restaurant Tex-Mex Americain,*" ordering pitchers of beer and toasting each other with wives, girlfriends, and children in tow. Sitting as far as possible from Matt's glare and Matthieu's whining that he couldn't afford to eat anything unless the team paid for it, I glanced around at the license plates, Alcatraz posters, and cowboy hats purportedly representing classic

American decor. The place looked like a Hard Rock Café had thrown up all over its walls. Bemused, I took Seb's recommendation and ordered the *Burger San Francisco*, wondering how my fair city had gotten the reputation for putting fried eggs on hamburgers with goat cheese.

CHAPTER 24: THE TRUE FRENCHMAN

During the week, I usually woke up early, tiptoe past Matt's mattress, and drink exceptionally strong coffee while studying for the CFA exam. Gazing out at the gently rolling Normandy hills, I brushed up on convertible bond convexity while thinking of ways to keep my job in provincial French baseball.

The team and I were both in tough spots. The win at La Guerche had emboldened Matt, and he began trying to exploit the power he had over the club as its best player, telling me bluntly on one car ride home that he had emailed Eric and Sylvain, demanding more money.

"It'd be different if I could just hand games over to you, right?" he said matter-of-factly as I drove in stunned silence. "But if I'm the only one pitching, I figured I could ask for more, you know?"

"Sure, man," I said with a forced coolness, collecting myself quickly to mask my discomfort. "That's between you and the team." I held his gaze for a moment to reinforce this debatable assertion before driving the rest of the way home, feeling equal parts anxiety, shame, and fury.

The next day, Matt and I drove to a Rouen internet café to check our email. Sorting through the messages that arrived in the days between internet café visits, I came across a delightfully unexpected one. "Kellogg School - Good News!" it started. I had earned admission to Northwestern's joint law and business program.

The unexpected good news created something of a dilemma. I had already cut a $1,000 deposit check to another school, but Northwestern offered a combined degree, and… Becky was going there. The decision, the most important one of my life so far, got impossibly complex if I factored in Becky. Suddenly, I faced a weighty decision in its own right, coupled with an implicit referendum on our relationship. I wanted some time to think it over without adding even more pressure by telling Becky about it, a mistake I would come to regret. I found myself interrupted by a call from Eric on my cell. I stepped outside to take the call out of earshot from Matt.

"Allo, Eric, ca va?"

"*Evan, I have to ask you something. It goes, between Matt and you?*"

I approached the question like I would a loaded pistol: with caution. "Oui, Eric. *It goes.* Pourquoi?"

Eric explained Matt's long email demanding more money. In our conversation, Matt had left out the part about telling the team how much more valuable he was to the Woodchucks than me. Eric said that he was afraid we had fought, that Matt wanted me off the team. Suddenly forced to convince *two* factions of my neutrality in their dispute, I repeated my mantra that it had nothing to do with me, wondering inwardly whether I could handle a second firing. If anything, I thought that Sylvain and Eric were on my side, but ultimately, they had to do what was best for the team.

If Matt gave them an ultimatum of firing the American and paying him more, or else…

"*Ok*, good." Eric replied, interrupting my thoughts. "*I was just afraid you were fighting. It will be fine. I will reply to Matt. You are right, this does not concern you.*"

Sighing with relief, I bid Eric adieu and reflected on our relationship, realizing that he and Fermin were my closest friends in France. Eric 'got it'; fundamentally, he understood that the game was to be played hard, but it was supposed to be fun. After each game, he knew that you were supposed to gather your friends and families together, have a few beers, and tease each other about how well or how poorly you played. The audible anxiety in his voice over the phone and his pained look anytime Matt threw a tantrum reminded me of my first conversation with Clement, who recalled Eric's campaign promise that if elected club president, he would ensure there was Budweiser at every club meeting. (His subsequent election demonstrates just how mightily the French struggle in transferring their sophisticated appreciation of wine to beer.) With his garbled Quebecois accent and *joie de vivre*, Eric would have fit right in on the Reds. It was among the highest compliments I could give a ballplayer.

We had really become friends on my second week in Normandy, when he took me and Matt to Dieppe, the site of the first Canadian/English raid on German-controlled France in 1942. Eric had served in a sniper unit back in Quebec, the same unit that participated in the raid, so his veteran status had made him the first historian with access to recently declassified internal English, Canadian, and French files on the raid. Essentially, we visited this enormously important WWII battle site with possibly the most qualified person on the planet playing tour guide, like hearing a lecture on jazz trumpet from Louis Armstrong. As we cracked a bottle of cheap red wine and broke out a baguette, ham, and cheese, Eric explained that the Germans had gotten wind of the raid, and instead of replacing the division on watch, they kept them in Dieppe and doubled up with a new division, dooming the Allied assault before it began. We spent the rest of the day climbing around German bunkers overlooking the impossibly steep cliff and exposed beach upon which the Allies attempted to land.

That Friday, we dined with the Jean-Luc branch of the Paturel family. Despite the previous year's scandals and his defection to Cherbourg, Jean-Luc still considered Matt a friend, and invited us for dinner at his house, where he poured us massive 'kirs' in 16-ounce water glasses. More than tripling the traditional French aperitif recipe of a splash of crème de cassis – a black-currant liqueur – and white wine, Jean-Luc impressively polished off four before dinner even started. We spent the evening joking and laughing with Jean-Luc, his son Charles, and daughter Laura, the past alleged transgressions apparently forgotten. As we drove home, Matt opined to me that such family dinners made him feel at home.

"That's what I miss, mate," he began, strangely personable and empathetic. "Feeling at home, part of a family. I don't have that here." For all his toxicity, I found myself feeling bad for Matt. Unable to speak a word of French, he was very much an overgrown kid, lost in a foreign land without family or friends.

Sadly, my relationship with Matt did not improve.

Meanwhile, my elbow still hurt like hell anytime I threw. During these dark times, my contact with friends back home kept me afloat. Greg at USF sent me an email telling me to trade the Australian and keep 'trying easy' at the plate. While his first suggestion revealed a basic misunderstanding of my power within the Woodchuck organization, the latter seemed to work, as I started lofting a few balls into the trees in batting practice. Most of all, Becky's phone calls every few days put a smile on my face, as I hunched over my cell phone whispering the day's news in fear that Matt might be listening next door. I pined for June, when the Woodchucks' schedule took a five-week break and Becky and I could resume our surprisingly resilient romance with a month of travel.

I felt that if I could *just make it to June* and the long break that ensued, I would be home free. With that much time off, surely my elbow would heal enough to let me pitch a little bit, getting Matt off my back. In the meantime, though, I felt like I had to make a move of my own. One bright Tuesday, I surprised Sylvain at his apartment in downtown Rouen. He ushered me in, asking what had brought me down the hill.

"*Sylvain, I need to talk to you. It's about my salary,*" I began. Sylvain looked stunned. Could *another* ballplayer be asking for more money?

"*I want to cut it in half. I don't want to get paid any more than I'm worth. I know the club is short on cash, and without me pitching, I don't want to take a full salary if I can't earn it.*"

Not surprisingly, Sylvain did not know what to make of this.

"*Evan! That's very gracious, but...*" he searched for the words. "*You don't have to do that. You're playing great! We're really happy you're a Woodchuck! It's not necessary to –*"

"*Please, Sylvain. I would feel more comfortable. Just half.*"

He laughed, a bit confused, but agreed. I felt a little slimy about it, because the amount of money didn't matter a lick to me; I just figured it would be harder to fire a guy if he was only making 150€ a month. French baseball really turned things upside down sometimes; I felt guilty for asking for *less* money.

That weekend, we awoke at 6:00 AM to drive to Saint-Lô, which lies on the border with Bretagne. All of the baseball teams in France so far had used English words for team names, but

Saint-Lô broke with the trend, calling itself the Jimmer's. Despite my repeated inquiries, no one could tell me what a Jimmer was. "*It's a mascot*," one Jimmer told me. Well, no kidding. Someone else insisted it was an English word for 'bear,' and the mystery remained unsolved.

The first game taught me a lot about Vince, a young guy I hadn't really gotten a good handle on. A skinny lefty with a taste for American hip-hop that began and ended with the Wu Tang Clan, Vince loped everywhere, like Matthieu a mess of baggy jeans and cockeyed Starter caps. Brooding and taciturn, he was roughly the same age as Matthieu, but his temperament could not have been more different. A classic southpaw, his goofy, self-deprecating sense of humor and comfort in his own skin stood in stark contrast to Matthieu's strained contrivances.

Relying on a sweeping curve and tailing fastball, Vince got in and out of trouble all day, managing to keep the ball down, and inducing a few double plays when he needed them. He gave up just one hard hit all day, a line shot two steps to my right in the fourth. I laid out, fully horizontal, but couldn't quite snare it. I fell hard on my left shoulder, my loud groan echoing across the field.

Down 4-0, I told Rafael that he would replace me if we failed to score in the seventh. Despite his rudimentary baseball skills, his Venezuelan nationality counted against the 'two foreigners on the field' limit specified by the Tres Lettres' protectionist regulations. Informed of this rule, Matt bluntly declared "Well I'm not fuckin' comin' out," so in the interests of keeping Rafael happy, I often pulled myself after seven innings to give him some playing time.

Rafael would have to wait; we rallied, plating two and bringing me up with one out and two men on. I lashed a line drive into right, scoring one run easily. I took too wide a turn through first base, though, and got caught in no-man's land between first and second as the first baseman cut off the throw and had me dead to rights, hung up in the baseline. It was a dumb misread on my part, but we made lemonade from lemons as I stayed in a rundown long enough to allow Seb to score a second run, tying the game at four apiece.

Vince kept slinging it. Inning after inning, this young, goofy kid just kept chucking that looping curve at baffled Jimmers, getting out of jams by the skin of his teeth. Every inning, he put two guys on, shaking his head and muttering to himself, then worked out of it with a pop-up or strikeout. I couldn't help but compare it to Matt's performance against the Hawks, trying to figure out which was more impressive; by the eighth, it wasn't close. Vince was an artist about it. As Sam McDowell once said, "It's no fun throwing fastballs to guys who can't hit them. The real challenge is getting them out on stuff they can hit." Matt had overpowered guys for seven innings, but Vince confounded hitters with soft stuff they could hit – *under*powered them, if anything – through nine. When he couldn't get the curve over for strike one, he would buckle down and run that two-seamer inside, breaking bats and eliciting exclamations of "MERDE!" from the Jimmers.

In one particularly tough jam in the ninth, still tied, I called time and visited the mound to check on him.

"Look Vince, you're doing great... but no shame in calling it a day. You're up to a hundred pitches- do you want to move to first?"

He stared back with a look of pure confusion, as if he hadn't heard a word I said. He seemed genuinely surprised to look up and see me standing next to him.

"{Puh!}" He shrugged, making the sound of a popping soap bubble popular among the French when they want to signal their disinterest. He grinned. "Non, ca va! *Listen, it's no big deal.*"

I cocked my head to one side and raised an eyebrow, holding his gaze. He chuckled, muttering "Non, non, ca va ca va ca va," making a shooing motion to speed me back to second base. A popup and a groundout later, we were back in the dugout. On the way in, I slapped him on the back, exclaiming in English that he was The Man. It seemed to translate even to Vince, whose limited English recognition came primarily from the

Wu-Tang lexicon, and he laughed and gave me a fist bump as we got ready to hit in the tenth.

But first, a word about the French.

The common American misconception about the French as effete cowards is bullshit, and I blame it largely on the Simpsons for coining the pithy, dismissive epithet of 'cheese-eating surrender monkeys.' This book is a memoir about baseball, not a treatise on cultural stereotypes, but permit me one paragraph to point out that going back to Napoleon, French soldiers time and again displayed lionhearted valor, often facing overwhelming odds. They had a rough couple of decades militarily – hey, anyone can have a rebuilding century, just ask the Boston Red Sox – due to failures of strategic leadership rather than weakness in the national character. Over the centuries, the true Frenchman has been at his finest when all hope is lost, fighting with a smile to certain death at places like Verdun with a perseverance and nobility that defines the country.

That was Vince: the true Frenchman.

He lacked Matthieu's INSEP pedigree, but I thought INSEP had it backwards. Matthieu was the better athlete and hitter, and had the superior work ethic, but curveballs like Vince's didn't grow on trees. Moreover, when the chips were down, and the opposing team started banging on the dugout walls and chanting to rattle him, Vince would chuckle and make a shooing motion, while Matthieu would blink back tears. Matthieu was the American *stereotype* of the French: a phony wannabe bully whose insecurity made him present a brave façade that belied his yellow underbelly. Vince was the real deal; Matthieu was hand puppetry outside the cave of actual toughness. If I was picking the Espoirs at INSEP, I'd take Vince every day of the week.

"Allo? ALLO!"

Aldo was shouting at me. I shook my head, dazed and lost in my thoughts, having forgotten that I was up next. Taking my cue from Vince, I shrugged and marched to the batters' box, strangely confident that I would play the hero with a base hit, then steal second and score, crashing the catcher into next week if necessary. I turned on an inside fastball and roped a line drive into left, then stole second on the first pitch, everything going to plan. Quentin then nearly made it all come true, smashing a groundball in the hole between short and third as I came barreling past the diving third baseman.

I passed the shortstop at full speed, his movements so slow that I knew I would be home free if the ball got past the third baseman. A realization dawned on me: I felt fast. I mean, Holy Shit Was I Fast. I was flying, and I knew in my gut that if Quentin's grounder squeaked through, I would score, probably standing up.

Time returned to normal as the third baseman made an incredible diving stop to his left, then jumped to his feet and nipped Quentin at first by a half step. It was a hell of a play, even if the replays later showed that Quentin was safe. (For the record, French instant replay consisted of me saying "*Eh, you looked safe. Were you safe*?" and Quentin replying "Oui.") But the Jimmers got the call and I was left stranded.

In the bottom half, Vince walked a player that had defected from Bois-Guillaume after last season's implosion, tired of the drama and constant losing. He promptly stole second, then tagged and took third on a sac fly to center, bringing up one of Saint-Lô's youngest players with two outs and the winning run on third. With a 1-2 count, the Jimmers put on the exceptionally rare hit-and-run with two strikes, two outs, and a man on third; disaster struck. The runner broke early from third, barreling towards home well before Vince had started his motion. All Vince had to do was step off and throw a batting practice fastball to the catcher so he could tag the runner to end the inning. Shoot, that's the easiest play in baseball. In fact, it's so easy that I recommend you try it some time. Just make sure that you do it in the tenth inning with the winning run bearing down on home plate, after you've pitched 9 2/3 innings under the hot Normandy sun, working out of jams every inning, facing 44 hitters and throwing about 140 pitches. So, yeah, piece of *gateau*.

After one of the most courageous pitching performances I've ever seen, Vince skipped a 59-footer, Matthieu dropped it, and we lost 5-4 on a walkoff steal of home.

We had so many opportunities to win it. If I spear that line drive, or Matthieu scoops Vince's low throw in the tenth, or we avoid two killer line-drive double plays earlier in the game, we come out on top. If Quentin's ground ball goes six inches to the left, and I come rocketing around third eager to make Rose/Fosse look like a fender bender in a Safeway parking lot, and we bring in Matt to close out the bottom half… It killed me to think about it. It killed me even more to remember that earlier, we *again* had the bases loaded with no outs and failed to score. That made three times this year: almost inconceivable from a statistical perspective.

A popular online statistical program shows that the probability of scoring zero runs with the bases loaded and no outs is 12.8%, making the odds of failing to score three consecutive times equal to 0.128^3, or approximately 0.21%. That was in the major leagues, where double plays are commonplace; given the weak defenses in France, I would wager that the odds of not scoring at all are less than one-third of that 12.8% figure. Even taking it at one-half produces a probability of failing to score three consecutive times of 0.026%, or less than three in 10,000 times.

The mind reels.

Not surprisingly, we dropped the second game. When two evenly-matched teams play a back-and-forth game like that to start a doubleheader, the loser always struggles to rebound in game two. We came out predictably flat, getting no-hit by their Venezuelan starter for six innings. The game droned on, far out of reach, as the heavens opened and the rain poured down. Matt pitched for a few innings after Quentin, but threw in the towel early when he decided it was a lost cause not worth his effort. Ironically, that capitulation by his idol forced Matthieu back onto the mound, where he again pouted and fought back tears, cursing at the rain and umpires for two miserable innings. Matt struck out to end the game and we limped home, dispirited and depressed, my parents' impending visit the following weekend providing the cloud's only silver lining.

CHAPTER 25: TEACH YOUR PARENTS WELL

The week began poorly, as the team's plans for housing fell through once again. Sylvain lined up an apartment, but the owner balked at two foreign ballplayers as tenants, demanding double the normal security deposit. Amidst that frustration, Matt and I worked on Eric's house in Neufchâtel before picking up Mathieu and Quentin from the train station. Class had ended on Friday afternoon, and they had decided to head directly to Bois-Guillaume for the weekend. No one else could put them up, so we headed back to Neufchâtel to watch *Platoon*, which prompted me to point out that Oliver Stone had never served a day in Vietnam and was prone to exaggeration. I thanked

Quentin and Matthieu – the lone representatives of France present – for leading America into that whole debacle, muttering "*hey, thanks for that handoff. Really appreciate it. Worked out great for us.* Merci."

After batting practice on Saturday morning, Matt and I coached the Bois-Guillaume Mini-Me's against Les Andelys. Only four junior Woodchucks showed up, making for a strong infield defense but little else. We forfeited the game, and made the mistake of agreeing to an informal scrimmage. The first pitch of this ill-conceived practice set the tone, as the LA catcher – a lefty, naturally[20] – failed to redirect *a called strike* from its unerring path towards his genitals. It never even grazed his glove, and he keeled over, emitting an agonizingly high-pitched "HEEEEEEEEEEINH!" as he collapsed into the fetal position.

I bit down on my cheek, choking back guilty laughter so hard that my stomach began to hurt and tears flowed freely from my eyes. The last thing I want to do

[20] For the uninitiated, no serious baseball team employs a lefthanded catcher, because they are obstructed in their throws to second and third by righthanded batters. Arguably, it's less because of the obstruction and more because any young lefthander with a strong arm gets made into a pitcher, but the proof is in the pudding; in over a century of major league baseball, only five lefthanders have caught more than 100 games.

is make fun of a 12-year-old kid, but I had never seen anything like this. I even turned to Matt, seeing the same bewilderment in his face; did that really just happen?

Sadly, it had, and the scrimmage mercifully ended after an hour. I caught a ride to Rouen, and met up with my parents on the Place du Vielle Marche.

"There he is!" my father cried as I turned the corner onto the square. "The pro ballplayer!"

A few tearful hugs later, we entered La Coronne, one of the oldest restaurants in Rouen, for a traditional dinner of Norman duck, which the maître d' introduced as "Dominique." Maybe it was the sight of watching my father order a "*martini gin*" in broken French, but seeing my parents provided just the tonic I needed. Like Alex and Jools before them, my parents put me at ease. Around Matt, I could never relax, and the atmosphere in our tiny apartment fluctuated precipitously with his mercurial moods. My parents' presence provided temporary relief, as they did their best to comfort me.

"Don't take any of that shit, Ev," my father bellowed.

"If he thinks he's so big league, tell him to look around. You're both playing at the same level, and you're both getting paid."

After finding to our astonishment that their hotel room featured a bathroom with a clear glass door – all the better to see you with, my dear! – we settled in for the night. In the morning, we cabbed up the hill to Bois-Guillaume to find the team in total disarray, with a shell-shocked Quentin and Sylvain whispering nervously in hushed French.

"*What's up, guys?*" I asked.

Sylvain shook his head, casting a furtive glance up towards the clubhouse. "*It is nothing, nothing,*" he whispered, his look clearly indicating otherwise. "*Can you talk to Matt?*"

I looked at Quentin, who smiled meekly and fled to attend to some suddenly pressing matter that would conveniently take him very far from whatever was happening. I got the story in pieces, first from Sylvain, then Eric, then finally from a ranting Matt in the clubhouse… none of which makes sense to this day.

Supposedly, upon leaving Neufchâtel that morning, Matt, Mathieu, and Quentin had somehow left the Woodsmobile trunk open, which doesn't really square, because an open trunk would be sticking straight up in the air: hard to miss. Because I stayed with my parents, Matt had to drive in that morning. On the autoroute, Quentin said he felt a draft, and upon realizing their mistake, they took inventory and discovered that Matt's backpack had fallen out somewhere along the way, and he had the bright idea of retracing their steps by pulling into the breakdown lane and flooring it in reverse. With his trademark rage boiling inside, he lost control of the Woodsmobile, crashing into the divider and mangling the passenger-side door beyond recognition. He lost it, turning to scream at the two cringing INSEP kids in the back seat before punching the rearview mirror in anger, dislodging it and sending cracks spiderwebbing across the windshield. His tantrum over, they drove the rest of the way in tense silence. Rolling my eyes, I climbed the stairs, wondering how to put this behind us and get everyone's heads together for a game we could win against a beatable PUC club.

I had barely poked my head through the clubhouse door before Matt turned his fury towards me.

"How the fuck did that happen? I mean COME ON! How can you not fucking know the boot is open?"

"None of you heard it fall out?"

"Fucking Hell! No, how did THEY not hear it? I had my headphones on! FUCKING HELL!"

Matt usually listened to house music before games – loud enough for me to hear on his headphones while I drove – so it made sense that he wouldn't have heard anything, The list of things wrong with the scenario is vast: why someone was wearing headphones while driving, how he didn't notice the trunk sticking vertically open in the rearview mirror, to say nothing of how no one immediately felt the kind of draft that results from… having an open trunk while traveling 140 kilometers per hour on the autoroute.

"That fuckin' kid! Christ, all my clothes were in there! My nice jumper! And my $400 jeans!"

"Man, that- wait, you have $400 jeans?" I recoiled, as Matt often cried poor because he hadn't worked in Oz during the offseason.

"Yeah, $400 Aussie! That's why I'm so fuckin' pissed!"

After futile efforts to calm him down, I went outside to survey the damaged Woodsmobile, maimed beyond repair. The collision had ripped a space about three inches wide between the doorframe and the roof, preventing the door and window from closing completely.

The team gathered in the dugout, the tension palpable. The other Woodchucks tiptoed nervously around Matt, who sat scowling at the end of the bench.

"You coming, Matt?" The team had started its communal run from foul pole to foul pole. The responsibility for Woodchucks-to-Matt diplomacy fell to me.

"I just can't be fucked, mate." He glared angrily out at the field.

We ran and stretched without him as I tried to calm everyone down. I looked around at the circle of ballplayers and saw everyone thinking different thoughts about the same thing. Quentin looked frailer and more nervous than usual, while Matthieu seemed to be working himself up to emulate Matt's anger. They both looked up to him, and in Matthieu's mind, he could do no wrong; if Matt was pissed off at the team for his bag falling out of the car he was driving, then Matthieu would be pissed off at the team too. Aldo played to win, so his competitive streak made him tolerate Matt's occasional tantrums. The others played for fun, and just tried to stay out of Matt's way and ignore him.

I aligned myself with the latter crowd; after all, *I* hadn't wrecked the Woodsmobile. I dutifully wrote out the lineup card, trotting to home plate to exchange lineups with PUC's coach, only to find something I had never seen in the game of baseball.

He was shitfaced.

He stumbled out to home plate, grinning with a mouth full of teeth stained purple with red wine.

"Oh, un... a-MER-ee-CAN!" he slurred. "BIEN-ve-NUE!!!" he added, gesticulating wildly. His face was bright red, and he lilted slightly as I shook his hand.

Shaking my head, I trotted back to the dugout to grab my glove.

"*Is he... always like that?*" I asked Eric, who diplomatically refused to answer, instead rolling his eyes.

"*Wow.*"

Despite the anxious dugout mood, we came out strong. I slapped a ball up the middle for a hit to lead off the first and immediately wanted to show off for my folks. I took two big steps off first base, then another, pausing as the pitcher eyed me from the set position. He stood stock still for a moment, then stepped off and fired to first base, where I slid in just ahead of the tag.

"SAUF!" the base umpire shouted.

I dusted myself off and grinned at my cheering parents, locking eyes with my father. He knew and I knew; I had this guy dead to rights, because he had already made two revealing mistakes. With a base stealer on first, a smart pitcher will wait before going to the plate, standing casually on the mound while the runner has to remain taught, ready to break in either direction. It tires out his legs. Second, experienced pitchers save their good pickoff move for when they really need it. This pitcher had only waited a few seconds before going right to his best move, and his eyes darted to the ground right before making it. It was like overturning his hole cards in Texas Hold'Em; I knew exactly what he had up his sleeve, and now I was going to steal second.

I took the same lead again, then extended it a half-step further. Seeing his right wrist straight instead of cocked, I guessed fastball. At the instant he picked up his left leg, I burst towards second, listening for the sound of a batted ball. The second baseman drifted into view, scurrying to the bag to receive the throw. Butterflies danced in my stomach, my brain shouting "I'M GONNA BE SAFE I'M GONNA BE SAFE AM I GONNA BE SAFE???" Starting my head-first slide, I saw him reach up to receive the ball from the catcher and apply the tag. "Here we go!" I thought as my chest crashed into the loose dirt around second, my fingertips reaching desperately for the safety of second base. His glove tapped my shoulder. I was pretty sure I had beaten it, but I rolled onto my right side to hear the umpire's call, carefully keeping my left leg on the bag.

Silence.

I looked around. Where the hell was the call?

Irritated, I watched the second baseman trot back to his position as the catcher lobbed the ball back to the mound. There was no call because there was no throw; the second baseman had just slapped his glove with his right hand to make me slide.

"Bush," I said to the smirking second baseman, not caring that he didn't understand. "Bush league," I repeated, shaking my head. That type of thing would get a guy knocked down in his next at-bat back home.

My father roared "All day, Ev! Don't stop there!"

Look; my dad taught me everything I know about how to play baseball. What was I going to do, ignore him? After he crossed an ocean to watch me play?

I took off on the very next pitch and beat the throw by a mile, sliding safely into third. The next hitter flew out to left field, and I scored standing up after stealing most of the diamond, pumping my fist and grinning goofily at my applauding parents.

"Way to go Evy-Baby!" my mother shouted as I high-fived Eric, Sylvain, and Seb. I hadn't heard her say that in years, probably not since high school. This is alright, I thought. Playing ball in front of my folks, getting base hits, stealing bases, and scoring runs. I can live with this.

Vince tired in the seventh, a problem because we had exactly nine players for both games; we couldn't warm anyone up mid-inning. He gave up a few runs with two outs, and then just missed what should have been strike three to end the inning. Instead, the ump called it ball four, and the next hitter crushed a hanging curve into the trees in left. Baseball's a game of inches… and he hit that one about 4,000 inches.

Suddenly down 8-6, we rallied for two in the bottom half to tie it, even as we ran out of pitchers. Matt hated coming in to clean up other people's messes, as he put it, and insisted on starting game two instead of coming in to close the first one. Lacking options, I turned to Quentin, who got rattled by the rowdy PUC bench's trash-talking and gave up three in the eighth. We lost

12-8.

Between games, my parents and I enjoyed a sandwich on the lawn behind the dugout, reveling in the rare Normandy sunshine. I called Matt over as he walked past, and he introduced himself to my folks before renewing his tirade about his lost clothing. After he left, my parents stared at me intently. I tore up a piece of grass and tossed it in the air, watching it scatter in the wind.

"Hey, what can you do, right?"

"Ev..." my mother began. "That's who you've been living with? He just- he didn't show the least bit of concern! Or contrition! He smashed up the car! And he's complaining-"

"I know, mom. I know. Like I said... what can you do?"

Somewhere, ages and ages hence, as I lay dying and my life flashes before my eyes, I think I will see a montage of all the baseball games I should have won, the tight matches that barely squeaked away in the end. I hope it's the opposite – all the close ones my teams have pulled off over the years – but I can't shake the feeling that I'll be like the poker players who never remember the big wins but can describe every tough beat in excruciating detail. Both games against PUC will be enshrined in that mental hall of shame, but game two will have its own dedicated wing.

Matt pitched well, entering the ninth up 4-3. Their foreigner led off, an American who played at Dartmouth. He grounded to Quentin at third, who promptly skipped it past Vince at first, putting the tying run on with nobody out. He advanced to second on a passed ball and took third on a ground ball that made for the second out. With two down, Eric went into the hole and made a sliding stop on his knees, but couldn't field it cleanly, his throw coming in a split-second too late to get the batter. Instead of escaping with the 4-3 win, Quentin's error left us tied us at four.

The league had a limitation on foreigners throwing more than nine innings in a weekend, so I was stuck when we failed to score in the bottom half despite Matthieu's leadoff double. I tapped Seb, knowing that he didn't really belong out there; very good shortstop, but he lacked control as a pitcher. A few walks and a hit batsman later, we found ourselves on the wrong end of a sour 6-4 decision, our second extra-innings loss in two weeks.

Painful.

Making the grapes even more sour, both games were among the worst-officiated games I have ever seen. The umpires completely lost control of the second game when Seb grounded a ball just fair down the line in the third, scoring me and Quentin. PUC's red-faced manager stormed out to berate the home plate umpire so long and condescendingly, I couldn't believe they didn't toss him. Screaming drunkenly with his 80-proof breath, he argued that the ball had first touched the ground in foul territory, and therefore had to be ruled foul even though it crossed third base in fair territory. For those of you who share this boozehound's unfamiliarity with the rules of baseball, his argument completely lacked merit; the fair/foul designation is made at the point when the ball crosses the third base bag. Seb's had done so in fair territory, so it was a fair ball, end of story.

Shockingly, the umps just sat there and took it as this intoxicated lout and his team heaped abuse on them, call after disputed call. The catcher took his efforts to frame pitches to a ridiculous extreme, holding the ball for – no exaggeration – five or six seconds on balls he thought were strikes. During my third at-bat, he actually stood up after two straight outside sliders missed, stepped into the left-handed batters' box, and turned to the umpire, exclaiming "*It's called a curve ball! It starts here and curves over the plate here! Have you never seen a curve ball before???*"

I couldn't believe it didn't earn him an ejection. Back home, a catcher might get a third of the way through the word 'curve' and he would be out on his ass. Either way, everyone in the ballpark knew that after not getting the call on two breaking balls away, they would try to bust a fastball in on my hands. I turned on the ensuing fastball and smashed it down the line in left for a standup double. I stole third and scored on a base hit as my parents hooted and hollered.

"That's my boy! Show'em the *right* way to play this game!" my father cried. It was all for naught, but at least I had put on a show for my folks.

The team threw a barbecue after the games, the sausages and beers cheering us up after two dagger-in-the-stomach losses. I felt a surge of pride at my parents' surprisingly coherent French, as they invited Aldo and his mother to visit us in Boston. My father didn't conjugate verbs well – or, frankly, at all – but the effort seemed to impress my teammates. We rode back to Rouen, my mother still marveling at Matt's behavior. I reiterated that was just the way it was. He was our best player, and we needed him, warts and all.

CHAPTER 26: I FOUGHT THE LAW

I bid my parents farewell on Wednesday after two days of showing them around Paris. My father's parting words lingered with me on the train back to Rouen. "Don't let any of that shit from Matt get you down, Ev. You just keep playing your ass off, and hopefully the others will follow your example."

That would be challenging against that weekend's opponent: crosstown rival Rouen, the pinstriped guys that dinked and dunked me into oblivion at Montigny. Saying 'the Rouen Huskies and Bois-Guillaume Woodchucks were rivals' is sort of like saying '*Les Misérables* is a book about a bread heist.' The full subtext requires an anthropological study of a decade of player movement in northern France, an economic analysis of French federal funding of Olympic sports, and an appreciation of good old-fashioned snobbery and spite. Ready?

The Rouen and Bois-Guillaume fields were separated by just a fifteen-minute drive up the hill from the Seine, but the clubs existed in totally different strata of French baseball. The Rouen Huskies were the 800-pound gorilla and frequent national champion, with a reputation for stealing the best players from other teams. (The club in Dieppe, for example, folded entirely when their best players left en masse for Rouen's greener pastures.) In fairness to Rouen, this is not simply villainy on the Huskies' part. I chatted with Josh Chetwynd, journalist and author of *Baseball in Europe: A Country by Country History*, and he pointed out that in European markets, like attracts like, and as in the U.S. or anywhere else, good ballplayers want to play with other good ballplayers. "It's often typical in European baseball for there to be a team that's dynastic," Chetwynd told me in an email, "because each nation has limited talent and many of the top domestic players tend to gravitate to each other. Think Draci Brno in the Czech Republic, the London Mets in the U.K., or Neptunus or L&D Amsterdam in the Netherlands."[21] In France, that meant if you were a good ballplayer from the north, you played for Rouen; from Paris, for Savigny; from the south, for Stade Toulouse.[22]

In contrast to Rouen's stately pedigree, the Woodchucks were the Bad News Bears, rough-and-tumble party crashers who had joined the elite division uninvited just eighteen months earlier when they shocked French baseball by winning the N1A championship years before they were expected to contend. They weren't ready organizationally, financially, or talent-wise, and Woodchuck players that had excelled at N1A in 2004 found themselves overmatched in the elite division in 2005. A lot of the Woodchucks' organizational disfunction resulted from that fluky 2004 win; had they gotten close a few times and then won the N1A a few years later, they would

[21] Email exchange with Josh Chetwynd, July 20, 2020. HBWT: come for the goofy French jokes, stay for the cutting-edge primary research!

[22] I thought that lopsidedness was bad for French baseball, because it stunted player development. Players get better by constantly being pushed, but having only three dominant teams meant that instead of challenges every weekend, the best French ballplayers just had four tough games a year.

have had more time to build their talent base and gotten their institutional infrastructure house in order so as to enter the elite division more prepared to compete.

That first year in the elite division (with Australians Matt and Ben) proved a complete disaster, with a steady drip of scandals, infighting, and embarrassing losses. They avoided relegation on the final weekend by edging PUC, but soon after, the Woodchucks' best young player, 16-year-old David Gauthier, decided he had had enough and defected to Rouen. I can't fault David or the Huskies for that; he was already on the Espoirs at INSEP, and if he wanted to make the most of his baseball career, Rouen objectively offered him the best opportunity. They practiced more frequently and more seriously, had a better facility, a bigger budget, more and better coaches, you name it. But you try telling that to my friend Eric after a few beers at the Underground, as he wistfully recounts the tale of helping a seven-year-old David put on a baseball glove for the first time, lending him videos of old Expos games to show him how to swing a bat. "*He was going to be the future of the club! The next generation!'* Eric would sputter, disappointment and frustration plain in his voice. For Eric, the Woodchucks were family, and the Huskies might as well have kidnapped his son.

Animosity between the two clubs went far deeper than one 'stolen' ballplayer, however. As Virginie told me in my first night in Normandy, Bois-Guillaume's sole organizational goal for 2006 was to avoid relegation to N1A; Rouen had a strong financial incentive to stymie those efforts and force the club's demotion. While each team pursued sponsorships from local businesses – as Bois-Guillaume had with the Resto Rock – the vast majority of funding for French baseball (and all other Olympic sports) came from the federal government. The umpires, the bats and balls themselves, the travel, and, yes, the salaries of imported foreigners like myself, it was all paid for by the Tres Lettres, making me technically an employee of La République Française. But while the funding came from the federal government, it was allocated on a région-by-région basis. Both Bois-Guillaume and Rouen played in the Haute-Normandie région, forcing them to split that région's budget; Rouen obviously preferred the good old days, when it received 100% of it. Rankled that Bois-Guillaume had narrowly avoided relegation in 2005, Rouen wanted nothing more than to ensure it in 2006, so that they could recapture the Woodchucks' share of the région's governmental largesse.

On top of it all, players around the league – many from Rouen – had discovered the blog I was writing at the time. It was on havebatwilltravel.com that I first told many of the stories in this book, albeit in a slightly more diplomatic, less brutally honest manner, knowing that people I played with and against might read it. (For example, I made barely any reference to Matt other than his performance in games, and friends back home told me they knew we didn't get along just from how little I talked about him.) But read it they had, and when I found the French baseball message board thread discussing my blog, the vitriol in the comments surprised me. Imagine all the worst aspects of the internet commentariat, then imagine it written by teenage and 20-something French baseball players, many of whom didn't like what I had to say about the competitive structure of French baseball, or the implications about the quality of French baseball if a mediocrity like me could roll over there with no collegiate baseball experience and compete successfully in the elite division. It felt like guys were coming out of the *woodwork* to talk shit about the American who had been cut by Savigny, then 'brainwashed' by bitter Bois-Guillaume players (a direct quote from the thread.) After reading a few posts, I felt defensive; after a dozen more, I just started laughing. The Woodchucks weren't going to replace me –I had played well enough that my future at Bois-Guillaume felt secure. Scrolling through petty screeds, I giggled, realizing that for once, I just didn't give a shit about a few baseballeurs getting Big Mad about little old me. I embraced it. Haters gonna hate.

Already simmering due to the financial motivations and bitterness over player movement in the background, the planning for that year's Challenge de France brought the tension between Bois-Guillaume and Rouen to a boil that summer. Like European soccer – ahem, *football* – French baseball had no one climactic

World Series, but rather, several different postseasons, all with their own respective levels of prestige and implications for the following season. Two teams would represent France in the European Cup (the baseball equivalent of the Champions' League) each summer; the league champion, who won the postseason tournament in October, similar to the MLB playoffs, and the winner of the Challenge de France, a mid-summer double-elimination tournament. Hosting the Challenge was an honor akin to hosting the Super Bowl or March Madness, and Huskies' executives had successfully petitioned the Tres Lettres to hold it in Normandy that year. The Challenge, however, required two fields, because the decision not to relegate PUC in 2005 had left nine teams in the elite division, each playing at least two games. Rouen had just one diamond, so in the offseason, Bois-Guillaume had graciously agreed to host half the Challenge's games. Long before I had ever heard of either team, their respective executive committees battled for months over funding, with Rouen demanding a greater portion of the tournament's governmental subsidies because it would host the finals. Day after day, every issue of scheduling, field preparation, and financing brought out the worst in the two clubs and the Tres Lettres, as I saw how the French elevate bureaucratic squabbling to an art form.

Amidst those tensions, we descended to Rouen that weekend for a doubleheader and promptly got waxed. We battled for a few innings before succumbing to superior talent, losing both games by double-digit margins. Down 8-3 in the second game, Matt yanked himself after just four innings, leaving Quentin to close out what Matt had deemed an unwinnable game.

We spent the next week preparing Bois-Guillaume's field for the tournament. The entire club – players, administrators, wives and girlfriends – pulled together to put Bois-Guillaume's best foot forward with new signage, concessions (pastries and crepes, of course), and seating for fans. On Tuesday, Matt and I borrowed an extra inflatable mattress from Eric so that we could stay at Aldo's apartment in nearby Bihorel, to avoid the daily drive from Neufchâtel during the tournament. As Matt barged past Aldo into his apartment and headed straight for the computer to check MLB scores, I apologized for the imposition, assuring Aldo that we would only stay a few days.

The tournament was set to begin on Wednesday, but we awoke that morning to find that the week's steady drizzle had turned to overnight thunderstorms, flooding the field. We gathered in the nearby recreational park used by the French equivalent of the Cub Scouts, where Eric waved me over.

"*The Lions should be here in a few minutes*," he said, gauging my face for a reaction.

"*Super!*" I said, mustering every bit of stoicism I could. "*I'll say hello when they arrive.*"

I collected myself as I jogged to the clubhouse to grab the batting helmets. It *would* be a little bit awkward, coming face-to-face with the team that fired me. The Lions trooped in one by one, each seemingly surprised to see me, their faces revealing their feelings.

Fabien: diplomatic courtesy.

Pierrick: apathy tinged with scorn.

Marc: playful excitement.

Dus: halfhearted discomfort.

Vincent: his face lit up, and he stuck around to chat. Joined by Marc and Sebastien, he asked how I was doing with genuine curiosity.

"It's good, Vincent," I declared. *"I like it here."*

"Really?" he responded, his cheerful smile betraying piteous disbelief. *Really? How could you like it here, in this backwater of the elite division, losing every weekend, with only one other English speaker?* I chuckled, realizing that while the losing sucked, it was the English speaker that was killing me.

After some small talk, we sat down to enjoy the lunch that Zoe, Monique, and Jean-Luc's wife Bénédicte laid out, no ordinary institutional lunch spread. Whereas in the U.S., you'd get dry pizza or greasy pasta, our volunteers had produced a feast. Each player received a quarter-chicken in white wine sauce, sides of diced radishes and carrots, and a cube of camembert for dessert. Soon the air filled with the sound of rapid French, cleats scraping on linoleum floors, and requests to pass the baguette.

After lunch, we traipsed out to the quagmire caused by 48 hours of steady rain, finding the field completely unplayable. The official from the Tres Lettres tried to bully Sylvain into proceeding, but Sylvain stuck to his guns against a much older, louder, bossier bureaucrat. Instead, we rescheduled a doubleheader for the next day, where we would play Savigny and then La Guerche back-to-back. Winning even one game would constitute an epic triumph. We had no illusions of making a play for the championship when we had won one game all year, so Eric had called on a pitcher from BG's second team to face Savigny, saving Matt, Quentin, and Vince for teams we actually had a chance of beating.

I hated the approach of conceding one game to play for another. It isn't terribly sporting, and it sure as hell isn't the American way of doing things. Outgunned and outmanned, though, the Woodchucks had to make concessions, so we brought up the cagey veteran Christophe from the second team. He had been instrumental in the Woodchucks' lightning-in-a-bottle 2004 N1A championship run, but the Lions didn't care, pounding everything he threw. Already down 8-0 in the second, Christophe served up a grand slam to make it 12-0, followed by a fly ball that Pierre misplayed into a double. You can tell when a team is on the ropes, I thought, and the Woodchucks were there. It's in their body language, how they groan a little each time the pitcher falls behind, or-

A burst of profanity interrupted my introspection. Matt had erupted in expletives when Pierre let the ball drop; Matt always cursed loudly at a teammate's error, so I had grown accustomed to tuning it out. This time, it kept getting louder as he ran in from centerfield.

"Matt, what's up?" I called out as he passed me at second base.

"Fuck this, I'm not putting up with this shit," he muttered. "Put in Sylvain, I don't give a shit."

"Man, come on, we've got to –" I began. Pointless; he was already sitting on the bench, staring out haughtily at the rest of the Woodchucks with an air of threatened violence. "*Aldo! To center! Sylvain! Left*!"

At second base, I fumed. I had never seen a ballplayer

– a *coach* – be so selfish and cowardly as to quit on his team in the middle of the game, let alone immediately after an error to show up his teammate. Matt felt his teammates were beneath him, and he would play only on his own terms. Suddenly it made sense why, with all the talent in the world, he was playing at the same level as a guy like me for 300€ a month.

That's the thing; I should have just grabbed him by the shoulders and said "Look at us. Look at our talent. *Obviously* we're gonna lose more than we win, but there's no reason to be an asshole about it. Make the best of it and play like you're playing for a title, that's what we should do." I didn't, because I couldn't. He had the team over a barrel and had already tried using that leverage to squeeze more money out of them. I felt I couldn't risk forcing a confrontation. I had become close friends with Eric and Sylvain, but if forced to choose between me and Matt, they would have no option. Now, the Reds would have been totally different: we'd rather toss the asshole and lose without him than win with him. Same talent level, same sport, same rules, and a totally different outcome.... Why?

Because we were getting paid. That's what I learned, more than anything, from playing with Matt. The game and your relationship with it gets all turned around when money enters the picture.

The game ended mercifully via the slaughter rule after five innings, and we took a short break before facing La Guerche, who picked up where Savigny left off, trouncing a Woodchucks team that seemed unsinterested in being there. Late in the rout, I slapped a Piquet slider through the hole on the right side for my only hit of the day. Typical of the day's events, Matthieu grounded into the rare inning-ending 1-5-3 double play: again, something I had never seen before on a baseball diamond. For those of you unfamiliar with baseball scoring, it requires runners on first and second, so that when the pitcher fields the ground ball, he flips to third base for the first out, and then the third basemen throws to first to nab the batter. It can only happen if the batter loafs to first base with the enthusiasm of a man heading to a root canal, as Matthieu had, 'running' like a man four times his age.

The next morning, we returned to a field that had

evidently hosted the Kentucky Derby and a ZZ Top concert overnight. The drizzle during the day's games had given way to torrential downpours, producing a swamp where the baseball diamond once stood, scarred with cleat marks from the dugout to the outfield fence. Even adjusting for the French (and particularly Norman) tendency to play in conditions considered unsafe back home, the idea of playing in that swimming pool was ridiculous. Sylvain, Matt, and I huddled quickly, agreeing that playing on such a surface would risk injuries for both teams and destroy the field, with no time for recovery before the following weekend's games against Senart.

There was just one problem; the Tres Lettres didn't give a shit about our field, and it was their decision. Technically, because the game took place during a league-organized tournament, the Tres Lettres' Technical Director had the final say. As he stormed up to a suddenly cowed Sylvain, barking orders and scowling underneath a meticulously groomed moustache, I realized that he intended to force us to play.

"Monsieur, monsieur! *We can't play on this field! It's unsafe, and it'll destroy the grass for the rest of the year!*" I said. I got halfway through the second 'monsieur' before he cut me off with a dismissive "Non, non," shooing me away with the insufferable arrogance of a bureaucrat entrusted with a modicum of power. Throughout my stay in France, I saw the French for what they were: good, honest, welcoming people whose unique way of life presented a refreshing change of pace from the American rat race. All of that cross-cultural goodwill vanished as I stared down at this petulant worm of a man, a real-life caricature of condescension and bureaucratic snobbery.

"Excusez-moi?" I asked. "EXCUSEZ-MOI???" I repeated, advancing on him and glaring down into his reddened, sniveling face. Eric grabbed my arm before I could lose my cool any further, and I turned back to the dugout imagining the headlines back home: 'American Ballplayer Suspended for Slugging Undersized French Bureaucrat Weasel: Welcome Home Parade at Noon.' Given the relationship between our countries at the time, it wouldn't have helped the French perception of

Americans as bellicose hotheads just spoiling for a fight.

Meanwhile, Sylvain and Eric's arguments fell on deaf ears. It was goddamn ridiculous given what I had seen during the day before, on a much safer field than what we currently faced. Players had slipped awkwardly on the slick infield surface, risking injury. Against Savigny, I had fallen ass-over-teakettle rounding third and barely made it back to the bag, crawling on my hands and knees to beat the tag.

Such plays had left telltale scars across the field, with huge puddles of mud replacing the grass around each infield position. With a series of home games coming up and BG's notoriously limited resources to repair a field that three days ago had been in its best condition ever, it made absolutely no sense to play a meaningless game and screw up the field any further. As bad as it looked, it sounded even worse, for across the field, one could literally hear air pockets bubbling to the surface under the intense rain pressure, something I had only heard as a child walking through salt marshes on Cape Cod. Though never a professional groundskeeper, my personal rule was that you probably shouldn't play on a field so wet you can *hear* it.

It didn't matter. The technical director insisted loudly that the game go on as scheduled. His words stretched the boundaries of my comprehension of French slang, but I had hung around enough ballplayers and malcontents to understand his profanity loud and clear.

"*I DON'T GIVE A FUCK ABOUT NEXT WEEK'S GAMES,*" the technical director shouted, "*I CARE ONLY ABOUT THE TOURNAMENT, AND THE GAME MUST BE PLAYED.*" Sylvain threw his arms up in disgust.

For the first time, I understood what I had heard from day one in Bois-Guillaume. It had been easy at first to dismiss their claims of persecution, of the league wanting the Woodchucks relegated to the second division. I had taken it with a grain of salt; in my experience, every bad team had an excuse for why they were bad.

But that did it for me. Hearing this asshole from the federation that oversaw the league, scheduled every game, and, most tellingly, determined INSEP player allocations (bestowing Quentin and Mathieu upon us)... it convinced me. Where I once had seen conspiracy theories and sour grapes I now saw a clear and unapologetic disdain for the weakling. Here was the official representative of the league saying that he 'didn't give a fuck' about our field, our future games, or our team.

It was precisely this kind of front-running and protectionism that would forever relegate French baseball to third-tier status. The Tres Lettres prayed for one team to go 32-0, protecting one favorite at all costs in the absurd hopes that they would go on to win the Coupe d'Europe or some other international tournament. The inferiority complex of the Federation produced preposterously skewed incentives. The Tres Lettres, in their own accurately translated words, 'didn't give a fuck' about developing players, or even the sport of baseball. In their perverse mindset, an underdog team squeaking out a win didn't mean they had overcome adversity; it meant that their designated future Olympian had failed, a devastating blow against the INSEP medal-producing machine. That protectionism of an already stacked deck made me want to light the whole goddamn thing on fire. It felt at times like we were playing two different sports; I was playing baseball, they were playing France.

"*Eh, Evan! It goes?"* Eric noticed me fuming on the bench, so he came over and put his arm around me. I spat and shook my head, suddenly feeling a long, long way from home.

"That guy," I half-shouted, pointing at the technical director and locking eyes with him, "is a Fucking Asshole." A few Woodchucks laughed. That had crossed the language barrier.

We convened briefly, and made the right call. I walked purposefully across home plate to the Senart dugout, and asked the first player I encountered in my best French "*MAY I PLEASE SPEAK TO YOUR MANAGER*." He pointed me to the older gentleman I recognized as the coach. I nodded, and asked him to step out from the dugout, at which point I told him that the Bois-Guillaume Woodchucks would not be bullied. He squinted. I probably translated it wrong, something like "*Monsieur, the Woodchucks will not be fricasseed.*"

Linguistic barriers be damned, I plunged forward, explaining that we refused to serve as the lapdog for the Tres Lettres, and intended to take the field at 1:30 in full uniform to declare a forfeit and formally protest any further games that day given the field's condition. I gave an insincere apology, and he said not to worry, agreeing that the field was unsafe.

As I walked to the clubhouse to make the symbolic gesture of getting dressed, the head umpire asked if I had seen the field. He was a little late to the party, and began adamantly arguing that under no circumstances could we play baseball on the field that day. He refused to put players in harm's way, and couldn't imagine playing as scheduled. "No shit," I muttered, then turned and pointed at the Tres Lettres official.

"*Take it up with him.*"

I knew that news of our forfeit had spread through the rec hall when I heard Zoe shouting.

"*Great 'Challenge,' Woodchucks! After all this work, TWO games! One slaughter rule! And then you just forfeit!*' she ranted. I couldn't blame her; she had pulled together the friends of the club and worked their asses off to prepare for the Challenge, and felt betrayed by the forfeit.

"Hey, what is she bitching about?" Matt asked.

"She's pissed that we're forfeiting. They put in all this effort to make crepes and print t-shirts to sell, and now we're not even playing," I said.

Matt lumbered over to Zoe, still shouting at a stunned room as she cleaned up, making exaggerated noise with each dirty pot or pan to demonstrate her disgust. He reached over to calm her down, but she wheeled on him unexpectedly. Recognizing the insincerity in his face, her eyes narrowed.

"*And you! You didn't even play the full game! You're supposed to be the coach, the best player! And you didn't even finish the game!*"

Matt recoiled, accustomed to players deferring to him out of necessity. The men of the club (myself included) had tiptoed around the enfant terrible all season, but Zoe had no fucks to give, and had no qualms in pointing out the emperor's nudity. I envied her courage to speak her mind, consequences be damned. Matt turned to me for a translation, but I had seen enough, and trudged over to the clubhouse to get dressed.

It was surprisingly difficult. My brain knew that the field looked like the day after Coachella, but my body still had the Pavlovian response of excitement from pulling on a pair of baseball pants, trained for over 20 years to know that meant baseball was afoot. This time, I had the stimulus without response. Even a rush of adrenaline cannot dry a slice of the Everglades in Normandy. We massed in the dugout as the head umpire argued passionately that the field was unplayable and games should be delayed. The technical director politely thanked him for that advice before declaring the official decision of the French Baseball Federation that the games would proceed as planned.

"*In this case, Bois-Guillaume will declare a forfeit in order to protect the field and the players you're supposed to represent,*" I said, and that was that. As I walked away, the Senart manager joked that they would have preferred to play, because the Federation would record the forfeit as a 9-0 loss instead of the 20-0 slaughter rule Senart expected; the higher run differential would help them in case of a tiebreaker. I stopped walking, turned, and locked eyes with him, counting ten awkward seconds until his grin faded and he looked away sheepishly. I stormed off to change back into street clothes.

Toulouse won in the afternoon, placing them in the semifinal against Savigny the next day. We hoped the rain would stop, to give the battered field a chance to recover. Naturally, it did nothing of the sort.

With the field under an inch of standing water, we performed the same choreographed tango as the previous day, the outcome determined long in advance. We argued the field needed time to dry out to play safely, the umpires agreed, and the weasel of a technical director ignored both of us, declaring play would resume.

With the CFA exam just weeks away, I holed up in the clubhouse with my study materials, resisting the urge to tell the technical director to stick his Challenge where the sun don't shine, which as it turned out, was Normandy. I came down to the field in the ninth to watch Savigny's new Canadian pitcher – an Evan Meagher replacement – close out a 6-4 lead. With two men on and two outs, Romain took two steps backward to field a routine popup before slipping on the slick surface and falling with a crash. (Whodathunkit? Oh, wait: everyone but the technical director.) That made it 6-5, with two outs and men still on first and second. The next hitter drilled a liner to left to tie the game. The runner on first base inexplicably rounded second and carried on toward third base. One of baseball's 'cardinal rules' involves making the third out at third base:

YOU ABSOLUTELY MUST NOT DO IT, EVER, UNDER ANY CIRCUMSTANCES, OR THE BASEBALL GODS WILL SMITE YOU.

The unforgivable blunder cost Toulouse when the home plate umpire declared that the runner from second had not yet crossed home plate when the tag was applied at third, ending the inning and the game. (It was close; the ump may have just called him out so he could get in out of the rain.) Meanwhile, Montpellier upset Rouen in the semis. The next day, the Barracudas beat Savigny 9-4 in the final at Rouen, a remarkable upset that I took as a positive sign. Upsets meant a weakening of the Rouen-Savigny-Toulouse hegemony, and that was good for French baseball. If it sent the Federation's bureaucrats to their fainting couches, too bad.

The French baseball world erupted in gossip the following day, as Toulouse's hulking Canadian centerfielder disappeared in a cloud of smoke. He played on Sunday, when Toulouse lost in the semis, and then on Monday – {poof} – he was gone, Keyser Söze-style. Juicy rumors swirled that he had left after discovering that the Federation planned to drug test all foreigners. He had spent some time in the Angels' farm system, and his Herculean physique and Popeye-like forearms made his XXL t-shirt look like a tank top. His home run to straightaway center at Rouen shattered the skies to bring rain, and the remnants of his blast off Pierrick in the semis at Bois-Guillaume landed just shy of the soccer field, most of it having burned up in re-entry.

CHAPTER 27: DEAR DOCTOR

With the Challenge over, Sylvain resumed his efforts to find us a place to live. Every morning, I drove to Rouen to meet him at the apartment that we always seemed *just about* to rent, and every afternoon, it fell through for some reason or another. Aldo had agreed to host us for the Challenge and the Challenge only – me on a futon in his living room, Matt on an inflatable mattress in his computer room – and two burly ballplayers living in his apartment was a big imposition on someone who cherished his privacy. Only I felt compelled to do anything about it; Matt declared after the Challenge that he refused to return to Neufchatel, happy to impose on Aldo until the season ended. Like fish, I knew that we as house guests would begin to smell after three days.

Thursday marked my 27th birthday, and I celebrated by meeting Sylvain downtown once again to rectify our living situation. Just five minutes before we planned to sign a contract to lease two small studio apartments – which would give me some much-needed isolation from Matt – Sylvain's cell phone rang. It was Virginie, beseeching us to hold off long enough to examine "another option," which turned out to be a few rooms in Tyler Durden's house from *Fight Club,* still undergoing major repairs for damage from some recent, unnamed bombardment. After we left, promising to "*consider it,*" I hurled my keys to the ground in frustration: sadly, the best fastball I had thrown in Normandy.

I caught an early Friday morning train into Paris, unaware that it would begin one of the most bizarre weeks of my life, a whirlwind whose lasting effects I would feel for decades to come. Upon arriving at St. Lazare, I walked to the Opera station to catch another train to the southeast corner of the city, where I would stay in preparation for the CFA exam the following morning. Lacking clean clothes, I picked up a cheap t-shirt and flagged a cab to INSEP, where Eric had made an appointment for me with Dr. Demarais, a physician specializing in elbow injuries. I immediately regretted my t-shirt purchase: a knockoff of the blue French national soccer jersey, "FRANCE" emblazoned across the front and goofy red-and-white stripes around the armpits. In the waiting room of the National French Athletic Institute, I overheard the athlete next to me discussing her silver medal in judo from the Athens Olympics. I looked like a goddamn clown, as if I had attended the Oscars wearing a t-shirt that simply declared "MOVIES".

Dr. Demarais (translated literally, '*Of the Swamp*') welcomed me into an examination room and began manipulating my elbow this way and that, declaring that I suffered from an inflammation of the ulnar collateral ligament. (Point at someone directly in front of you with your right arm fully extended, then touch the bottom inside of the right elbow closest to your left side with your left hand; that's the UCL, more or less.)

The UCL is the Voldemort of ligaments. Those three letters (out of a doctor's mouth) rank up there with 'you're being audited' and 'you have the right to remain silent' in terms of phrases a pitcher never, ever wants to hear, because a torn UCL does not heal on its own. It requires Tommy John Surgery – or 'Thomas Jean,' as it's known in France – named after the first pitcher ever to have doctors remove a healthy ligament from elsewhere in his body (or from a cadaver donor), thread it through where his UCL used to be, and connect it with screws to his humerus and ulna bones. After two solid years of constant, painful physical therapy, a Tommy John patient *might* pitch again, but it's always a season-ender, and sometimes a career-ender.

To verify that I hadn't torn the UCL, he sent me to have an "IRM": *Imagerie par Résonance Magnétique*, or MRI. All of our conversations existed in a strange lingual netherworld between English and French, layman and physician; I started out apologizing for my French, he began in English, I persisted in French to demonstrate effort, he fluctuated between the two, and we finally settled on a confusing blend of Franglais.

My heart soared when he said I wouldn't require surgery, and might even pitch within a month. I almost hugged him; at last, someone could fix the excruciating pain in my elbow. Demarais prescribed mesotherapie, which involved minor injections below the surface of the skin. It sounded to me like a cortisone shot, so I asked in mangled French whether it was similar.

His jaw dropped, and he recoiled as if I had asked how they would kill the puppies whose blood they would inject into my elbow.

"*Oh no, no. Cortisone is a steroid!*"he replied, aghast.

"*Oh, I... had no idea. I'm sorry- we use cortisone to reduce pain and swelling in the States. Will this reduce swelling and pain like cortisone?*"

*"Of course! The mesotherapie will reduce your pain and swelling and get you back on the field before you know it!"*he said, smiling eagerly.

Thrilled with my newly optimistic prognosis, I walked down the Boulevard Poniatowski, reveling in my good fortune. I was young, soon to be healthy, and playing professional baseball in France. Now I just had to do what I did best: crush a standardized test. I chose a quiet restaurant for dinner to clear my head, and enjoyed an exceptional meal of oysters, braised short ribs, and a dessert of chocolate mousse and calvados, Normandy's famously potent apple-brandy.

I wandered back to my hotel, where I made the regrettable decision to check my email one last time on the hotel's free *huit filles* before going to bed. As usual, a hundred emails streamed into my inbox upon connection. One from my father read "Va avec Dieu, mon fils. You will destroy the exam, just like the others. Get a good night's sleep." I skimmed the rest until I reached the last; it was from Becky, sent just a half hour earlier.

My heart sank. Becky had called Kellogg and they had told her about my acceptance, and she was devastated to find out that I had been keeping it from her. My mouth went dry, and I lilted to one side as if struck by a right cross when I read the final line.

She was breaking up with me.

I stared at the ceiling for eight hours, never sleeping

a wink. What is there to say? I was in love, for the first time, and yet had somehow fucked it all up. My alarm at 7:15 AM more annoyed than awakened, as I had watched with irritation as 7:01 turned into 7:02, 7:02 into 7:03, and so on in a maddening march towards the moment I would have to get up and pretend to be ready for an exam. I showered in a daze and staggered off to the test site, where I powered through the morning essay section purely on adrenaline. I avoided a heavy lunch, trying to concentrate on questions of bond market liquidity, option-adjusted spreads, and the equity accounting method instead of how I had screwed up the only relationship I ever cared about.

The exam over, I took the train back to Rouen, where Matt greeted me with two pieces of irritating news. First, the new apartment had fallen through, so we remained stuck at Aldo's. Second, Matt declared that I would play first base on Sunday against Senart.

"Look mate, your arm just ain't cutting it at second, right?"

It was asinine, but I didn't have the energy to fight him. Moving me to first would downgrade two positions defensively; we would have to move Pierre to second, and he had a strong arm but limited range and a damning inability to pick up ground balls, while I had never played first base in my life. I had made just one error all season at second – in front of my parents against PUC, of course – but I knew better than to introduce facts into the conversation. Fine, I thought, first base. What's the worst that could happen?

I pulled on my stirrups on Sunday, and it felt like turning the key in the ignition of a car whose lights had been left on all night; the engine whimpered before giving out. For the first time in my life, playing baseball seemed like work. I ran extra warmup sprints, trying to get my head in the game, but it did no good; I played like dogshit. I busted a bat named *Sic Itur Ad Astra* ("Thus One Journeys to the Stars"), which exploded into a well-earned retirement after 20+ hits in France (more than half my total all season). I took a called third strike some 18 inches off the plate in the 8th, possibly the result of the differences between the rules-defined strike zone, the French strike zone, and the French strike zone for foreigners. (Every foreigner I knew complained that strikes against them were balls against French hitters, unless the pitcher was also foreign. In my estimation, there was absolutely truth to it, but it wasn't worth complaining about. We were getting paid and they weren't, so of *course* the umps held us to a higher standard.)

Vince continued his streak of quality starts, going seven-and-a-third innings and settling down nicely after serving up a 2-run dinger in the first. He gave up just one more run the rest of the way, but we couldn't get the offense going, which I pinned squarely on myself. I took my first 0-fer in France, and when your leadoff hitter goes 0-for-4, you're not going to win a whole lot of games in any country. We lost 3-2, our sixth loss by just one run.

Between games, I wandered to the grass behind the dugout where the Woodchucks congregated for lunch and tried to get my head straight. Pierre's father noticed that I hadn't brought anything to eat, and graciously offered me a quintessentially French lunch of ham, bread, and salad. I thanked him profusely, and between the rustic lunch and our breezy conversation about France's upcoming presidential election, I started to feel like I was getting my head in the game. Unfortunately, in the very first inning, I did just that.

With one out in the top half, I held a runner on at first when the batter hit a sinking line drive at Pierre, playing second for the first time per Matt's decree. Playing close to the second base bag in case of a stolen base, he snared the liner on one hop, tagged the bag, and turned to throw. He didn't realize that the hitter never left the batter's box, apparently thinking that Pierre had caught it on the fly. Pierre needed only to toss it softly to me for the inning-ending double play. Instead, he unloaded as hard as he could, launching an errant missile that skipped about six feet in front of me.

I spent a good portion of my life as a shortstop or third baseman, silently cursing out first basemen that lacked the courage (or, in retrospect, foolishness) to stay down on throws in the dirt to make a scoop. It drove me crazy when first basemen simply waved at a low throw instead of digging it out of the dirt. Having already made a nice scoop on a low throw from third in the first game, I did what I always heard coaches shout at first baseman: stay down on it. Unfortunately, the field at Bois-Guillaume was a treacherous one, especially in the soft dirt by first base, pounded flat like a veal *paillard* by runners leading off the bag. The ball caromed off a divot in the first baseline, skipped up over my glove, and crashed into my nose with a sickening crunch. The world went silent.

Rivers of blood. Fountains of blood. *Torrents* of blood, spewing forth from my nose before the ball even fell to the ground in front of me. Think of the elevator doors opening in *The Shining*, to get some idea of the carnage that materialized suddenly on the Woodchuck's infield. At shortstop, Seb's face contorted in horror as I wandered over to pick up the ball, dazed like the armless infantryman in *Saving Private Ryan*. As the world suddenly switched back from silent film to Dolby Surround, I heard Matthieu screaming "UNE! UNE!" from behind home plate. Retrieving the offending ball, I wheeled and flipped to Quentin, who had sprinted over from the mound to cover first when he saw the ball bounce away from me. I realized things looked every bit as bad as they felt when I raised my head to flip him the ball, revealing my newly rearranged face; Quentin's jaw dropped, his eyes the size of basketballs. Years later, I still take some pride in having finished the play, just your routine, run-of-the-mill 4-3-broken nose-1 double play.

I staggered off the field as Sylvain frantically called the paramedics. First base looked like a murder scene, and as I collected my belongings to jump in the back of the ambulance – something of an overreaction, I thought – I saw Aldo using a push broom to sweep the blood off the basepath, like one might sweep a porch after heavy rain.

If you ever want to get some funny looks, walk into a hospital in Normandy wearing the uniform of a sport no one understands, with metal cleats that create a disconcerting click-clack, click-clack with every step, looking like *Carrie* on prom night. After verifying my insurance status (the Tres Lettres insures all ballplayers at the elite level), the doctor took a quick X-ray before proudly declaring his diagnosis: my nose was broken. It recalled the overdose scene in *Boogie Nights*: "Oh, you think so, doctor?"

You learn something new every day, and on this particular Sunday, I learned not only that I had no place playing first base, but also that the French don't believe in local anesthesia, even while stitching up a jagged cut on the bridge of my nose that made me look like Frankenstein's monster. Not wanting to disgrace Americans and ballplayers everywhere, I sat in stoic silence, generally trying to pretend that I was tougher than I am. I soon sported three gruesome stitches on a horrifically swollen nose, with twin black eyes that lent me a Rocky Raccoon look.

The surgeon discharged me with instructions to return after ten days to have the nose set, and to avoid playing baseball for a month. Zoe picked me up and drove me back to the field, tutting over my disfigurement. Upon arrival, we discovered that we had lost the second game – drum roll please – 26-0. I would like to think that I could have made a difference, but even in my prime, I was never worth more than 22, maybe 23 runs per game. I showered carefully and headed out to find the '*Pharmacie de Garde,*' French for 'open on Sundays and holidays.' Naturally, that day – a

Sunday! – was also a holiday, something about worker's rights. Go figure! Apparently, responsibility for serving as the Pharmacie de Garde rotates each week, and a phone hotline explains which one is on duty. Unfortunately, the hotline's message is delivered in French at the speed of 'cattle auctioneer', and so after much misunderstanding and much driving around, I finally located the on-duty pharmacy. I will give you two guesses as to whether it was actually open, and the first one doesn't count. As such, my painkiller for the evening was not the prescribed Ixprim-325, but the self-prescribed Laguvulin-16, with a dosage of four fingers... for each hand. An oft-overlooked sedative/analgesic, it got the job done, went down smooth, and was remarkably affordable on that side of the pond.

I stopped by a Kebab shop for dinner, and treated myself to an extra serving of basbousa. I lived in France according to 'Summer Camp Rules': first kid to camp gets the top bunk, no pissing in the shower, and so forth. In this case, Summer Camp Rules meant that if you broke your nose during afternoon activities, you got extra dessert. Between getting dumped and shattering my nose in a less than 48-hour span, it might not have been the *worst* weekend of my life, but I've certainly had better, like the time I ruptured my kidney playing high school football, or nearly impaled myself on a prominent fountain during an ill-advised early-morning scooter ride in college.

My nose's throbbing agony woke me the following morning when the Lagavulin wore off. I wondered briefly what the other guy looked like before remembering my misadventure at first. Staggering to the bathroom mirror, I saw a man who had gone seven rounds against Marvelous Marvin Hagler. The blackish-purple skin around my eyes had swollen enough to obstruct my vision, and the stitches protruding from the ridge of my nose foretold a grisly scar. I winced, remembering what had distracted me enough to take a ball in the face: Becky.

I blew it, I thought, as I gingerly washed the few scab-less portions of my face. I had violated her trust, losing one of very few people who kept me afloat during the last few months of turmoil. I stumbled to

Aldo's kitchen, brewed a pot of strong black coffee, and watched the sun rise. By the time I heard Matt stirring in the computer room, I knew what I had to do.

He brushed past me on the way into the kitchen and grunted.

"How you feelin', mate?"

"I'm alright," I started cautiously, assuming that my injury would only invite Matt's mockery. At the very least, he probably wouldn't ask me to play first base again. "I have to use the computer."

Twenty minutes later, I returned to find Aldo and Matt at the kitchen table, preparing to work out. Aldo's eyes widened as he surveyed the carnage.

"*My friend... It goes?*" he gasped. *"It does you pain?"*

"*Yes, it goes, it goes. You?"*

"We go to Bois-Guillaume to work out. Do you want to join?"

"No, thanks. I need to pack... I'm going to San Francisco."

CHAPTER 28: BACK TO CALI

The day before my flight home, Aldo drove me, Matt, and the two Americans playing for Rouen (Cy and Royce) to Caen to visit the D-Day beaches. It was June 6th, the 62nd anniversary of the Allied landing. It lent me some perspective on the stress I felt from living with tantrum-throwing man-child, the anxiety of knowing my next paycheck depended on me getting three base hits each weekend, and my suddenly tenuous relationship with my girlfriend.

Ex-girlfriend.

You think you have problems? Walk out onto Omaha beach at low tide, as it was when the first American (and British, Canadian, New Zealand, and so on) soldiers arrived to stiff resistance. Gasp at the impossibly long sprint they faced, up the sand to steep cliffs where the Germans lay waiting and rested. Try running it; even without a 50-pound pack on your back, it takes several exhausting minutes that will make you feel thankful that they did it so you don't have to. Downcast though I felt, I appreciated the good fortune that made my visit to Normandy involve baseball and not bombardment. As we watched octogenarian veterans decorate the graves of fallen comrades in the sprawling American cemetery above Omaha beach, I reminded myself; it could be worse.

That weekend, the Woodchucks played Savigny, a team enjoying a very different season. The Lions were battling Rouen and Toulouse for the league title, while the Woodchucks battled only for the right to avoid relegation. The only thing the two teams had in common was... me. It was a game I had circled on my calendar ever since that strange string of events in April sent me from Savigny to Bois-Guillaume.

It was also a game played without me, as Wednesday found me in the international terminal at the airport in

Amsterdam, waiting for my connecting flight to San Francisco. Sometimes, mistakes that hurt people you care about leave you no choice but to hop on a plane and fly 6,000 miles to apologize in person, complete with stitches and a broken nose. Put differently, I had to go see about a girl. Sure, I wanted to play Savigny, and even knowing that they had blown the Woodchucks off the field three straight times – once with me on the mound – I knew that even a shocking upset would make no difference in the grand scheme of things. I could go 4-4 with three dingers, or I could go 0-4 with four ugly K's, and it wouldn't change anything. It wouldn't change their opinion of me as a ballplayer, it wouldn't change my opinion of Savigny, and it wouldn't change what happened; maybe it was for the best.

On the long flight home, my mind focused on more pressing matters. What the hell was I doing? Would Becky take me back?

I had sent a few hasty emails to arrange a place for me to stay in case things didn't work out with Becky, and borrowed a car from a former co-worker: the same

1972 El Dorado rag-top convertible in which I had picked up Becky for our very first date. I was pulling out all the stops. I cleared customs and took a cab to Pacific Heights to pick up the cherry-red behemoth, drove downtown, and parked in an alley just outside Becky's workplace on Kearny Street, where I waited for her to leave work.

Becky and I first met at a wedding; I knew Marc from Stanford, and she knew Hillary through a mutual friend in San Francisco. The four of us had become inseparable, often playing spades and drinking scotch late into the evening. When I booked my flight to SF to surprise Becky, I had called Hillary, hat in hand, pleading for her help. As I stood there on Kearny, the stereotypically frosty San Francisco summer wind forcing me to turn up the collar of my old motorcycle jacket, Becky thought she was heading to North Beach to meet Hillary for an after-work cocktail.

Instead, she found me.

Our eyes locked as I offered up silent thanks for Hillary's subterfuge. Becky did a double-take; just minutes before I was her ex-boyfriend, a continent away. Now I was in the heart of San Francisco's financial district, leaning up against the passenger side door of a 35-year-old Cadillac, with a look on my face somewhere between an apology and a proposal.

"You're... here." She whispered.

"Uh... yup."

Hey, I never said it was poetry. In fact, for all my preparations, I hadn't put a lot of thought into what I would say when I finally saw Becky. This unpreparedness made for an awkward reunion at first, but I eventually convinced her that Hillary wasn't waiting for her, and drove in silence back to her apartment in the Marina. I told her I loved her, that I couldn't imagine not having her in my life, and that I was sorry. She said... ha! She said that she was glad I was sorry. But she also said that she loved me. After a draining four hours, we kissed and made up. The grand gesture had worked, and we spent the rest of the weekend seeing friends and eating delicious San Francisco burritos.

While stateside, I took a few orders from

Woodchucks back in France: Skoal chewing tobacco, MLB The Show for PlayStation, among other things. Following the advice of a bodybuilder who read my blog, I ordered a powerful joint balm that promised to increase the circulation in my elbow and help me return to the mound. When it arrived, I found a bottle marked with pictures of horses and references to racing injuries. Shaking my head, I realized I had ordered an equine analgesic… and I didn't care. If smearing racehorse juice on my elbow let me pitch sooner, I would do it three times a day, even if it did burn like hell. Which it did.

On my last night in town, I surprised Becky with a reservation at Gary Danko, an impossibly expensive restaurant near Ghirardelli Square. When the chef brought our caramel mousse cake for dessert, the drizzled chocolate ganache on the plate spelled out "See You In Chicago, Kiddo" in an elaborate cursive font. Becky turned to me, perplexed.

"Does this… mean what I think it means?"

I couldn't hold back my ear-to-ear smile. "Yes, it does. I'm going to Northwestern with you."

Her face lit up, and we hugged for a long time. She wiped away a tear, and we ordered champagne to celebrate as I explained how I had come to the decision two days earlier, while wine tasting with our friend Ganek.

"Must have been some good wine."

My plans for the rest of the summer, once blurry and vague, now came into sharp focus. The Windy City would be home for the next few years, and I would have to figure out the overlap between school starting in late august and the season's climactic playoffs not ending until October. First, I had to worry about getting back to France, a voyage that took me one car ride, two airplanes, three buses, two metro lines, and one high-speed train. Some 36 hours after leaving San Francisco, I rang the doorbell at Aldo's apartment, where he and Matt were thrilled to see me, or in Matt's case, at least the Skoal that I had brought back with me.

After an all-too brief nap, Matt and I drove to Mont-Saint-Agnan to meet with Sylvain. Before leaving, I counted up the bags of Red Man and tins of Skoal remaining, noting by simple subtraction how many

Matt had grabbed. Sylvain took us to see our new apartments, single rooms in a dilapidated dorm on the campus of a local university. The difficulty we had faced in finding an apartment – combined with Sylvain's warning that they were "very small" – had me wondering just how bad the place would be. The rooms measured roughly 7' x 13', including the bathroom and shower, or approximately 35% smaller than the Cadillac I borrowed in San Francisco. The paint peeled off the walls, and cobwebs spread through the corner by the ceiling.

"*This is great!*" I said, turning to Sylvain. Matt grunted and headed upstairs. Not only had Sylvain procured us housing, ending our six weeks of imposing on Aldo, he had managed to find rooms on two different floors.

"*This is REALLY great!!!*" I repeated to Sylvain, who responded with his trademark gap-toothed grin. Sylvain's first year as club president had not gone entirely smoothly. Between the constant losing, the noxious clubhouse atmosphere, and the headaches from the Challenge, he faced a thankless, overwhelming workload. He did the job for free, and only played a few innings at the end of lopsided losses. For all his efforts, he got only surly reproaches from a cantankerous Australian and second-guessing from guys who enjoyed the fruits of his labors (and vastly more playing time) but didn't want to put in the effort to help. Not surprisingly, he lit up anytime anyone recognized his efforts.

"*I'm glad you like it,*" Sylvain said, beaming. "*You will stay here for two weeks, then move into another apartment in Rouen. It's not bad, no?*"

"Goddamn right it's not bad!" I said in English, reaching out to give him a fist pound. "*Great work, Sylv.* Merci."

Proving that you can't satisfy all of the people all of the time, however, controversy raged over the team's travel plans to Toulouse. We wanted to avoid the debacle of our Montpellier trip, where last-minute price increases nearly doubled the cost of train tickets, so we traveled in the ultimate budget option: a minibus. It only fit nine players, but we could only find eight players. For home games, we often relied on second-team players like Stephan and Eric Fournier to fill out the roster, but they couldn't sell their French wives on driving eight hours to Toulouse and eight hours back just to play baseball. One by one, I called Bois-Guillaume's N1B (the level below N1A) players and begged them to help us out, knowing that even if one agreed, they would be completely overmatched at the elite level. Desperate, I called Pierre's brother Yves, who played on Bois-Guillaume's *third* team. That was all the way down in Régionale, a level where a middling American high school team would go undefeated.

We met at the clubhouse and began loading the equipment as my teammates razzed me. They had placed bets on whether Becky would take me back.

"*With your nose like that, we figured there was no chance!*" Eric bellowed.[23]

---

[23] User error had actually made my nose worse; in my disoriented state at the hospital, I misunderstood the doctor to have said 'come back after ten days,' when in fact he had said 'within ten days." When I finally came back, there was nothing he could do; the broken bone had set, crookedly. Later that winter, the day before my last final exam, I got a torrential nosebleed that went on for four hours, ultimately forcing me to the ER, where the doctor determined I needed surgery to reset the broken bone, straighten my crooked schnoz, and repair my deviated septum. He also asked me more than five times whether I was a recreational drug user, because that kind of damage usually only results from snorting a LOT of cocaine. After each denial, he would give it a few minutes, then revisit the topic: "It's okay, I'm not going to tell the Dean. It's just... former investment banker/pro athlete? You definitely fit the profile."

"*Yeah, yeah, yeah,*" I said. "*Screw you guys. Oh, hey, Pierre, how are you?*"

"Bien, et tu?"

My jaw dropped, and I turned to the other Woodchucks; it had to be a joke. Pierre's voice had fallen – no exaggeration – three full octaves in the nine days I had been gone.

"*Uh, I am, uh...*" To my right, I saw Eric duck behind the driver's seat, choking back laughter. "*Are you alright, Pierre?*"

"Yes. I'm fine."

I couldn't handle it anymore. The elephant in the room was just too big.

"*Pierre...*" I gave up on saying this tactfully. *"What the fuck happened to your voice, Barry White?"*

The other Woodchucks burst out laughing. I wanted to be more subtle, but this was something else; Pierre, the voice that could crack glass, suddenly sounded... normal.

"I don't know, Evan. Before, I could talk like this, but

only for a short time, and it hurt my throat. All at once, it stopped hurting," he said in a rich baritone. Well, tenor, anyway; let's not get carried away. "*So I just started talking like this all the time."*

I didn't want to over-celebrate it, because that would draw attention to just how awful he had sounded before.

"Hell yeah!" I exclaimed, high-fiving him. Again with the subtlety.

Eric drove the first three hours out of Rouen, handing off to Aldo and then me. Most French highways have a speed limit of 110 kilometers per hour (~68 mph), but driving from Neufchâtel to Bois-Guillaume had made me comfortable at 145 (90 mph). Despite driving a souped-up Peugeot convertible himself, Aldo found this speed distressing.

"*Eh, buddy! What are you doing? You'll kill us all! Slow down!"*

"THANK YOU FOR YOUR ADVICE, ALDO." I replied. I slowed to 140, eliciting laughter from a few teammates. Several subsequent efforts to get me to slow down

resulted only in more snarky expressions of gratitude for his wise counsel, and he eventually gave up as Eric, Seb, and I chuckled. Near the end of the 500-mile drive, I overheard the terrible twosome of Matt and Matthieu speaking in hushed tones.

"I won't be here next year, I do not theenk," Matthieu began in English. "But it has been good for me, I get to play, get experience."

"Yeah..." Matt's voice trailed off. "You should go somewhere else, somewhere they don't lose every weekend."

"I wheel," Matthieu responded. "Maybe Montpellier. That team is like, party time."

I stewed in the driver's seat, listening to my teammates talk about how they were too good for the Woodchucks. I cast a sidelong glance at Eric, feeling grateful to find him sleeping and therefore oblivious to Matt's sedition. The other players dozed or had headphones on, so only I had heard the two Matts talking shit about them. My knuckles clenched around the steering wheel. I wanted to bring the bus to a screeching halt, drag both of them out of their seats and leave them on the side of the road, even if it meant a forfeit and team mutiny. Sighing, I reflected on the tragic factions on the Woodchucks. On one side, we had Matt and Matthieu, cancers with loyalty only to themselves. On the other side were me, Sylvain, Seb, and Eric, trying to keep the ship afloat just long enough to make it to the tournament and avoid relegation to N1A. In the middle was a loose affiliation of lifetime Woodchucks who played for fun like Vince and Pierre, some N1A holdovers like Stephan and Christophe, and Aldo, a fanatical competitor who marched to the beat of his own drum. These factions clashed on everything from travel arrangements to which dugout to claim. With only nine players, we needed to keep all three groups happy enough to show up, or we risked forfeiting. We were stuck with each other, one big dysfunctional Woodchuck family trying to make it through the season.

After a familiar stay in a Formule 1, we drove to the Toulouse field, among the best I had seen in France: no goofy cutout infields or concrete mounds. As we unloaded our gear in the parking lot, a quarrel flared up between Matt and Eric, reaching a boiling point before I could rub the sleep out of my eyes and intervene.

"NO!" Matt shouted. "THAT'S NOT IT. WHERE IS THE PAPER? THE PAPER YOU HAVE TO FILL OUT!"

"It's this!" Eric responded, his hands raised as if being mugged. He offered the necessary paperwork required by the Federation meekly, desperate to avoid a fight. "Here it is!"

"THAT'S NOT FUCKING IT!" Matt started again, excoriating a helpless Eric.

"Matt! Hey, buddy!" I interjected as soothingly as I could from the bench behind the driver's seat, where Eric looked at me with eyes pleading for intervention. "It's okay. Relax, man. Relax. I'll take care of it." We couldn't afford to have Matt sulk his way through 18 innings against a team as strong as Toulouse.

"Shut the fuck up!" Matt screamed over his shoulder at me. "I'm not talking to you." He turned back towards Eric and resumed shouting.

I felt backed into a corner. I was always tiptoeing

around Matt, knowing that if push came to shove, the Woodchucks needed him more than they needed me, but I also knew that I couldn't let him bully me in front of the other players, who looked around furtively, like children watching their parents fight. Matthieu cowered in the corner, refusing to look up, while Pierre sat frozen next to me, worrying that he was in line of fire should the situation escalate. *Take a stand here or lose their respect for good,* I thought. *Whatever respect you still have.* I took a second to compose myself and choose a volume level that would make it clear I meant business without pouring gas on the fire.

"Matt," I began. He ignored me, and continued berating Eric. "MATT." I repeated, louder this time. He turned. "IT IS TIME THAT YOU START SHOWING ME SOME FUCKING RESPECT."

He drew back, surprised at the opening of a new front. "Shut up! I'm not talking to you!" he shouted, and turned back towards Eric, but not before glancing back in my direction to see if I would respond.

"LET ME MAKE THIS PERFECTLY CLEAR, MATT: DO NOT EVER TELL ME TO SHUT UP AGAIN, OR I WILL

GET OUT OF THIS BUS AND WE CAN SETTLE IT RIGHT FUCKING HERE." I jabbed my index finger towards him. We locked eyes, mine narrowed to slits. My heart thumped like Ginger Baker on a bass drum as I sized him up; he had height and weight on me, but he was a bully and something of a coward. Flashing back to four years of living with collegiate wrestlers, I decided that if I could take the fight to the ground, I might negate his size advantage. *Maybe.*

"Don't point your finger at me like that!" he shouted, and for the first time I thought we might actually throw down right there in the parking lot. At the very least, I had diverted his attention from Eric.

"YOU HEARD ME." I said, jabbing my finger again and locking my eyes on his. We stared each other down as I prepared to brawl with my co-coach. My heart raced for an interminably long second, then another, before he muttered something about 'fucking off' and stormed off toward our dugout.

I lowered my index finger and took what seemed like my first breath in hours, my efforts to hide my relief hampered by the adrenaline pumping through my veins. I was shaking. I grabbed the bucket of baseballs and my duffel bag, dropped them off at the dugout, and sprinted to the outfield to burn off nervous energy. As I stretched in centerfield, Seb sauntered over with his usual Cheshire grin.

"*Thanks for doing that,*" he said, chuckling. "*And thanks for not getting in a fight!*"

I shook my head. I liked Seb a lot. Only he had kept his composure during Matt's outburst, rolling his eyes and trying to calm Matt down without taking it personally when the Australian snapped at him. Cool as a cucumber, as always.

"*No problem. I'm an adult. I can work things out without screaming and crying.*"

Seb grinned again. Then he slapped me in the face.

Actually more of a glancing blow off my shoulder, it still took me by surprise until I realized he had tried to swat one of the 'moucherons' (midges) that swarmed the muggy, swamp-like Toulouse field. I turned back to Seb, winding up as if I planned to smack him right back, before we both started laughing and continued our warm-up with the moucherons.

Relentless, tenacious, and impossibly numerous, the moucherons orbited every player like a horde of tiny satellites. They love few things in the world, and the lists starts with eyes, ears, and noses. Most of all, they love exposed wounds: can't get enough of them. Sadly, my face offered all of these attractions, so I spent the day doubling as a dipteran Disneyland. I swallowed three or four of them just warming up in the outfield.

Matt had never wanted to take the time to fill out the lineup card before, but this time, he grabbed it from the umpire and penciled me in at leadoff, but playing right field, a petty retribution for our confrontation. I sighed, briefly contemplating changing the card and sending Pierre back out to right. It would unquestionably make us a better defensive team – the switch made us weaker at both positions, just like against PUC, as I was a worse outfielder than Pierre and he was a worse second baseman than me – but instead accepted this trifling revenge for standing up to him in the parking lot. It was better than getting punched in my already shattered face, I guess.

Between only having nine ballplayers, the lingering antipathy between Matt and the rest of the team, and the 37-degree Mediterranean sun (I'm not sure of the conversion to Fahrenheit, but it felt like roughly 240 degrees), no one expected us to put up a fight against 17-3 Toulouse. They especially didn't expect us to make any noise in game one against the ace of the French national team, Samuel Meurant, but as Cardinals great Joaquin Andujar once said, you can describe baseball with one word: "joo never know." (The self-described 'one tough Dominican' was a great pitcher, but a lousy mathematician).

We came out energized, playing inspired defense behind a suddenly confident Quentin. He kept Toulouse's mashers off-balance by pitching in reverse: throwing his big, looping curveball early and going to his fastball once he got ahead in the count. Still jetlagged from my transcontinental flight, I foul-tipped a third strike to lead off the game, but took a fastball off the elbow in the third inning and stole second and third to ignite a three-run rally. The tension in the dugout slowly dissipated, replaced by enthusiasm and camaraderie as Eric rallied the team with cries of "Allez les boys!"

Quentin threw his best game of the year, spotting us a wholly unanticipated 3-2 lead to start the bottom of the sixth. Sensing a rare opportunity to knock off a league titan, I broke our mutual, hostile silence and asked Matt to warm up and try to close out an improbable victory. In the convoluted lineup juggling necessary whenever we changed players with only nine people, Matt went from center to the mound, Quentin from the mound to third, Yves from third to right, I from right to left, and Aldo from left to center. Just trying to explain (in French) all these shifts to the official scorer took me five solid minutes.

Matt cruised through the sixth, putting us nine outs from stomping into Toulouse against the consensus best pitcher in the country and stealing a win. I forgot any lingering resentment over our blowup, tantalized instead by the prospect of pulling off such a coup. I confess that during blowout losses, I sometimes found myself secretly rooting against Matt, in the hopes that it might temper his arrogance and make him a better teammate. It always made me feel dirty to root, even subconsciously, against a teammate. This time, I just wanted him to shut Toulouse down so we could escape with an upset win that would shock French baseball. The truth would be even more impressive than the headline, as we were essentially playing with only eight players; in three at-bats, Yves had had seen 11 pitches without touching a single one, while making two errors at third. And yet we clung tenuously to a lead until the seventh, when Matt allowed a walk, a sacrifice bunt, and a double to knot the game at three. After a scoreless eighth, extra innings loomed.

Meurant settled down after the third, using a lively fastball, big looping curve, and tailing changeup to set us down in order. I understood the debate raging around the league as to who was better, him or Piquet. Meurant was tough, real tough, but I gave a slight edge to Piquet, if only because he controlled the mound better, seemed more aggressive, more... American. He talked trash, stared hitters down, and jawed with umpires. Would have fit right in on the Reds! Meurant seemed cooler and more methodical, the Bob Feller to

Piquet's Bob Gibson.

I think my opinion was colored by the fact that I handled Meurant easily; I squared him up twice but came away empty, robbed by stellar defensive plays on two well-hit balls up the middle. With the game tied in the ninth, I needed a base hit by any means necessary. I dragged a bunt towards third, a beauty that died halfway down the baseline as I exploded out of the box with all the energy I had left. My legs pumping, I tracked the first baseman's eyes to anticipate the throw's arrival. A tall, skinny Algerian kid from INSEP, he stood about four inches taller than me while weighing 50 pounds less, and he suddenly leaped toward me when I was just steps from the bag, his raised arms exposing his rib cage. The bunt had been perfect and there was no play at first, but the third baseman unwisely tried to rush it. The wild throw pulled the first basemen directly into my path, his lanky outstretched frame recalling a defenseless wide receiver with the strong safety bearing down on him.

Already at top speed, I couldn't stop or avoid contact. I ducked to protect my fragile nose, my shoulder plowing into his unprotected ribs with a sickening crunch. The collision spun him like a top, and I turned to see him fall awkwardly on his back, knocking the wind out of him. I grimaced, feeling culpable, but not enough to prevent me from taking second base as the ball bounced out of play and he lay prone, the trainer attending to him.

He rose to his feet as I realized that this was our chance: our fastest runner in scoring position with just one out. We just needed a base hit from Seb or Matthieu, and then a scoreless ninth to pull off the impossible. I stepped off second and thought about stealing. Meurant threw hard and was quick to the plate, and the catcher had shown his strong arm, but I thought I could take third.

Whap!

I ate a face full of dust.

Meurant evidently had the same thought process, and whipped a pickoff throw to the second baseman. I dove back instinctively, barely beating the tag. Stealing third would be harder than I thought. I resolved not to take the bat out of Seb's hands.

He slapped a soft flyball to the right fielder for the second out. I tagged and took third. We needed a base hit from Matthieu.

"Come on, you son of a bitch," I muttered to myself as Matthieu stepped into the batter's box, his pre-at-bat routine lacking its usual performative swagger. "Prove it. Show us you don't belong here. Just one goddamn base hit, and you can write your ticket anywhere in the league."

"Shit, I'll buy your damn train ticket myself," I added. It wasn't a terrible matchup for Matthieu, who hadn't grown into his body yet – hell, he was just 16 years old – and so lacked power, but had decent hand speed and a compact swing. (His swing tended to get long when he swung for the fences, but he had enough respect for Meurant – maybe too much – that he was unlikely to let his swing get long and loopy.) For Matthieu, Meurant was tough but not overpowering, no tougher than a half-dozen guys I used to bang heads with in San Francisco. Just a little flare into right, or a seeing eye ground ball, and we would have the lead.

As Billy Beane said in *Moneyball*, sometimes it helps to be dumb in this game: dumb enough to ignore the specter of facing the legendary Sammy 'Mayday' Meurant and step into the box confident you'll barrel one. Seb and Eric could summon that irrational confidence, but too often the INSEP kids were victims of their Tres Lettres' education.

At INSEP, the Federation told the Espoir kids like Matthieu they were the best in the country, but only in their age group; the Federation held up older players like Meurant as the gold standard to which to aspire. With Matthieu, that held him back; weaned on the Tres Lettres' mythology (and respect for the very elders we now needed Matthieu to disrespect with a base hit), he built Meurant up in his mind, taking himself out of at-bats, giving himself comfort that there was no shame in striking out against the 'best pitcher in France.' He might as well have started with an 0-2 count.

Matthieu popped meekly to second, happy simply to have avoided a strikeout, and the window of opportunity closed with me stranded at third. On the jog back to the dugout, I wished that we could have redirected some of the disrespect Matthieu regularly showed to me, Eric, Seb, and Sylvain toward Meurant, even if just for one at-bat.

We walked a tightrope into extra innings, as the heat took a devastating toll, occasionally forcing me to call time to untie and re-tie my shoes just to hide my dizzy spells. Matt labored through the ninth and tenth innings without giving up a run, but the bottom of our order couldn't push anyone across. In the 11th, Matt gave up a base hit, a walk, and a deep fly ball down the line in right that fell just fair past a hapless Yves, scoring the game-winner easily from second without a throw. Another walkoff defeat.

We had an uncanny ability to find new gut-wrenching ways to lose close games. It made, count 'em, *seven* games lost by one run, three in extra innings. A few bounces here and there, and instead of 5-17, one game out of last place thanks only to the four forfeit wins from Senart and Savigny, we could have been 12-10, shocking the league by clinging to the final playoff spot. We just didn't have the horses. We weren't unlucky; if anything, we had gotten all the lucky bounces just to make those games close in the first place. It seemed greedy to ask for still more luck to actually win them, but the heart wants what the heart wants, and my heart wanted a victory or two to show for it.

In the second game, we had absolutely no one to throw. Quentin and Matt had pitched in the first game, and our usual horse Vince hadn't traveled with us due to his high school graduation exams. Seb courageously trotted out to the mound, settling down after walking the first three hitters on 13 pitches, but we never got closer than 4-2. After a quick cold beer with the Toulouse team, we started the long drive home with the dubious comfort of knowing that we had played our best baseball of the year, taking arguably the best team in the league to 11 innings against their ace, but it still hadn't quite been enough. Our #8 and #9 hitters went a combined 1-for-16 with 12 strikeouts across the two games, and combined with Matthieu's pop out, that cost us a possible win.

CHAPTER 29: NO PARTICULAR PLACE TO GO

As we left Toulouse, I felt calm, reassured by the ensuing four-week layoff that would let me travel around Europe, and more importantly, escape my insufferable teammate. The minibus atmosphere turned festive as Eric tuned in to France's World Cup match against South Korea. Never a huge soccer fan, I nonetheless found myself caught up in the excitement. If ever there was a time to be in a foul mood, it was then, after 19 innings in scalding heat, my muscles setting like concrete in the cramped minibus. Instead, I felt like we finally bonded as a team. You had to be there, but we had a moment, the sun silhouetting an ancient Roman aqueduct in the hills over Toulouse, with a group of six smelly French ballplayers (plus one Yank, one Canuck, and one Aussie) belting out La Marseillaise[24] at the top of their lungs, where I realized with a smile and an "Allez Les Bleus!" ("Go Blues", the French national team nickname), that this whole French baseball thing was a pretty good gig, the long drives, short pay, and gut-wrenching losses notwithstanding.

For months, World Cup fever had gripped the country, and even the French athletes that preferred baseball weren't immune. France had one of the best teams in the world, always a threat to win it all. They last pulled the feat off in 1998, stomping Brazil in a match that even French diehards acknowledged had featured a disproportionate number of calls in favor of "Les Bleus." In 2002, they lost to Senegal, getting their comeuppance from a former colony, as Matt loved to remind our French teammates. Stung by that shocking first-round upset, the French seemed a little apprehensive in the summer of 2006, as evidenced by a recent heated talk show with the topic of discussion

---

[24] The French national anthem. I have to say, it's pretty good.

"Les Bleus: Faut-Il Y Croire?" ("The Blues- Should One Believe in Them?") The roundtable featured a who's who of former players, coaches, and one long-haired comedian who concluded his commentary by pulling out a guitar and singing a romantic ode to Zidane.

Ah yes, Zidane. His name dominated the airwaves throughout the spring, as he announced in a tear-soaked farewell interview that he would retire after the World Cup. The captain and consensus best French player over the past decade, his balding image was emblazoned in Mao-sized portraits over every town we passed through. News of his retirement met with caterwauling and tearful remembrances, well-timed in conjunction with a biopic on his life story. Sadly, France would ultimately lose in the finals to Italy, with Zidane earning an ejection over an ill-advised blatant head-butt into the chest of an Italian defender.

We finally arrived back in Normandy after midnight. I disappeared before sunrise, locking my duffel bag and leaving early to avoid further interactions with Matt. I caught a train into Paris and a flight to Cork. I won't bore you with details of my travels, except to say that in

Dublin, I procured a ticket for both Gaelic football and hurling, a sport so impossibly violent that I cannot help but imagine that a few lacrosse players were once sitting around, trying to find a way to maximize an already dangerous game's potential for carnage.

"You know, I love Lacrosse, but I just wish that our sticks were blunter and more lethal, and we could use them to strike our opponents more indiscriminately."

"Absolutely. Lacrosse is great, but I hate that goalies actually wear helmets and we can't tackle, cross-check, slash, or trip."

"Let's invent a sport to circumvent such safety precautions!"

The conversation could only result in Hurling. If you love the grace of the floor routine or the pageantry of equestrian, do not come to a hurling match. If you like watching players smack each other with wooden hurleys (sticks) so hard that their impact on wrist bones and teeth rings out across the field, you will not go home disappointed. Meanwhile, I found Gaelic Football everything that an ugly American like myself thinks soccer ought to be: scores in the twenties, titanic collisions, and the ability to use one's hands.

After traveling through Galway, the picturesque Aran Islands, and Belfast, where the locals assured me that they loved visitors and saved their visceral hatred for one another, I flew to Bristol on the west coast of England. Convinced that I could handle driving on the left side of the road, I rented a car so I could see Stonehenge on the way to London to meet Becky. It was easy on the freeways, but devilishly difficult in urban areas, given that the steering wheel's position on the right side of the car meant I had to work the stick shift with my left hand. As I approached the Hertz drop-off location near Victoria Station, I turned onto what I thought was a one-way lane separated from the rest of the street by a decorative wrought-iron fence. I glanced at the fuel gauge, knowing I would have to fill up before dropping off the car, only to look up and find myself staring at a massive double-decker bus bearing down on me, its horn honking and driver waving and screaming with such enthusiasm that I can only assume he wasn't welcoming me to London.

White-knuckling, teeth-clenching, heart-pounding terror consumed me as my life flashed before my eyes. I fumbled with the stick shift, cursing its counter-intuitive reverse layout. Seconds from impact, I slammed it into first gear and rocketed out of the oncoming bus's path just inches before a catastrophic collision would have made Matthieu's pop out against Meurant my last frustrated thought on this green earth. Shaken *and* stirred, I pulled the car into the Hertz location, mumbling as I retrieved my luggage.

"Sir!" the attendant pleaded with me in a thick Indian accent. "Sir, you need to refuel the car. It is very expensive to have us fill up the petrol chamber!"

I laughed. "You can charge me whatever the hell you want, man. No *way* I'm going back out there."

I met up with Becky, and we drove a new rental car north to dine with Alex and Jools. We then flew to Barcelona and enjoyed a romantic overnight train to Pamplona, where we arrived just before the running of the bulls. We followed some Americans to the center of town, where I bought a red scarf and a white t-shirt to match the local uniform, and meandered down to the course entry point. Just before the legendary run started, we ducked into a sidewalk bodega, where my Spanish proved sufficient to order "Una cerveza grande, por favor." With the light Spanish beer and the sight of a nearby David Ortiz t-shirt bolstering my courage, I stood and waited as loudspeakers dotting the fenced-in route blared safety instructions in six languages, imploring people to stay down if they fell so as to avoid tripping up other runners.

An alarm sounded, announcing the bulls' release some 200 yards above us. With each passing second, more and more runners starting the *Encierro*[25] at my location began descending the wood-fenced path towards the bullfighting ring at the end. There is something powerful and intoxicating about standing your ground as hundreds around you flee, waiting for something unfathomably dangerous to overtake you. Steady… STEADY! Suddenly, the last holdouts in front of me turned, and I knew it was time to run faster than I had ever run before, faster even than the Quiet Storm. I took off in a dead sprint, arms pumping, feeling *alive*.

---

[25] The Running of the Bulls.

Some 50 yards later, I glanced to my right, only to see a massive bull galloping past me as if I were standing still, well within arm's reach. My eyes as big as baseballs, I hurdled a pile of fallen runners, relieved they had heeded the broadcasted instructions and remained prone. The bulls passed me in a blink, and I jogged triumphantly to the bullfighting ring. After a few minutes of scanning the crowd, I spotted Becky, who waved, smiling and clapping at the festival around us.

From Pamplona, we traveled back north through Bayonne to Paris, where Becky flew to her own adventure in Kenya. We would meet up in Amsterdam two weeks later, after Bois-Guillaume's doubleheader against familiar foes La Guerche. The unorthodox French baseball schedule had given me four weeks off before these two games against The Great Piquet, then *another* four weeks off before a doubleheader against Saint-Lô, then finally the postseason relegation tournament. I had played well for the Woodchucks, hitting about .380 and playing a nearly errorless second base, but even I knew it wasn't enough. French teams signed foreigners to *pitch*, and the Woodchucks were no different, having signed me entirely on the promise of that snapping curve I showed them in Savigny. When I couldn't pitch during the regular season, the Woodchucks only *kept* me in the hopes that my elbow would recover in time for the postseason.

George Plimpton postulated that "The pitcher is happiest with his arm idle. He prefers to dawdle in the present, knowing that as soon as he gets on the mound and starts his windup, he delivers himself to the uncertainty of the future." With all due respect to George, whose writing helped inspire my French adventure, that was bullshit. Never in my life had I felt so impatient to pitch as I did upon returning to Bois-Guillaume. With excitement and a little trepidation, I pulled Aldo aside at the beginning of that Wednesday's practice to test my arm. He set up about 70 feet from me and threw me a pretty good heater, with a little zip on it.

"*Whoa, buddy, a little closer, eh?*" I wasn't ready to air it out right away.

Aldo advanced 20 feet as I palmed the ball in my

glove, contemplating the task before me. I did some quick mental arithmetic; 20 years of playing baseball, minus four years in college, an average of 16 games per year including travel teams and Babe Ruth league, plus practices, maybe 200 throws per game or practice... add it all up, and I had probably thrown a baseball almost a half million times in my life. I didn't have to reinvent the wheel here, just pick it up and let it go naturally like those hundreds of thousands of times before, and hope to hell that it doesn't hurt.

I wound up, pulled the ball back, and lobbed it to Aldo.

Not bad, I thought. I didn't throw it dart-style, as I had done to baby the elbow since Savigny, but my delivery was far from natural. Aldo and I fell into that familiar rhythm, catching and throwing, catching and throwing, my confidence growing each time I let the ball go without hearing a shriek of protest from my elbow. I never reached 100% velocity, but it would have to suffice. Fear of injury made it hard to control the ball, though. Baseball requires the most finely-tuned proprioception – perception of the body's position in space – of any sport in the world, and my brain's ongoing preoccupation with re-injury prevented me from finding a consistent release point, leaving me with no idea where the ball would end up. Worse, I couldn't make the ball cut or run. I threw one gentle cut fastball, and immediately upon release, received a clear message from the elbow: 'Hey buddy; don't even *think* about doing that again.' I iced it that evening, applied my equine joint balm, and hoped for the best.

That night, I answered a call from Eric Fournier, asking if I would help him work on his house.

"Sure, Eric. No problem." I hesitated, knowing that Eric and Matt didn't get along terribly well. This Eric only played on the elite team when we needed bodies, so he didn't feel as invested in placating the volatile Aussie. *"Do you want Matt's help too?"*

"Eh, no, I do not think so." Awkward silence. Then laughter.

I helped paint the room he was remodeling for his baby son, complimenting him on reusing the turn-of-the-century exposed wood beams. Like Eric Coutu, he had purchased a decrepit Normandy barn, over a century old, and done a great job refurbishing it, retaining the aged beams to create an intimate, rustic look. Curious how he would protect the vintage wood, I racked my brain for the French word for 'lacquer,' and decided to guess by just French-ifying the word 'preservative.'

"*So... are you going to put a* 'preservatif' *on the wood?*"

His nonplussed giggles made it clear; I had guessed poorly. Hm. I knew 'preservatif' was a word. I had heard it used, but I couldn't place exactly where.

"*A* preservatif*, non? That which one puts on the wood to protect it?*"

"*Oh, oui, le* varni*, OK*!!!" he roared with laughter, using the correct word for varnish. "*Preservatif, that's totally different.*"

I realized my mistake.

Preservatif is the French word for condom.

Oops.

CHAPTER 30: STUCK IN LA GUERCHE AGAIN

The odds of a baby born at the Boston Lying In Hospital ever visiting La Guerche – France's answer to Hanover, New Hampshire – have to be on the order of 1 in 10,000, or 0.01%. The odds of visiting twice should be more than .01% squared; statisticians would argue that anyone who visits once has a higher chance of visiting a second time, but they obviously never actually made the trek out to Bretagne, because anyone familiar with La Guerche would agree that one visit is the surest way to prevent a second.

That's actually not fair, as La Guerche-de-Bretagne is lovely, albeit so remote as to be 'not-so-much-in-the-middle-of-nowhere-as-on-its-periphery.'

We would visit the rural commune once again facing a ballplayer shortage, exacerbated by the French custom of vacationing in the south for the summer, Aldo's work schedule, and Vince's ankle injury, which cost us his steady six innings on the mound.

The goodwill from our game in Toulouse had worn off in the ensuing weeks, and we piled into cars, tiptoeing around another one of Matt's vitriolic moods. Having spent four listless weeks hanging around Rouen, he couldn't wait to skip town and travel through Italy with Cy and Royce, the USF ballplayers from the Huskies.

That lousy *ambience* spilled over to the field, where we came out listless and apathetic. With Matt once again uninterested in filling out lineup cards, I moved myself back to second (after stumbling around the outfield at Toulouse), and enjoyed my second five-hit weekend of the year. Two came off Piquet, the only bright spots in a pair of lopsided losses. We drove home in silence, save for an outburst from Matt when we stopped for gas. He cussed out the entire team, shouting that we didn't deserve him and he shouldn't even waste his time. As usual, his tirade met with tired, stony faces of Woodchucks players eager only to get home, except from Matthieu, who egged him on. On the second leg, I sat with Seb, Sylvain, and Eric, who was almost in tears watching this cancerous foreigner destroy the teams' sense of camaraderie.

"*It's not right,*" he began. "*This team... it was never like this. We always played to have fun, to enjoy friends. Not just to complain, just to play for the money.*" The despair was raw and palpable.

"*I know, Eric. I know.*" I put my hand on his shoulder. "*You can't let guys like Matt and Matthieu... listen: they do this on purpose. They're like the kids who tear the wings off butterflies. They just insult everyone to feel better about...himself. Uh... them. Uh...*" Suddenly very emotional, I had forgotten the word for "themselves. "*You understand me? Matthieu went, what, one-for-fucking-nine today?*"

Eric nodded. He didn't resent Matt like I did. He loved anyone who wore the grey and black of the Woodchucks, even Matt. I realized that Eric was a better man than I, because I had lost all patience with Matt's bullshit.

"He's not a Woodchuck," I continued. "*I wish we had more guys like you, and Seb, and Vince, but we don't. Matthieu is here for himself. Matt too. We need those guys for the play-down, but that's it. Just remember: we only have to put up with their bullshit a little longer. For the Woodchucks, for Bois-Guillaume. That's what's important."*

Eric nodded again. Matt's verbal assault on him in Toulouse notwithstanding, Eric got along better with the Australian than I did, but he couldn't hide his frustration.

"*Evan, I'm glad you're here, my buddy."*

"Me too," I replied.

The next day, I called Kayvon, my best friend of over a decade. We went to high school together, were college roommates, then lived together in San Francisco. Along the way, he provided me sage counsel in my frequent times of need. He was the best friend a guy could have, loyal to a fault, and one of the smartest guys I've ever met.

I used an international calling card to catch him at work, eschewing small talk and launching immediately into the noxious atmosphere, how Matt had done everything he could to suck the joy out of playing, and how he tried to extort more money from the team on account of my elbow injury. The venom poured out of me, pent-up resentment flowing into the receiver.

"What do I do, man? The whole season is about this play-down; that's the only thing that kept our heads up all seasons, because we knew that even if we got smoked in April, it wouldn't matter if we stepped up in September. So here I am, with this asshole for a roommate – the biggest clubhouse cancer I've ever seen – and he's the other fucking coach! Now I'm supposed to start at Northwestern on August 28th, before the play-down even starts. Sure, I have some frequent flyer miles from work, but not enough to buy all those expensive flights across the pond... and can I even do that? Fly back and forth every weekend? Should I even bother?"

Kayvon listened. Took it all in. Working for a major investment bank, he was in the middle of a 100+ hour week, and every minute he spent talking to me was another minute in the office, another minute after midnight he would go home.

"You know what, Ev? *Fuck* that guy. I mean it, *fuck'm*. This is *your* story, this is what *you* wanted to do, and I saw you make all these sacrifices for it. So *fuck* him. You gotta close this shit out, dude." He took a deep breath. "You're a closer, right? Close. This. Shit. Out."

A warm breeze blew up the hill from the Seine. I shook my head, and chuckled.

"You're right. Screw it. You're right."

He laughed right back.

"That's what I'm talking about. Now get your shit together. This is gonna be awesome."

I hung up, feeling a lot better. As usual, Kayvon was right. I had told Eric and Sylvain that I would help Bois-Guillaume 'jusqu'au bout': to the end. Pulling out my calling card once more, I called Becky's travel agency. Within 20 minutes, I had booked five consecutive round-trip tickets from Chicago to Paris, leaving every Friday at 5:55PM Chicago time, returning from Paris on

Monday morning. I had some frequent flyer miles from work, but not enough to pay for all five, so I dipped into my savings and purchased the remainder in cash. Of all the silly things I have done – like leaving a stable six-figure income to make €300 a month playing baseball – this was by far the most nonsensical.

I felt better right away.

Mounting the stairs to our filthy apartment, I found Matt watching television in his room.

"Hey, I'm bouncing. See you in a couple weeks." He grunted, never turning away from the television. "By the way, just booked my flights back from Chicago." Now he turned back, an eyebrow raised. "Yeah. I'll be here throughout the playoffs. Later."

I grabbed my bag and marched off to the train station, feeling a certain sense of minor triumph. Matt had exploited his status as the team's best player, lobbying to get me off the team, but I had outmaneuvered him. Despite his best efforts, I would finish the season as a Woodchuck.

With another four weeks off, I took a train to

Luxembourg and traveled through Belgium and Amsterdam en route to a reunion with Becky. First, however: Saint Sixtus. On that first plane from San Francisco, I had read an article in one of the airline rags about Belgium's more than 100 breweries. Beer aficionados elevated the six trappist breweries over all others, with one standing out as the world's finest, hardest-to-obtain beer: the Westvleteren 12 from the Saint Sixtus Abbey near Poperinge, Belgium. Beer Advocate rated it the world's finest, its reputation growing to legendary proportions given its exclusive availability at an adjacent café. Somewhere over the North Atlantic, I knew what I had to do.

I rose early in Brussels, eager to start my mission. Poperinge required a long train ride, so I skipped breakfast to maximize my time at the abbey. It took much longer than expected, as I hadn't anticipated the train stopping at every town in West Belgium, towns like Zottegem, Denderleeuw, and the unfortunately christened Leper.

In Poperinge, I asked the train's engineer how to find the abbey, which required a 15-minute walk to the square, where I rented a bicycle and rode north to taste the world's finest beer. I idled pleasantly up the hill, my first thought concerning Belgium's serene beauty, its endless fields of barley punctuated only by occasional turn-of-the-century farmhouses.

My second thought was 'Damn, but this place sure smells of cow shit.'

I soldiered on, turning left at a sign pointing me to Saintsixtusabdj (TheBelgiansseenoreasontopunctuacewordswithspaces), where I saw the abbey in all of its glory. I pedaled up to the abbey and the adjacent café, finding it, to my profound dismay, closed.

I had to catch a 3:45 train the next day to meet Becky in Amsterdam, but I had come too far not to taste the nectar of the Gods. I grumpily pedaled back to town, returned the bicycle, and hopped on the train back to Brussels.

The next morning, I awoke even earlier, catching the first train. Once again, I walked into town, this time with the speed of Americans marching through western Belgium some 60 years earlier with greater purpose than mere beer consumption. I rented the same bicycle from the same shop, but my voyage north to the abbey exhibited none of the carefree, Newman-in-Butch-Cassidy-and-the-Sundance-Kid spirit of the day prior. This time, I attacked the hills like Lance Armstrong, muscling up them like the Cutters in *Breaking Away*. My calves burned with lactic acid as I turned onto the straightaway, where the abbey rose out of the fields like a beer-soaked oasis. To my relief, the café's outdoor patio teemed with visitors, who witnessed me fist-pumping and raising my hands in triumph as if I had won the Tour de France.

Following the advice of professional beer tasters, I started with the lightest beer, the blond Westvleteren 6, before moving onto the brown 8 and the holy grail of the brown 12. The blond was creamy and spicy, and potent at 5.8%. The brown 8 was fruity and surprisingly crisp, packing a punch at 8.1%. Finally, the Westvleteren 12... sublime. Checking my watch, I realized I would never again have the opportunity to order the world's finest beer, and waved off the waitress asking if I wanted the check; non, Madame, another 12, s'il-vous-plait. I nursed it as long as I could before paying the bill and staggering back to my bike. I turned onto the alley leading to the main, realizing that I… was hammered. Four beers don't sound like a lot, but when they have an average alcohol content of about 9%, they equate to about 12 Bud Lights. I drove Popeye-style back to the small town, one eye slammed shut to keep the world from spinning, hanging on for dear life. Miraculously, I arrived in one piece, and reached my train just in time to make it back to Brussels, grab my luggage, and catch the high-speed rail to meet Becky in Amsterdam. We saw a Rolling Stones show before flying to Florence, traveled by train from Rome to Bari, where we took a ferry to Croatia. We traveled up the Dalmatian coast to Split, flew to Budapest, and took a train to Prague before I flew back to Paris, ready for my last week as a resident of France.

This fantastic voyage has but one story worth mentioning. In Korčula, a walled island city off the Dalmatian coast, we arrived at the train station and agreed to stay with one of the local entrepreneurs offering a spare bedroom for rent. He insisted that it was a ten-minute walk from downtown. We piled into his Yugo, our eyebrows rising as the drive took some 35 minutes. We finally arrived in a desolate backwater of the island, at least an hour's walk from downtown, in a room that reeked of cat piss. Despite our pleas to drive us back, that he had deceived us as to the proximity of his home to downtown, he refused, rubbing his fingers together shouting "Petrol! Petrol!", in an attempt to extort gas money for the ride back to town. Furious, we refused, recognizing a situation where he held all the cards, leaving us powerless to exact any retribution whatsoever.

Unless you write a book. To Andelka Borovina at Sv. Anton, Korčula, 20262, Croatia, phone number 011-385-020-715226: Jebo ti pas mater, ubit cu te, pa te mrtvog jebat. I'm not sure what that means, but an online translation site indicated it was unforgivably vulgar.

I feel better now.

As soon as I arrived back in Rouen, I called Eric. He seemed on edge.

"Evan, have you heard from Matt?"

Silly question, really.

"No, Eric. What's up?"

"We emailed him to verify that he would play against Saint-Lô... he never responded! We don't know if he will come!"

"Don't worry. I'm sure he will play. He knows he won't get paid for the month otherwise, so-"

"No, Evan, that there is the problem! He asked to be paid in advance for the month of August so that he could travel!"

Oh. Well in that case, you're fucked, I thought.

"You do not think that he would not show up for games for which we already paid him, do you?"

Awkward.

"Eric... I'm sure he will play," I lied. *"All the same... I think we should make sure we have nine players without him for Saturday, just in case."*

"Oh, la la." Eric sighed, audibly distraught. Desperate to cheer him up, I divulged something I probably

shouldn't have, something I should have kept under wraps until the last possible moment, just in case I couldn't deliver on it.

"Eric..." I inhaled sharply. "*My elbow feels good. I... I think I can pitch. Just an inning, you know? We'll see.*"

"Ohhhhhhhhhhhh..." he exclaimed. I could almost hear the smile on his face. "FANTASTIQUE, mon ami!!!"

CHAPTER 31: BACK IN THE SADDLE

There's something about a pitcher's mound.

So far as I know, it's the only ground in any sport elevated above the other players, accentuating the singular control its inhabitant wields over the outcome of the game. The goalie, the point guard, even the egomaniacal quarterback must all stoop to the same altitude as their less glorified compatriots. Not so the pitcher, who exists literally on a different plane than all the other players, floating above them with exclusive access to the field's high ground, the captain at the ship's helm.

The saga of my summer in France centered on my physical inability to return to that place of stature. In

April and early May, throwing caused such explosive pain that the possibility of season-ending Tommy John surgery seemed very real. Forget France; as weeks turned to months and the pain remained, I worried that I would never pitch a baseball again.

On August 20th, 2006, some four months, 18 days, two hours and 40 minutes after stepping off the mound in Savigny, I climbed back up the hill and let it loose. It happened at the tail end of a pair of whuppings from Saint-Lô, in our second-to-last weekend of regular season games before the tournament. Surprising only me, Matt never showed up, so trailing 8-2, we had to squeeze some innings out of Eric. He closed out the sixth, seventh, and eighth, and insisted he could handle the ninth, but I decided to give it a go. If not now, when?

I warmed up cautiously, watching for the slightest tension in my forearm. Like a Russian nuclear engineer firing up the uranium tubes the day after Chernobyl, I ran a tentative systems check. Fastball? Ok, 60% maybe, but no pain. Slider? Can't quite snap it off, but it'll run a little. Curveball? Too afraid to snap the wrist and throw it properly. I couldn't muster the courage for the Yellow Hammer, so I resolved to make do without it.

New territory for me; with the Reds, I got by more on guts and overpowering stuff then finesse. Suddenly, I found myself weaponless, robbed of velocity and the Yellow Hammer, Popeye without his spinach. I hopped over the baseline out of superstition and strode to the mound, trying to project the confidence I lacked. Never particularly religious, I nonetheless thought of all the impressive cathedrals I visited throughout Europe, looking up at the sky for help.

The artifice was gone; as a Red, I ended my warm-ups with a backstop salute, my best fastball off the backstop to show the hitters I was throwing hard and wild enough to be scary. After 140 days off, I lacked the arm strength; it would have arrived on a lob, amusing instead of intimidating. Catching the ball from Stephan – playing catcher only because Matthieu had emulated his role model's selfishness and no-showed on us – I turned towards the outfield, pretending to adjust my jersey while actually giving my elbow a good talking to.

"Come on, you (expletive) (really foul expletive.) Do what the (expletive) you're supposed to do, just throw the little white ball into the imaginary square, don't (expletive) (expletive) about it, let me get through the next three outs. (Gratuitous and unfathomably foul expletive)."

It didn't listen; I walked their leadoff on five pitches, realizing to my chagrin that I would face the heart of the order, which had gone something like 26-for-40 that day against Woodchuck pitchers far healthier than me. I got lucky, inducing a pop-up for the first out, then teased their #3 hitter with a sneaky little slider. Fear of re-injuring my elbow prevented me from really snapping it off, so it skated a little bit, but he rolled over on it and grounded to me on one hop. I flipped to second for out number two, things suddenly looking up. Feeling nervy, I started the next hitter with a curveball that broke more than either of us expected, and he waved at it feebly for my first swing-and-a-miss. I followed with a sinking splitter away, which he chunked off the end of the bat, a can of corn into right. Pierre ran for ages but couldn't quite get there in time, putting runners on first and third with two outs after giving up my first base hit in France...

... in late August. If you told me in March that I would allow my first base hit in August, I would have envisioned a very different story than the one you have read.

The next hitter smacked a 1-2 slider on the ground directly to Seb at shortstop; miracle of miracles, I had escaped the inning without any damage. I took two steps toward the dugout only to see Seb fumble it after 18 exhausting innings in the sun, scoring an unearned run, but I ran a fastball in on the hands of the next hitter for an inning-ending groundout. I looked up at the sky, savoring the moment.

I spent the next week with one foot in each of two worlds. In one, I managed a French baseball team, running practices and calling ballplayers to make sure that we could field a full squad at PUC without Matt. In the other, I filled out student loan forms, met a roommate online, and rented an apartment in downtown Chicago. The dichotomy left me frazzled, as I prepared frantically for Monday's touchdown in the

Windy City – some four days after the 'required' orientation events began – while marshalling the Woodchucks for a doubleheader against a team I despised more than the Yankees. PUC's behavior in our games in May galled me, but I felt distracted as I packed up my belongings, knowing well that my six-month romance with France drew rapidly to a close. After Monday, I would return only on weekends, a series of 48-hour trysts that couldn't possibly maintain my long-distance relationship with *La Patrie.*

I would miss the bread, the wine, the pastries, and the kebabs. Most of all, I would miss the generous, welcoming people in Bois-Guillaume who made me feel at home. Never let anyone tell you that the French are rude, aloof, or anti-American; it's bullshit. They are a proud, hospitable people who know how to live.

Over six months, I had learned a few French words that were just overwhelmingly superior to their English equivalents. ('Feu d'artifice,' for example, literally means 'fire of artificiality': vastly more elegant than '*fireworks.*' 'Stupefiants' means narcotics, but literally, it's '*things that stupefy you.*') The relevant one here is 'mal du pays,' which means 'homesick' but literally translates as '*pain of the country.*' Simply put, I missed America. For all its faults, all its crappy croissants and weak coffee, I missed it terribly. I wanted to watch Red Sox games. I wanted to call a taxicab without worrying that the driver would hear my accent and try to rip me off. I wanted to drink American beers, eat hamburgers, and watch movies without subtitles. With all apologies to France, I wanted to go home.

Life abroad means living in a world without proper context, or any context at all. Every social norm I knew disappeared the day I arrived at Charles De Gaulle, and I found myself thrust into a world where the only certainty was my identity as an outsider. It was hard enough for *me*, and I spoke functional (if heavily accented) French. I could only imagine what it was like for Matt, or the two Americans with Rouen, who spoke nary a word. I can understand their inclination to retreat within their own worlds, an isolated zone of normalcy where they rolled neither their "r's" nor their own cigarettes and didn't sit down to shower.

At the end of the day, I think you have a choice: either throw yourself headlong into the culture – do as the Romans do and savor the confusion – or wall yourself off and pretend you're still in Boston, or Sydney, or wherever you call home. I chose the former, and while I never did get the hang of the sit-down shower, I had grown to appreciate France's potent cheese, calvados, and occasional outbursts of historical revisionism. I had seen France the best way possible. Between the exchange rate, the cost of Parisian hotels, and the big-city resentment of tourists, the average trip to France is far too abrupt, too centered around Paris to get your money's worth. Far better to come for six months or a year, find a job that pays Euros, and take advantage of life's leisurely pace. You'll make friends like Eric and Seb, who show you things missing from the tour books, and teach you to appreciate the unique French perspective on life, America, and Lance Armstrong.[26] *That's* the way to do it. Given my impending schedule of 48-hour visits, I found it ironic that six months in the country convinced me that

[26] It turns out they were right all along about Lance.

France is a *fantastic* place to live... but I wouldn't want to visit there.

I reflected on such matters in the dingy apartment Sylvain had finally procured for us on the Avenue de L'Yser, a main thoroughfare connecting the university to the train station, when my cell rang. It was one of the USF infielders playing for Rouen, who had traveled to Italy with Matt over the break. We had only hung out a few times that summer, but they were both good guys, very good ballplayers. I bounced downstairs to give him the tins of dip he had requested, finding him surprisingly disheartened.

"Everything ok, man?" I asked, handing over the Skoal.

"Yeah, I guess..." he responded unconvincingly. "It's a drag, man. I'm ready to go home, but we've got this playoff." I nodded, understanding completely. Rouen would be playing in a different tournament, where the prize was a championship title rather than avoiding relegation, but our homesickness was the same.

"How was Italy?" I asked. He exhaled out of the side

of his mouth.

"Man, your friend Matt? Dude, he's fucked up. He bailed on the bill for dinner in Rome, then decided to hang out with some friends in Switzerland. We never saw him again."

"That guy sucks," he added, as I nodded ruefully. What could I say?

The next day, my team drove into Paris for my last games as a resident of France. Matt never showed, and sensing his imminent absence, Matthieu again decided to take the weekend off too.

"*Why isn't Matthieu playing?*" I asked Seb on our drive into Paris.

"Didn't feel like it." He sighed, and I considered that maybe I had been a little hard on Matthieu. Granted, he was a horrible teammate who disrespected everyone on the team, and he exhibited filet mignon arrogance while turning in ground chuck performance... but in a lot of ways, it wasn't his fault. First, ground chuck wasn't bad for a kid who was just 16 years old, facing much more seasoned ballplayers. Second, his youth

made him emotionally and physically immature and in need of a role model, and in that, I obviously failed him. He certainly wasn't going to emulate the 'pretty good' American with the bum wing, or the grizzled old Quebecois. That left only Matt. It would have been a bigger surprise if Matthieu *hadn't* acted like an asshole. Underlying it all was an insecurity I recognized all too well; Matthieu suffered from the same cognitive dissonance that I had faced growing up: of being simultaneously 'pretty good' but 'not good enough.' On the one hand, INSEP was telling him (and the rest of Team Espoir) that he was the future of the sport in France… but then they sent him to Bois-Guillaume, the team everyone expected to get relegated. The message was nuanced, but it clearly got through to Matthieu; the Tres Lettres didn't yet think enough of Matthieu to let him take up a spot on a bona fide contender like Toulouse or Montpellier, where he would get more consistent quality coaching and training. 'You're among the best!' they seemed to say, 'but you're kind of the worst of the best.' Matthieu understood the Tres Lettres' unspoken willingness to let him sink or swim on his own, and he took his frustration out on the

Woodchucks, deeming us beneath him.

That was fine. We would go into battle without the Matts, with guys like Eric, Seb, and Vince: Woodchucks for life. In game two, I lined a ball off the pitcher's kneecap hard enough that he had to leave the game, stole second, and advanced to third, down by nine runs. Recognizing my last chance to steal home in France, I took a big lead off third and broke for home. I got a good jump off the righthanded pitcher, sliding into the left side of the plate just ahead of the tag.

"OUT!" the umpire screamed.

I turned to argue; I had waited for months to swipe home, and had finally done it, but the ump had already turned his back. What's another bad call in a season full of them? Bottom line, we weren't going to win that game, and we might have that same ump in the playoffs: better to avoid antagonizing him. I stormed back to the dugout, resigned to my frustration. (Winners don't complain about calls, so I try to avoid it at all costs... but if there's one blown call in my life that grinds me, this is it. I was safe by a half a goddamn mile.)

We lost both games, ending the regular season not with bang but with a whimper. I could barely look the addled PUC coach in the eye during the post-game handshake, blanching at the memory of his team's embarrassing behavior months earlier. Sylvain dropped me off in the Marais, at the apartment of my friends Sierra and Miklos, where I prepared to fly to my new home in Chicago.

CHAPTER 32: SWEET HOME CHICAGO

The ensuing weeks presented an overwhelming maelstrom of orientation events that felt like the first week of college all over again. I watched as my classmates made friends and poor decisions on whom to sleep with, and drank too much at the weekly happy hour, cheekily called 'Bar Review.' Everyone was thrilled to be there, eager to flaunt their intellect, and we immersed ourselves in the standard first-year law courses of Contracts, Criminal Law, Civil Procedure, and Torts.

I couldn't concentrate. Sure, it was exciting, but my thoughts remained fixed on a hard luck baseball team in the corner of France. The gravitational pull of real life would soon suck me back in; I couldn't earn 300€ a month and drive around in the Woodsmobile forever. Hell, I would even have to shave. For months, I had steadfastly refused Becky's pleas to trim a four-inch goatee that spiraled out of control, raising eyebrows when I showed up at Northwestern Law next to bright-eyed kids fresh out of undergrad, eager to forge a path to the Supreme Court.

Having missed all three Monday classes, I survived until Friday's flight back to Paris. After just two weeks in the States, barely enough to overcome jetlag, I faced five weeks of a ridiculous schedule that had me boarding the same 6:00 flight every Friday and returning on Mondays. As I sat on the tarmac at O'Hare, I placed a final call to Eric to verify that Matt had come back for the tournament.

"Allo! *Ah, Evan, super! It goes?"* he exclaimed.

"*Yes, of course it goes, Eric!"* I responded. "*Did Matt ever come back? Will he play this weekend?"*

"Oh, yes, but no! Matt returned, but we are not playing this weekend! Did Sylvain not email you? There

was a declaration of postponement two weeks ago for rain, so we begin the play-down next week!"

I nearly coughed up my airplane peanuts.

"We don't play this weekend? Really?" I couldn't simply walk off the plane then and there, because it would forfeit the return ticket I needed several weeks later. To avoid the exorbitant premium for flying in on Friday and back on Monday five weeks in a row, my travel agent had booked a series of overlapping round trips. For example, one Chicago-to-Paris trip started on Friday, September 15th, with a return flight on Monday, October 2nd, while another separate itinerary (on another airline) had me leaving September 22nd and returning October 16th, and so on. This meant that at any point during the tournament, I would be 'in the middle' of three or four different itineraries. Not surprisingly, this gaming the system for cheaper fares was prohibited by airline policies against what they called 'back-to-back ticketing', and my travel agent was upfront with me that it was risky. If I got caught, they might cancel my remaining itineraries without refund, but on a shoestring budget, I had to cut corners to keep

the crazy adventure rolling, even if it meant bending a few rules.

As a result, I had no choice but to fly to Paris, well aware that while flying to France for 48 hours and two baseball games shows a questionable grip on reality, flying to France for two baseball games that won't even happen merits institutionalization. I landed at 8:00 AM and took the train to meet Miklos and get the key to his apartment in Le Marais, a Paris neighborhood featuring a curious combination of strong orthodox Jewish and gay populations. When I arrived, I found not Miklos but a gay pride parade that made San Francisco's Castro Street look like a Republican convention. I dialed Miklos a dozen times from a nearby payphone, shouting into his voicemail over the droning house music blared from each passing flatbed truck full of gyrating young men with rippling abs and slicked back hair.

Miklos arrived a bit later, apologizing for having turned his phone off. He led me to his fourth-floor walkup, where the faint strains of the gay pride celebration wafted in through the kitchen window. I liked Miklos immediately. Without even meeting me, he had offered his apartment for the weekend, simply because he had been dating Sierra, a brassy American friend from college. Most importantly, he drew my attention to his refrigerator just before leaving, earning my everlasting appreciation.

"Eat whatever you want. There's eggs and cheese and stuff if you want to make breakfast. Oh, and you've got to try this."

He reached into the fridge, retrieving a sausage the size of a rolling pin.

"Try this," he said, gesturing with the glistening, fat-jeweled sausage. "My mother sent it from Hungary."

I spent six months in France trying not to offend its inhabitants. I lauded their coffee and cheese, forgave their daytime television, and gave my tacit (if reluctant) approval to their curious economic system, hoping to avoid becoming, in their eyes, the ugly American. That all went out the window the second I tasted the Hungarian sausage from Miklos' mother, smoky and sinfully fat-encrusted. I will no doubt alienate countless French friends when I say that it was the finest delicacy I tasted in France. My God; you just have to taste it.

It is impossible to imagine a more gratuitous waste of time than a first-year law student, presumably concerned with his grades, flying to Paris for an already-cancelled baseball game. Nonetheless, I did just that, reassured only by the fact that I had bought this particular flight with frequent flyer miles and by the inexpensive shawarmas available nearby at the famous *L'As du Fallafel.* I spent an absurd weekend drinking red wine and reading Civil Procedure cases in Le Marais, waiting for Monday's flight home.

CHAPTER 33: ON THE ROAD AGAIN

I stumbled off the plane at 2:30 PM in Chicago, bleary-eyed and feeling like I had been hit with a pillowcase full of doorknobs. The time change was already killing me after just one back-and-forth weekend trip, even without playing in a doubleheader with an immediate post-game train to Paris. My professors grilled me following Monday's absence; who did I think I was, skipping classes so soon in the ostensibly important 1L fall semester?

I sleepwalked through the week, finally recovering from the weekend's jet lag on Thursday, just 24 hours before flying back to Paris. This time, I had a secret weapon, having stopped by Student Health Services for an Ambien prescription. A week earlier, I had arrived as the sun rose over Charles de Gaulle at 9:00 AM local time, with my internal clock at 2:00 AM Chicago time. I had stayed on Chicago time for the rest of the weekend, going to bed at 5:00 AM and waking after noon, which worked only because I didn't have to play 18 innings on Sunday. Knowing I would need to acclimate rapidly to play well, I started taking two Ambien on the tarmac at O'Hare, around 1:00 AM Paris time.

Dreams about the Rouen Huskies haunted my drug-addled sleep. The Tres Lettres had dictated that 12 teams would participate in a 10-game round-robin tournament: five from the bottom half of the elite division attempting to avoid demotion, and seven from the top of the N1A division hoping to earn promotion, with Rouen's N1A team presenting a curious exception. Because they already had an elite team, Rouen's second team couldn't possibly advance, but it performed well enough in N1A to earn entry into the tournament.

Rouen's N1A team was "second" in name only. Rouen's ravenous poaching and stockpiling of all the good players from other teams – they had a handful of players from last year's Woodchucks squad – left them stacked with talent at every position. They enjoyed an embarrassment of riches, particularly from the perspective of a Woodchucks team struggling to field nine players each weekend. Given Rouen's wealth of talent and incentive to see Bois-Guillaume demoted, we knew they would send quality players from the first team to play in the N1A tournament. Naturally, who did we draw as an opponent in the first round? Rouen.

We arrived late after a tornado warning delayed our departure in Chicago, but the Ambien had done the trick, and I felt rested and ready. I noticed at the baggage carousel that someone's suitcase had burst open in transit, spilling its contents onto the floor for anyone to see, revealing a set of blue padded handles. Could it be? Yes. A Thigh Master.

That's gotta be embarrassing.

Matt had returned to Normandy just in time for the playoffs, and Quentin and Matthieu stayed with us on Saturday. They had taken a much longer long train ride up from Toulouse, where the Tres Lettres had relocated after the French government kicked them out of INSEP on account of baseball losing its Olympic status.[27] As they watched a movie in Matt's room, I tried to piece together a paper on defamation for my legal composition class, poring over cases in a dingy French apartment without working ceiling lights. Just the way Joe Morgan prepared for big games.

Vince started game one, looking rusty after months off due to vacation and his ankle injury. He left fastballs up in the zone, and Rouen had enough good hitters that even their second team feasted on them. All summer, I had no choice but to use an exceptionally slow hook with our starters. With just four pitchers to get through 18 innings, I couldn't pull a guy early just because he didn't look sharp. The outs had to come from somewhere.

The playoffs required a more aggressive approach, so with six runs in and only two outs in the first, I called time, walked to the mound, and took the ball out of Vince's hands. For the umpteenth time, I had to call on

---

[27] The journalist in me feels compelled to point out that this was just what Quentin and Matthieu told me; I didn't go factcheck it. Maybe French baseball was never kicked out of INSEP, and they were just messing with the American? Google seems to confirm that the Federation left INSEP around 2007 or 2008, and established two baseball 'hubs', in Toulouse and Rouen, naturally.

Eric to stop the bleeding. As always, he pitched his heart out, and as always, it was in vain. Any time we had to yank Vince in the first and have Eric throw more than two innings, we didn't have a frog's chance in a blender.

Tempers flared in the seventh, when Rouen's excitable shortstop stole second up by nine runs. In the U.S., that would get noticed, to say the least. The fielders might not say anything, but a few innings later, the base-stealer would take a fastball in the ribs, to remind him of the unspoken rule that you don't steal with a big lead. Apparently, it's a little different in Australia; the rule is decidedly spoken.

"Why the FUCK are you running up by nine runs, mate?" Matt bellowed from shortstop. The runner looked at me, bewildered and stammering, understanding Matt's tone of voice if not his words.

"*The Australian is upset that you stole with a big lead,*" I translated. Having suffered through countless unjustified Matt tirades, I decided to enjoy the one time he was in the right. The French kid's eyes opened wide, and he apologized with an eyebrow-raising explanation, which I then translated for Matt's benefit.

"Matt, he says they just want to get the lead to 10 runs so they can slaughter rule us as fast as possible." I could have put a little more polish on the translation so it seemed more diplomatic and less insulting, but I didn't care enough to put in any effort on the kid's behalf. The stolen base grated on me the same way it had Matt, and besides, Matt was pitching game two. I knew from experience that he pitched better angry.

In the sixth, a peculiar umpire's call killed a rally and cost us a run. With one out, Seb on second, and Matthieu on first, Matt hit a ground ball in the hole to the shortstop's right. Seb took off for third but slowed down as the ball passed him, narrowly avoiding contact with the batted ball but allowing his natural progress to third base to put him in the shortstop's line of sight. The shortstop fielded it cleanly and flipped to second to start the double play, but the pivot man threw it into the dugout, scoring Seb. Fresh off a dressing down from Matt, the shortstop started whining loudly to the umpires that it was unfair, and that Seb had interfered with his ability to field the groundball. (This strained credibility given that he hadn't bobbled the ball.) After a brief conference, the Scottish home plate ump ruled Seb out for runner interference on account of his attempted distraction, ending the inning and disallowing the run. (He had already called Matthieu out on the force play at second base, for the second out of the inning.)

"Sir! He didn't touch the ball!" I said in English, jogging in from my third base coach position. "The shortstop wasn't interfered with; he fielded it cleanly! Besides, interference is a dead ball-"

"*No, I- I- I- I have made this call once before, in an international-*" he stuttered in broken French tinged with his Highland brogue.

"It's fine, you can speak English," I told him.

"The ru-runner-" he stuttered again, now in English.

"THAT CALL IS FUCKING BULLSHIT AND YOU KNOW IT!!!" Matt screamed, sprinting over from first and gesticulating wildly like George Brett during the pine tar incident. "HE NEVER TOUCHED THE BALL!!!"

"No, I- I have made this-"

"HORSESHIT!" Matt exclaimed again.

Matt and I were... *mostly* right. The French made a point to claim they played strictly by MLB rules[28], and those rules technically grant the umpire discretion to declare interference if he feels the runner has interfered with the fielder's attempt to make a play. (From a practical perspective, it's awfully tough to justify that judgment in this case, where the fielder picked up the groundball without incident.) In the 30 years of organized baseball that I've played, I've seen this situation over and over again, and even in situations where the runner clearly *and successfully* attempted to distract the fielder by stopping, I never once saw an ump declare runner interference unless the runner made contact with the fielder or the ball.

Except, of course, in this game, against Rouen.

I'd argue – hell, I'm arguing it right now, 14 years later – that the umpire made a terrible judgment call, but he had the right to make the judgment call and

---

[28] They *kinda* do. French rules differ from MLB by restricting the number of foreigners on the field, the number of innings they can pitch, and the number of players that can change teams during the year, not to mention permitting composite bats and a ball with higher seams than MLB. The proud fallacy of using MLB rules is an oft-repeated mantra in France, but it's mostly bunk.

declare runner interference. What he got unequivocally wrong was the rule's application; runner interference results in a dead ball. Once he declared that Seb had interfered, Seb was out, and play should have stopped. Matt should be awarded first base, Matthieu second, and play should resume with two outs. This is not up for debate; it's black-and-white, end-of-discussion. By preserving the out produced by the shortstop's flip to second – the result of play that continued after the runner interference call – the umpire simply conjured up a false double play where none could have occurred under the rules of baseball. Simply put, he blew it.

Matt and I were inarguably right on that count, but the umpire simply reiterated that he had made his decision and the inning was over. I didn't want Matt to get the heave-ho from the second game, so I shepherded him to the dugout, trying to calm him down.

"COME ON BRAVEHEART!" Matt shouted on the way, which cracked me up. Laughter seemed out of place given our dire situation, and Eric turned to me quizzically for an explanation.

"Uh... Matt just compared the umpire to Mel Gibson." I started laughing harder.

"I... see." Eric said, rolling his eyes. (Just a few weeks earlier, Mel went on a drunken anti-Semitic diatribe during a DUI arrest, so it was a pointed comparison.)

However terrible, that call paled in comparison to one that went against me in the seventh. The pitcher left a 1-2 curveball low and inside, and I pulled my stride (left) foot up in the air to avoid it, but it bounced and hit me in the rear (right) foot: the only one touching the ground at the time. I tossed my bat to the dugout, and took two steps toward first before hearing "BALL! BALL!" I stopped and looked back at the umpire, bewildered.

"You did not make an effort to get out of the way of the ball. It's a ball, you will not go to first."

Stand up some time and pretend you're about to swing a bat. Lift your front foot as if trying to avoid a pitch. Now jump off your rear leg. Notice anything? It's impossible. Your rear leg is planted. It has 100% of your weight on it. I had never seen a more bizarre call, but I shrugged it off and singled to left before being stranded at second.

Our 17-6 loss inspired a decidedly foul dugout mood. I was a newcomer to the fractious Rouen-BG rivalry, but longtime Woodchucks like Aldo and Eric chafed under their perceived condescension from Rouen for years. They considered it one thing to lose to Rouen's elite team, but losing to the second team gave them what Whitey Herzog called 'the red ass.' They were pissed off and they wanted blood. As Matt lit a cigarette, I stalked the dugout, playing instigator.

"*You see the way they stole bases late in the game? That would never happen in the United States, or you'd take one in the ribs...*" I bellowed, picking up steam. "*These guys don't think much of us. They just figured they would come in here and kick our asses, no problem.*"

Aldo snarled, and normally mild-mannered Pierre curled his lips into... what was that? Did we just get a sneer out of The Voice? We might make a ballplayer out of him yet.

"*FUCK THESE GUYS!*" I continued, now rolling. "*Let's fucking DESTROY them!*" I hadn't tried to give an inspirational speech all year, preferring calm positivity to emotional exhortations... but shit, it was the playoffs! With only four weekends left in France, I saw no downside in letting it all hang out.

I had planned on starting Matt, if only to put the fear of God into Rouen's shortstop, but Quentin pulled me aside unexpectedly. All season long, he had rarely showed emotion outside of occasional frustration.

"*Evan... I feel really good,*" he said, with a look of confidence I had never seen from him. "*My arm feels strong. I can start.*"

Taken aback, I cocked an eyebrow.

"*How good?*"

"*Really, really good.*" A grin crept over his face.

"*Okay, kid.*" I said, slowly talking myself into it. "*You've got the ball. Short leash, though.*"

"*What?*" Apparently, the idiom didn't translate well.

"*You get into any trouble, I'm going with the*

Australian. Capiche?"

"*I won't get into trouble.*"

I nearly had to yank him in the first, but Quentin worked out of some jams and gave us three solid innings. He had been a good soldier all year long, a Southern boy on the Team Espoir at INSEP, exiled to the frozen north of Bois-Guillaume by the Tres Lettres. Like Matthieu, it was clear to everyone that 2006 would be his first and last year with the Woodchucks, but unlike Matthieu, he had taken his posting to the Woodchucks in stride, without fake braggadocio or contempt for the organization. Now, when we needed him most, he was stepping up for the Woodchucks, and showing a little swagger besides. My heart soared with pride.

Quentin pitched courageously, keeping Rouen's impressive lineup off balance and scattering a few hits before tiring in the third. I turned it over to Matt with two runners on, who gave up a couple Rouen base hits to score those inherited runners, putting us down 4-0. I had my scrappy, ugly game working, and sparked rallies in the 3rd and 5th innings by drawing a walk and earning first base with a hit-by-pitch, respectively. I stole second and scored both times, helping us cut the lead to one.

I led off the sixth, still down 4-3. Matt was making Swiss cheese of the Huskies' hitters, forcing them to bring in their Canadian to close us out. That's right: Rouen paid two foreigners to play on their *second* team. I tapped the plate with the bat, feeling a mix of confidence and urgency: 'arrogance and fear,' as Crash Davis would say. Drop a bunt down, take a fastball in the ribs, or smash a ground ball off someone's glove; didn't matter, I just had to get on base.

I ran the count to 3-2 and fouled off three pitches before the Canadian missed inside, the ball grazing my knuckles on a checked swing. I stole second on the first pitch, and had to hold up at third when Aldo seared a line drive to left, hit too hard to score me. Aldo stole second without a throw, and we had men on second and third with nobody out. Seb hit a slow chopper to third base. I took off on contact, barreling down the third baseline and expecting the third baseman to make the scoop and come home with it. At last: a collision at the plate! I saw it unfold instantaneously in my mind's eye: I would be a step late, forcing me to try to splatter the catcher all over the backstop to dislodge the ball. Two steps from home plate, already in Rodney Harrison 45-degree-angle-to-the-ground bone-crushing mode, I noticed that the catcher was still holding his mask in his right hand. No play. Smash-up canceled.

I didn't find out what happened until Eric explained it to me in the dugout. The Canadian playing third – *another* salaried player who floated between the two teams – had been practicing at Rouen's field when someone on the bench called his cell to tell him 'hey, the game is close at Bois-Guillaume, we need you', but he hadn't had time to don his spikes before jumping in at third base. Bois-Guillaume's crazy cutout infield meant that when he stepped to his right to field Seb's chopper, he did so on the always wet Normandy grass. Wearing sneakers instead of spikes, he slipped and fell ass-over-teakettle, allowing the ball to trickle slowly into left field. I scored without any ultraviolence, and Aldo came chugging in behind me to give us our first lead of the weekend. Hell, it was probably Bois-

Guillaume's first lead over Rouen in a decade; about time we got a little home cooking from that infield.

Suddenly up 5-4, we put together what I had waited for all year: a Woodchucks Bat Explosion. After Matthieu struck out, the Huskies' pitcher intentionally walked Matt, but Quentin immediately made them pay with a single into right, scoring Seb. Two walks loaded the bases with two outs, and I found myself muttering 'come on, Vince, just stick the bat out and drop one in the gap.'

From my lips to God's ears. Vince blasted a high fly ball into the left-center gap, scoring two more runs; the rout was on! We batted around in the sixth, adding another one in the seventh to make it 9-4, a fantastic development for two reasons. First, it allowed us to relax and have some fun with a big lead, something we hadn't done all year. Second, and perhaps more importantly, it really, really pissed off the Huskies. They started badgering the umpires and throwing equipment, with one guy getting ejected for arguing balls and strikes. The idea of losing to Bois-Guillaume – even Rouen's second team – proved such an anathema to them that they totally lost their composure.

Now, I don't like to hold grudges (oh wait; I do), and I am not the type to rejoice when the mighty have fallen (oh wait; I am), but there was something about watching Rouen bicker amongst themselves and with the umpires that made me feel good to be alive.

Now is probably as good a place as any to point out that I liked almost all of the Huskies I met, even the guy who stole up by nine runs. Honestly, they were good ballplayers, and they just wanted to win championships; I could never hold that against them. We were just on the opposite ends of things. Rouen had been the big bad bullies in Normandy for decades, the vastly superior team who looked upon the upstart Woodchucks with bemusement at best, condescension at worst. They didn't respect us... but candidly, the Woodchucks hadn't done a whole lot to earn their respect on the field, especially not their glass-armed American who could barely make the throw from second base. I'll admit that while I was there, it grated on me that they tended to hoard 30 of the best 100 players in France in a sport where they could only use nine at a time, while we Woodchucks struggled to field a full roster most weekends. As I look back years later, my views have mellowed here, because it was human nature; good ballplayers want to play with other good ballplayers, and they want to improve as much as they can. Growing up, all I wanted was to improve as much and stretch my limited talent as far as possible. Had I been born in northern France, that would have meant training at and playing for Rouen. It would be hypocritical of me to condemn others for doing exactly what I would have done.

That said, I was a company man. My paycheck[29] said Woodchucks on it. Outside the lines, I could like and respect Rouen, but inside the lines, I hated their guts, so as Matt kept throwing goose eggs, I took no small amount of pleasure in watching their frustration mount at the prospect of losing to their clownish cross-town rivals. Matt struck out the last two hitters in the ninth to seal a lopsided win, as I let out a roar of satisfaction and fist-pumped at second base. We went through the postgame handshake line, the

[29] My metaphorical paycheck; Bois-Guillaume paid us in straight cash, homie.

Woodchucks' ear-to-ear grins contrasting sharply with the Huskies' embarrassed grimaces. Second team or no, they knew: they just *weren't supposed to lose* to guys with BG on their hats.

On the day, I had three walks and got hit four times; in the back, on the knee, in the shoulder, and on the foot. It wasn't really what French teams paid foreigners to do – just get on base and steal bags – but it got the job done, even if it did make me feel like I had reached the "Rickey Henderson with the Red Sox" phase of my career. I didn't care; for the first time all year, we felt like a *team* during the postgame celebration. We took team photographs that caught even the two Matts smiling. Guys sang in the shower, played pranks, told old army jokes, and made fun of Eric's Quebecois accent. It was the best we had felt all year, and one of my greatest regrets from France was that I couldn't stick around to enjoy the joviality; I had a train to catch. I showered and said my goodbyes, caught a ride to my apartment from the Huskies – like I said, good guys, even in defeat – and jogged to the train station.

In retrospect, I can pinpoint Vince's walloped two-run double as the season's turning point. All year long, teams had bullied and disrespected us, with good reason; we didn't play well enough to demand respect. The second that goofy lefthander – pizza delivery guy by trade, Woodchuck for life – stuck the bat out and drove a ball into the left-center gap, everything changed for the Woodchucks. We had stood up to the bullies, and got to thinking that maybe, just maybe, we could win another three games and avoid demotion. David had found his sling.

CHAPTER 34: TORN & FRAYED

I visited an orthopedic surgeon in Chicago, who verified that I had played all season just a few millimeters of connective tissue away from needing Tommy John surgery. Near the end of our consultation, he dropped the hammer on me.

"With time, this will heal," he said, in that stern doctor's voice that unapologetically attempts to scare patients into compliance. "But I have to tell you; you can't pitch for at least six months, period. You'll tear it the rest of the way, and it's already pretty far gone. Your insurance doesn't cover Tommy John surgery[30],

[30] Unless you're a major league ballplayer, Tommy John is considered elective surgery, because no one HAS to throw a slider. My student insurance at Northwestern would never cover it, so I started pricing out surgical tourism

so…" he trailed off with a pregnant pause.

"Unless you're willing to pay out of pocket, it would end your baseball career."

I inhaled sharply. So that was it.

One inning, I thought. One stinking inning pitched. That's all I could give the team that pulled me back from the abyss in April, when I thought my tour in France was over. One lousy, measly inning. All summer long, I thought if I could only make it to the fall, my elbow would heal, and I would come out of the Woodchucks' bullpen throwing fire. It never happened; my elbow never healed. I had let them down.

I left the doctor's office depressed, and stopped for a beer at one of the three kinds of bars Chicago had in abundance – Irish bars, sports bars, and Irish sports bars – feeling pretty low. My cell phone rang.

"Hello?"

"Dude, you are FUCKING AWESOME!"

"What?"

---

options in Mumbai, where I could get it done for under $10,000 USD, including the flights.

"You guys are gonna do it. You're gonna pull it off!" It was Kayvon. He had read the blurb I posted on my blog about our improbable victory over Rouen, and evidently, it had brightened his day.

"I don't know, man. I just got some bad news about my elbow...."

"Fuck that, dude. You said yourself you just needed four wins. You've got four games against crap teams, plus two against that team you already beat once. Dude, you're gonna do it!"

His enthusiasm was contagious. Maybe he was right. Our win on Sunday put us in the driver's seat; all we had to do was hold serve against Marseille and Compiegne, and even if Montpellier and La Guerche swept us, we would probably come out with four wins, enough to avoid relegation.

"You know what, man?" I asked. "You're right. We're gonna pull this shit off. Hey, what size cap did you say you wore?"

Another week, another frantic rush to O'Hare, this

time bringing goodies. No French supplier carried quality baseball hats, so Eric had asked me to get some embroidered with the interlocking 'BG' logo in Chicago. The caps safely tucked away in the luggage hold, I popped two Ambien: the ballplayer's little helper that helped reset my internal clock each weekend. Still, three weeks into the playoffs, the jet lag took its toll. I walked around Chicago each week in a fog, stumbling in and out of law classes examining the minutiae of Supreme Court rulings. Disoriented and exhausted, my body staged a full-scale revolt, shutting down less important functions like 'remembering the court's holding in *Robinson v. California'* or 'not tripping on the steps into the classroom.'

We faced Montpellier again, on that crazy elevated artificial turf field, so I took a train directly from Paris to the south of France. On the ride, I hoped that the warm weather would loosen us up, and the positive camaraderie from our upset of Rouen would allow us to upset the much stronger Barracudas, as we nearly had in May. The problem with having such a large talent discrepancy against your opponents is that you have to play an A or A+ game just to keep it close, and you need them to turn in a B- or worse to actually beat them. There's no margin for error. Anything less than your best is a recipe for a blowout.

We delivered far, far less than our best.

I had one of my better weekends, going 4-for-7 with a couple walks and four stolen bases, but it didn't matter. The rest of the team just had an off day, and the Barracudas mercy ruled us twice. Matt started game two and served up a sinking line drive into left; Aldo dove for it, but the ball bounced just in front of his outstretched glove. Matt exploded in anger as the ball rolled all the way to the left field fence on the all-dirt outfield, allowing the batter to score standing up with an inside-the-park home run. As much as he complained about the French preoccupation with personal statistics, Matt was furious that the scorebooks would show him allowing a dinger on a soft liner into left.

The sense of capitulation in the dugout demoralized me, particularly from the usual suspects of Matthieu and Matt. I had flown 4,000 miles, and while I didn't expect to beat the Barracudas, I at least expected the other eight guys to go down fighting with me. Instead, we rolled over in both games as soon as we fell behind.

I walked to the locker rooms only to find that a football game had broken out. The presence of baseball in France never failed to amuse me, but the sight of the Montpellier Mustangs playing American football within sight of the Mediterranean blew my mind. Eric joined me, and we watched from an elevated vantage point by the locker rooms, as I pointed out the Power and Belly formations from my own high school football days.

"*You played football?*" Eric asked.

"*Sure. Starting outside linebacker my senior year.*"

"Were you good?"

"*I mean, I was...*"

I had been pretty unremarkable.

"*Nah, not really.*" We laughed, and I left to shower.

Once clean, I plopped down on the team bus next to Eric. He grinned mischievously and reached behind his bag to produce a stolen Heineken, which he handed to me.

"*A gift from the Montpellier football team,*" he said, eyes twinkling. "*They wouldn't mind giving a beer to a real American football star, no?*"

I smiled back.

"I guess not, my friend."

CHAPTER 35: WHEN THE LEVEE BREAKS

Another week passed in a blur as I struggled to keep my eyes open in class, while eager law students poured themselves into the ritual of their 1L year, knowing that their first semester GPA would determine their attractiveness to the large firms paying the highest salaries. With no desire to practice law, I felt detached from the rat race. My first semester grades would be terrible, the result of spending five weeks jetlagged and exhausted, and I didn't care. With the Woodchucks 1-3 in the tournament, I focused solely on winning three more games to avoid demotion. It was my obsession, driven by lingering guilt over my failure to contribute on the mound. I wanted – desperately – to feel like I had earned my paycheck.

This obsession overtook my everyday interactions with classmates. On Thursday, my roommate Tyler asked "Hey, Ev, who are we playing this weekend?"

"Marseille, man, second division team we need to blow out, send a message. Don't know much about them, but-"

"Dude, I was talking about the Patriots." Tyler also grew up in Massachusetts, so we shared a love of Boston sports franchises. "Who are the Pats playing?"

"Oh... I don't know. Dolphins, maybe?"

I drifted in and out of classes, consumed by one thought: three wins. THREE WINS. The rain delay had shifted the playoffs back one weekend, making my first of five weekend trips irrelevant. I called my travel agent again, hoping that despite the complicated web of overlapping itineraries he had booked for me, I could book an additional flight back out to Paris for the weekend of October 15th, now the final weekend of the tournament.

"I'm sorry, Evan. It's impossible," he said. "No airline will allow me to book such a flight. It would take a new itinerary."

"What's the cheapest we could do it?" I asked.

"Hold on." His keyboard whirred in the background.

I had cost-of-living student loan proceeds sitting in my bank account, to cover rent and meals and maybe one more flight to Paris if we could do it cheaply. *Come on, under five hundred,* I thought. *Under five hundred. Under five hundred. Under five–*

"One thousand, nine hundred ninety-four dollars."

That simplified the decision considerably; I would miss the last weekend of games. I had just two more doubleheaders in France, during which we needed at least three wins to guarantee Bois-Guillaume's survival. Our best bet lay in sweeping Marseille, then squeaking one out against La Guerche or Compiegne during the final weekend, which I would miss. Without placing too much emphasis on my own absence, I knew that was unlikely; Compiegne had dominated N1A with the help of some strong foreigners, so we couldn't assume a win there. To be safe, we needed three wins over the next two weekends.

I was wired all week with nervous energy. Even after running eight miles on Friday morning, I had to take an extra Ambien to fall asleep as Air France flight 051 pulled away from the gate at O'Hare, seven months after I first left for France, six months after I no-hit the Woodchucks.

Time flies, huh?

When I finally got to Rouen through my now familiar fool's march through French public transit, I received a text from Eric; we weren't sure if Marseille was actually going to show up. Apparently, they had forfeited two games to La Guerche on Sunday, simply because La Guerche was so far out in the sticks that Marseille chose to save the train fare. As we say in Boston, 'you can't get they-ah from hee-yah.'

In a nod to my new life in Chicago, I hit the books Saturday night, crashing at Seb's nearby apartment so that Quentin and Matthieu could stay with Matt at our apartment more comfortably. A week earlier, I had slept on the couch while the three of them piled into one bed, a bit much even for three guys with a combined age under 60. In the morning, Quentin used his phone to play his new favorite song – *Ridin' Dirty* by Chamillionaire[31] – roughly 4,200 times. If you haven't heard this particular masterpiece, it ranks among the worst rap songs ever to attain popularity. Its lyrics deal with operating a motor vehicle while intoxicated or in possession of narcotics, and they remained stuck in my head for the rest of the day, along with Quentin's barely intelligible efforts to sing along. It went something like this:

"Zey see me row-leen... Zey Haiti.... (mumbles a few words in French) cash me rye un-dur-ree!!!"

Marseille finally arrived, and proceeded to take up almost the entire hour remaining before game time with a 45-minute batting practice. Meanwhile, Seb said his shoulder was sore, so I lent him the horse juice I smeared on my elbow to get through each game.

"AAAAAAAH!" he screamed moments later. "*It*

---

31 https://www.youtube.com/watch?v=CtwJvgPJ9xw&ab_channel=ChamillionaireVEVO, for what it's worth.

burns!!!!"

"*Of course it does,"* I shot back, "*what did you think I was rubbing on my elbow every weekend, suntan lotion?"*

I watched calmly from the Bois-Guillaume dugout as the Meds went through hitter-by-hitter, leaving us just a few minutes for a hurried BP. Back home, this would draw retaliation, like a hitter getting plunked; you can't big league the home team and expect to get away with it. The Marseille Meds clearly had no disrespect in mind – they were just totally disorganized – but I didn't care. I was already on tilt and eager to use any hint of disrespect as fuel for 18 innings.

When we exchanged the lineups at the beginning of the game, I leaned in aggressively toward the opposing team's coach, asking what their 'Meds' nickname meant.

"*It's an abbreviation of the Mediterraneans, because we're next to the sea,*" he responded with a big smile.

"*Oh,"* I responded, stone faced, never blinking. "*Like the Metropolitans of New York."* He nodded.

"*I get it.*" I said, still scowling. "*Clever.*" I kept staring, his eyes revealing confusion. He looked down, paused, then looked back at me, checking to verify that I was joking, only to find my eyes still locked on his.

They were good guys, these Meds – I could tell just by talking to them – but I didn't want to acknowledge it. I had drawn a paycheck all summer to help the Woodchucks accomplish one thing, and the Meds unfortunately stood in the way of it. *Screw them*, I thought, ignoring a pang of guilt for my hostility towards ostensibly likeable guys. I needed to ignore their amiability; I needed to hate them.

The wind blew in steadily from left, a breeze that grew stronger throughout the day. I felt good, fueled by my contrived antipathy towards the Meds, but a little bit... slow. I felt tired, somehow weaker than when I started the season. I grimaced, knowing that all my hard work at Velocity with the Quiet Storm had slowly frittered away. I was – (gasp) – getting old.

We fell behind 2-0 in the first, but responded by knocking their starter out of the game to take a 3-2 lead on my RBI double in the bottom half. In the fourth, we tacked on a few more when I pulled a ground ball past a diving shortstop, swiped second, and scored on a single to center. I led off the sixth just as the sun poked through the Normandy clouds, and finally – FINALLY – got into one.

Hitters dream of this pitch, a cup-high fastball on the sweet spot of the bat. It rocketed over the centerfielder's head to the deepest part of the park, one-hopping the fence as I coasted into third with a standup triple, leaving me just a dinger away from the cycle. It was easily one of my hardest-hit balls in France, second only to the seed I hit against Pierrick.

We batted around, extending our lead to 11-2, tantalizingly close to the 10-run rule that had victimized us so often throughout the season. Other teams had slaughter-ruled us so frequently that it still haunts my dreams like an unconfessed murder, but for once, we found ourselves just one run away from inflicting it on our opponents.

After our run of buzzard luck, I didn't mess around with victory in sight. Emboldened by his strong performance against Rouen, Quentin had again asked to start, and with the game arguably in hand, he asked to continue and maybe go the distance. In any other game I would have considered it, but I smelled blood in the water, and refused to risk a sure win.

"*Quentin, you pitched great... but I have to go to Matt. He closes it out, we win, and we save your arm for the next game.*" We both knew it was a lie; he was done for the day. He shrugged, and smiled.

"Okay, boss." His wry grin resonated with me for weeks, and I came to recognize it as the smile of a player coming of age. As Matt warmed up, I found myself glancing over at Quentin, seeing a ballplayer who had only begun to blossom. His best baseball lay ahead of him, and I should know, because that morning's lethargy had convinced me that mine was behind me, at some indeterminable date in San Francisco, when I was still full of piss & vinegar, youth & optimism.

What a drag it is getting old.

Matt struck out the side on 10 pitches. Guys like Matt were the real difference between the elite division and N1A; in the elite division, you faced *foreigners*, and they threw *hard.* Marseille might as well have been facing Pedro Martinez. Seb scored on a double in the seventh to invoke the slaughter rule, and we pulled one win closer to avoiding relegation.

The typical nonsense erupted between games, with Matthieu griping about meal money or a ride from the station, some perquisite that Sylvain supposedly should have provided to the INSEP kids. This kind of bitching had persisted all year, with me playing the unenviable role of trying to calm both parties in my strained French. Goddammit, but it was tiring. Here we were, coming off a dominating victory, the exact time when spirits should be running high, and instead, Matthieu wanted to throw it all away over a matter of 10 euros. I couldn't take it, still too wired up, even after nine innings of baseball had taken some of the spark out of me.

"*Matthieu,* SHUT THE FUCK UP." I knew he understood me despite his limited English. "*It's going to work out, Sylvain will arrange everything like he always does. Don't worry about bullshit like train fares... worry about game two, because we need to win,* mon ami."

I glared at him, my adrenaline spiking again. A nasty little part of me wanted him to push back, escalate into the physical confrontation I had dreamed about for months, even while I knew that kicking a 16-year-old's ass wasn't a really good look, particularly when we were teammates. He shrugged, mouthed something that was probably disrespectful, and slunk back to the other end of the dugout.

"*And get your arm loose,*" I spat after him. "*We may need you to pitch a few innings.*" I was adding insult to injury, knowing that Matthieu's bravado broke down into tears only when he took the mound. Six months of his posturing had worn thin, and I wanted to force him either to put up or shut up.

He shut up.

With the situation finally calmed, we started Vince against a soft-balling right-hander that gave us fits. Even in the heat of a close game, already piqued by Matthieu, and determined to cultivate competitive disdain for our opponents, I couldn't help but like this

Med pitcher. He was irrepressibly upbeat, constantly encouraged the fielders despite their occasional blunders behind him, and generally seemed to enjoy the hell out of himself. '*Man, you gotta get a load of this!*' he seemed to say with each pitch, eyes wide with excited disbelief. '*They're letting me pitch a BASEBALL game!!!*' I loved his unabashed enthusiasm; without exception, my best friends in baseball always exhibited something similar. Other than Eric and Seb, that attitude had been all too rare among the 2006 Woodchucks.

He tied us in knots with his slurvy breaking stuff, and the Meds staked him to an early lead before my single up the middle scored Pierre to tie the game at three. Vince finished the fifth without incident, and while we batted in the bottom half, he told me he felt strong and ready to continue.

I have always despised managers who played to stats, leaving faltering pitchers in for an extra inning in the hopes of getting them the win, but I had a soft spot in my heart for Vince. He had thrown more innings than anyone else for the Woodchucks, even Matt, bringing that 75-mile-an-hour junk from the left side week after week, gutting things out when they invariably went awry. He grew up a Woodchuck, wearing the B-G logo since age eight. Through all those tough games, good outings and bad, through his 10-inning gut-punch against Saint-Lô, his 3-2 loss against Senart, and his near misses against Montpellier and PUC, he always gave the Woodchucks all that he had.

And he hadn't gotten a single. Goddamn. Win.

Let the record show that in the top of the sixth, I fell victim to that same obtuse thought process I have criticized a thousand times in Red Sox managers. I sent Vince out for an extra inning, hoping that he could escape without a run and we could scratch one across to get him the lead before the big Australian came in to shut the Meds down.

The Challenger Launch. The Bay of Pigs. Skipping Michigan and Wisconsin in 2016. You get the picture; it was, in retrospect, a horrifyingly bad decision.

Vince walked the leadoff man, then gave up a Texas leaguer into shallow center. Vince should have gotten away with it, because the runner at first held up halfway just in case Seb could snare it. The ball fell just past Seb's outstretched glove, but our streetwise shortstop scooped it up on one hop and fired to me at second... and I dropped it. I just plain dropped it. Adding insult to injury, the umpire shouted (in a seemingly intentionally exaggerated French accent), "Ou-ut: NON, SAFE! SAFE!"

Le Sigh.

The next time you want to feel terrible about an obvious mistake at work, hire a French umpire to announce it to the world. Trust me, you'll seethe over it for weeks. Rattled by just my second error of the season, Vince loaded the bases with another walk, and gave up a sac fly to put us down 4-3. A wild pitch advanced the runners to second and third, when something bizarre happened, something I had never seen before in 20 years of baseball.

Matthieu was playing catcher. After corralling Vince's wild pitch at the backstop, he saw that the lead runner had taken an overly aggressive turn around third, and tried to pick him off by whistling a throw to third base. As always, we were short on ballplayers, so Sylvain was filling in at third. He slapped a tag on the retreating runner just a beat late, then turned to flip the ball back to Vince on the mound, a lazy, routine lob that he tried to retract the second he had released it. A sudden gust of wind – I *swear* I'm not making this up – had blown dust from the baseline up into Vince's eyes, and he ducked to avoid a ball that would otherwise have caused the second broken nose of the Woodchucks' season.

The ball dribbled past Vince toward first. Recognizing the chaos on the field, the runner on third alertly scampered home, increasing Marseille's lead to two. Vince then served up a base hit that made it 6-3, bringing up familiar looks of resignation on the faces of the Woodchucks around the infield.

No, I thought. No fucking way we're losing to these guys, not like this. I called time – "Monsieur, arretez, s'il vous-plait" – and jogged to center field, where to no one's surprise, I found Matt boiling over with rage.

"Jesus fucking CHRIST, mate! What the fuck is this bullshit?" He was not wrong. The toss from Sylv to

Vince was no one's fault, but it was so embarrassing that Matt's hostile cynicism was for once merited. I had to go into salesman mode.

"Look, man, I know... That was goddamn ridiculous, but listen..." I began begging. "We still have a shot at this. You only threw 10 pitches in the last game, and..." I paused for emphasis, ignoring the home plate umpire's cries that I to return to my position so the game could continue. "*We. Can. Win. This. Game. Matt,*" I said, jabbing the same index finger that nearly started a fight with him in Toulouse. "We can do it... if you close this out. We can score four runs off these assholes!"

The world reeled around me. Matt rolled his eyes, gesturing at the infield as if to say 'for THIS bullshit?'

I hated this act of begging someone to do the right thing.

"Please, Matt... *Please.* We need this win to survive ... We're already down three, and we only pull this out if you blank these guys the rest of the way."

"Please." I added, reeking of desperation.

"Fine."

My heart soared as he jogged in toward the mound. I felt euphoric, until I realized that he couldn't score runs from the mound, and we still trailed by three. We still needed to score four runs in three innings, a feat we had recently accomplished for the first time all season against Rouen.

It was never easy in Bois-Guillaume. From the day I arrived, we had to battle not just for every run, but for every baserunner.[32] We never had the talent to just smash a three-run jack to tie it; we had to do it the hard way, pitch-by-pitch, inning-by-inning, grinding out every at-bat one at a time. We tacked on a run in the seventh, and then another in the eighth when Eric singled in a run. Matt continued to dominate, but we needed runs, entering the bottom of the ninth down 6-5. Who led off? Well, me, of course.

---

[32] It recalled the great line from MLB coach Rich Donnelly about managing in the minors: "I managed a team that was so bad we considered a 2-0 count on the batter a rally."

CHAPTER 36: ALL DOWN THE LINE

I took a curveball away, feeling the same confidence I felt against Rouen; I was getting on base, no matter what. Inside fastball for a ball, slider away for a strike; he ran me to 2-2, then threw me a meatball out over the plate. My bat slashed through the zone, and I exploded out of the batter's box in case I hit the ball on the ground.

I didn't. I popped the ball up, and the Meds' second baseman easily handled the can-of-corn for the first out. All those days in San Francisco, waking up early for two hours of batting practice, were preparation for *this moment*: an at-bat late in the game where my team needed a run, where I had to get on base.

And I popped it up.

I slumped back to the dugout. If we didn't sweep Marseille, we just couldn't get there, wouldn't win the necessary four games to remain in elite. I had never heard the peculiar combination of French and English curse words that spewed forth from my mouth. Without question, it was the worst I have ever felt on any baseball diamond in my life, worse than getting fired, worse than striking out against Langone.

Seb singled to left as I plopped my sorry ass down on the bench. He took second on a passed ball. I didn't even consider the idea that we might still have life until he took third when Matt slapped a knee-high fastball past a diving second baseman.

Suddenly, we had the tying run just 90 feet from home plate with one out. Two outs left in our season, as far as I was concerned, so I glanced down the bench for a possible pinch runner. You see, Seb received a lot of gifts in the genetic lottery; he was funny, handsome, and likable, a ladies' man and a good hitter to boot. He had a good sense of humor, showed smooth hands at shortstop, and spoke the best English of all the

Woodchucks. But for some reason, Seb inherited the footspeed of a three-toed sloth missing two toes; it made no sense that one of the team's best athletes would be its slowest runner, but then, a lot about French baseball didn't make sense.

No one. I looked at the bench from the third-base coach's box and saw no one. There were no *people* there. Even for a home game *in the playoffs,* we had just nine Woodchucks, all of them already in the lineup; we had no subs. For better or for worse, we were stuck with our slowest baserunner at third, our season hinging on his ability to score on a fly ball or wild pitch to tie the game.

I called timeout, ostensibly to speak to Matt at first base when I really just wanted to draw the infielders away from Seb at third so I could speak to him alone after I returned from my trip across the diamond. As I had hoped, the third baseman and shortstop followed me toward Matt at first and stopped to linger near the mound, encouraging their pitcher; my silly gambit was working. I made some nonsensical small talk with Matt at first about maybe bunting, ignored whatever jaded feedback he might have given – to this day I have no idea what he might have said, as I was never in the first place paying attention to him – then jogged back to third, my heart pounding in my chest. Paranoid that the third baseman might be right on my heels, returning to his position before play resumed, I didn't dare glance at Seb as I strode back to the third base coach's box, muttering "I don't care where it is: you tag and score on any ball in play."

I turned, sighing with relief when I saw the third baseman still near the mound, talking to his pitcher. "You understand, Seb?" I repeated, slightly louder. I was so wired up I had spoken to him in English.

"Mais bien sur, mon ami." He said, flashing that Cheshire grin of his. And why wouldn't he? Seb had learned early in life that his smile could get him out of trouble with his mother or into trouble with the women of Normandy, so no reason not to use it to calm down an increasingly jittery American with just two weekends left in France. *Shit, man,* it seemed to say. *It's okay. We're havin' fun, aren't we?* Seb always had chutzpah, always kept everything in perspective. I loved that about him.

"Fine," I responded tersely, again in English, unwilling to waste time translating my thoughts into French before the third baseman came back within earshot. "I'm just saying: No waiting for a base hit. You're *scoring*, pal." I said, gasping from the pressure.

For months, I lectured on the importance of situational hitting at Bois-Guillaume. We just needed a fly ball or a ground ball to the right side to tie the game. So what did Matthieu do?

Of *course* he came out of his shoes trying to crush the first pitch he saw into the stratosphere, whiffing badly. He swung for the fences again on an 0-1 slider that never even sniffed the strike zone. I cursed silently. He was quickly down 0-2, trying to avoid a rally-killing strikeout.

Like I said, I had played baseball for 20 years at this point, but for the second time that game, just as the Woodchucks needed a miracle, something happened that I had never seen before. Matthieu waved defensively at a breaking ball, just barely getting a piece off the end of the bat. The first baseman circled behind the bag into foul territory, hoping Matthieu's popup would stay in play. Seb returned to third base; he was the slowest guy I had ever seen under 300 pounds, but he had the baseball intelligence to return to third base just on the off chance that the first baseman caught it and... I don't know, fell down? Was struck by a falling piece off a 747? Had a heart attack? Seb would finish third in a race against a pregnant woman, so tagging up seemed unlikely, but he tagged nonetheless. The first baseman drifted back, back, back and to his left, battling the sun before making an impressive basket catch that brought him right up against the chain link fence just beyond the dugout, his shoulders turned away from home plate such that I could read the number on his uniform from my third base coach's box.

Seb started running.

I admit, I cursed again under my breath as this lead-footed Frenchman took off for home. I tried to wave him back to third like Carlton Fisk waving the ball fair in Game 6[33], but Seb plodded homeward. Just as he

---

[33] https://youtu.be/n4P3n2TCgEE?t=202, if it's possible not to know such a thing.

neared the midpoint of his 90-foot sprint, the first baseman heard his teammates' shouts, turned toward home, and unleashed a bullet to the catcher, poised to tag Seb out.

Everything happened in slow motion... especially Seb. The ball arrived right as he dove headfirst, a cloud of dust enveloping him as the catcher applied the tag that would determine the Woodchucks' season. Seb slid on his belly, fully extended, and he rolled onto his side to see the umpire cross his arms and extend them outward, shouting "SAFE!!"

SAFE!!!

ALIVE!!!

I've hit walkoff home runs, I've won championships, I've won playoff hockey games in overtime sudden death... but I've never seen the kind of jubilation that awaited me as I leapt atop the pile of Woodchucks covering Seb at home. Seb? A guy who ran like he had concrete in his shoes, scored on a foul pop-out to the first baseman? To tie a must-win game in the final inning? *Are you kidding me*? The Woodchucks hooted and hollered in the dugout as play resumed, hugging and high-fiving the most unlikely of speedsters for his season-saving dash.

The euphoria wore off when we realized it wouldn't mean anything unless we tacked on another run. Quentin grounded out to end the 9th, and we went into extras. Fortunately, Matt showed up when we needed him, annihilating Meds hitters for the next two innings, blowing the fastball past them and then embarrassing them with his hard, knuckling splitter for K after K.

That brought me up to start the bottom of the 11th, visions of a glorious walkoff jimmyjack dancing in my head. I took a slider off the plate – they were definitely giving me more respect than I deserved, determined not to let the American beat them – before dropping a weak flare into left for a base hit: not so glorious as a homer, but I'll take it. The first baseman teased me good naturedly at first – "*You imagined a HUGE hit, not that little shit, didn't you?!*" – and I couldn't help but smile.

"*Huge hit in the scorebook, my friend!*" I responded. These Meds were tough to dislike.

All those drills training with Velocity came to this: steal second or die trying. Goading the pitcher into a pickoff attempt, I took a long lead, but he didn't offer; the instant he raised his left foot, I took off for second and slid in head-first without a throw, 180 feet from victory with nobody out.

The Meds congregated on the mound before deciding to walk Seb to set up a potential double play, bringing up our best hitter – Matt – with a runner in scoring position and nobody out. I wiped my dirt- and blood-stained hands on my pants, pleading for Matt to slap a ball through the infield to score me and win the game.

Matt struck out.

We still had a chance: just one out. We needed a base hit from Matthieu, one measly base hit. Drill a line drive into center? I'm scoring from second base. Pull a ground ball past the shortstop? I'm scoring. Jesus fucking Christ, whatever you do, Matthieu, I'm scoring.

Instead, the worst-case scenario unfolded before me. Matthieu tried to pull an outside fastball, producing a tailor-made inning-ending double-play groundball to the third baseman. With Seb at first, I was forced to third, so I took off sprinting from second base, hoping that the third baseman would boot it and leave everyone safe. No such luck; he fielded it cleanly, just as I was about ⅔ of the way to third base. I stopped dead in my tracks about ten feet from him; if I continued, he would only need to tag me for the second out and then throw to first for the inning-ending double-play.

Then he made a big mistake. Huge.

He hesitated.

It wasn't much – just a fraction of a second – but it was enough that now, if he took the three steps to his right to tag third base to retire me on the force play, it would be too late get Matthieu at first. It's still what he should have done; forget the double play – as soon as he hesitated, it was no longer an option, so don't get greedy – just take the sure out at third and trust your pitcher to get the next batter and end the inning. Instead, he pumped once in my direction, panic jumbling his decision-making process as he realized I was too far away to tag, then threw to second base to initiate a doomed double play at second and then first.

The millisecond that the ball left his hand, I jolted back into a dead sprint. We had caught a break: no WAY they were turning that double play, I thought, and I shortened my steps so I could hit third base hard and explode homeward, my ankles dorsiflexed just like Velocity had taught me to maximize the force each step imparted upon the earth. Matthieu had decent speed, so even if they got Seb at second, the second baseman's throw to first would be far too late...

...too late to get Mathieu at first to end the inning...

...maybe late enough for me to score?

My brain processed all of this as I tore around third base, hoping that maybe the second baseman had dropped the ball, or thrown it wildly to first, or that somehow, he might just not see my 220-pound frame barreling home with the winning run. *That's* how my dad taught me to play baseball; always force the other guy to make the play. If you're going to make a mistake, make it an aggressive one. *Be bold, even if you're facing Langone.* My dash home was a wild gamble that would backfire if the second baseman handled the throw from third to retire Seb for the second out,

quickly realized that he had no play on Matthieu at first, and

saw me sneaking home... all in enough time to make a strong throw to the catcher to tag me out.

I barreled home, eyes locked on the Meds' catcher, watching for the second baseman's throw to arrive. If it did? I would have to splatter the catcher so violently they'd be picking pieces of him out of the backstop until Christmas. I watched the catcher closely; it would just be a question of whether he could hold onto the ball when I trucked him.

And I watched, my arms pumping furiously, my tunnel vision narrowing to a six-inch target on the catcher's chest where my shoulder would initiate impact.

And I watched. Hammer time. I leaned forward, into the crash position. Three steps to impact. Two steps.

My target left the bombsights. The Meds' catcher vanished, walking off towards the Marseille dugout. I stomped home plate as it washed over me; we won.

Holy shit, we just won.

We're 3-3 in the playoffs. *We just won!*

The second mob scene of the game met me at the dugout as I pumped my fist, howling with pure euphoria. Aldo greeted me with a shout and a two-handed high-five, and Eric wrapped me in a huge bear hug. The 1664 tasted better than ever, as we toasted our victory right there on the field. Our goofy grins still hadn't faded when Eric dropped me off at the station for my train to Paris. I slid out of the passenger seat and turned back to him.

"So we need one more, right? One more win to avoid descending?"

"One win," he said, beaming. *"I think one win will suffice."*

"We're gonna do it next week, Eric," I declared, reaching out for a fist pound. *"We're gonna beat Piquet."*

"I hope so, my friend." We bumped fists and then snapped our hands back while flaring the fingers out

wide; I had taught the Woodchucks to 'blow it up' like we did on the Reds.

"See you next week, Evan." Eric said, laughing.

CHAPTER 37: DON'T TOUCH MY BAGS IF YOU PLEASE

Ever since August, I had practiced my story in case one of the United employees or customs officials noticed my frequent commuting to Paris. My heart raced with each check-in, terrified some check-in clerk would detect my verboten overlapping itineraries. What would they do if they caught me? Kick me off the flight? Cancel my itineraries going forward without refund? Arrest me, with French guard dogs clenching their teeth around my forearms? Looking back, the anxiety I felt each time I had to clear airport checkpoints that autumn makes it all the more impressive – or worrisome, depending on your perspective – that the airlines never detected my subterfuge. Between my racing pulse, shifty eyes, and stuttered, evasive answers to security questions, I couldn't have seemed more like a smuggler or terrorist if I tried.

To my relief, they again let me on the plane to Chicago without incident and I started preparing a memo for my legal writing class. The next day, I visited Becky at a Kellogg happy hour, weakly making up for how little time my schedule allowed for me to see her. She introduced me to a dozen friends, one of whom had come to Kellogg from a software company in the Bay.

"Oh, wait," he said, eyes wide. "You're the Have Bat Will Travel guy?"

"Uh... I guess so." Apparently, he and his coworkers had read my blog, particularly the post about the 40-meter dash at Velocity Sports.

"We thought we could outrun your 4.81 forty time, because we have a bunch of guys who ran track in high school. One Friday, the entire company went to a nearby high school and timed each other. Our fastest guy only ran a 4.98 on a hand timer." He gave me a dap and nodded with respect. Somehow, the image of a small software company testing themselves against my 40 time put a hop in my step for the rest of the week.

I took the bus to O'Hare on Friday, marveling at the season's symmetry; I would play my last games in France against Antoni Piquet and the La Guerche Hawks, the same team I faced Opening Day with the Lions in March. Strangely, between those two games with the Lions, four with the Woodchucks during the regular season, one in the Challenge, and two more in the playoffs, nearly a quarter of the games I played overseas were against Piquet.

A flood of emotions came over me as I boarded my last flight: sadness and nostalgia, certainly, but also relief, joy, and pride. The whole absurd exercise had been about making something happen, overcoming the inertia that the world imposes on our (often unrealistic) dreams, and being able to say that once upon a time, I had been a professional ballplayer.

And it happened. No matter what, I had made it happen, the real and surreal blending for seven unforgettable months that proved sometimes frustrating, often challenging, and always interesting. On Sunday, my career as a professional baseball player would officially end.

In the meantime, we needed a win.

Eric emailed me that morning, explaining that at 3-3, the Woodchucks controlled their own destiny in the tournament. We needed only to squeak one out against the Hawks, the only elite team we beat during a regular season where four forfeited 'wins' masked the true horror of our 5-25 record.

Eric closed his email with an invitation. "Eh-von,*"*he wrote, "*It has been my pleasure to play with you this season. I know that this is your last weekend, and Virginie and I invite you to dine with us on Saturday. You can stay with us, and we'll drive to the game in Bois-Guillaume. OK?"*

I awoke just as we touched down in France. Eschewing my usual route, I headed to the Latin Quarter to meet Miklos and Sierra. They had almost single-handedly made my back-and-forth jaunts possible by lending me Miklos' apartment as a launching pad to the airport on Monday mornings. To thank them, I had smuggled contraband gifts from home at Sierra's request, the finest that America could offer. Sierra lived in a third-story walkup, above a stretch of pubs and late-night dives where moped-riding hipsters and taxi drivers tended to congregate in the wee hours, smoking cigarettes and chatting loud enough to interrupt her beauty sleep. Lacking Americans' fascination with firepower, Parisian toy shops did not the sell high-powered squirt guns I brought from Chicago, each with sufficient range to scatter the night owls by delivering a liquid message that they were unwelcome. Sierra and Miklos opened the packages with glee, each finding a surprise addition: a Bois-Guillaume ballcap, with its impressive interlocking BG logo.

"Without you guys, I never could have pulled this off," I said, surprised at my own emotionality. "I want you to have these. You guys are honorary Woodchucks, as far as I'm concerned."

"You mean the team that lost, like, every game?"

Sierra responded.

"Fuck you. But yeah. That's the one." I laughed, and we shared a group hug before I left to catch the metro.

I headed to Rouen and met Matt in our dingy one-bedroom. He grunted.

"I'm crashing at Eric's place tonight," I told him, "Make some more room for the INSEP kids. See you tomorrow. One more to go, huh?"

"I guess. Two weekends to go, but if you go fuck off for next weekend, maybe I'll do the same."

I saw the future clearly. The team had already paid Matt for those games, so he would happily bail on another doubleheader with the money already in his pocket. He would refuse to play unless paid more, extorting the team when it needed him most. Forget the bank accounts or vehicles; *that* was the difference between us. Matt thought of baseball as work, preferring to collect his pay and go home as soon as possible, while I would actually pay to play baseball. Given how much I spent on airline tickets, I nearly had.

Eric honked his horn outside, and I put the

matter out of mind, skipping downstairs to greet him with a bear hug. We drove out to his house in Morgny-la-Pommeraye, chatting about La Guerche and Piquet.

"*He irritates me,*" Eric began. "*I don't like his attitude, always putting himself above other players,*" he added, becoming animated. "*He thinks he's bigger than the game, bigger than the umpires!*"

"*I don't know, Eric...*" I shrugged. "*I like him. He's intense, and a little, uh, how do you say* 'chippy'*? Like in hockey. After games, he always seemed nice enough. You know what? He's the kind of guy that you hate on the other team, and love to have on your team. I respect that.*"

Agreeing to disagree, we pulled into the driveway, where Virginie greeted me with a warm hug and a kiss on each cheek.

"*Eric is making his famous steak with black mushrooms- do you know them? The trumpets of death?*"

I shook my head as Virginie explained that these rich, black mushrooms had stems that opened up like the mouth of a trumpet.

"I brought you a gift, Eric," I said, changing the subject. *"I know we both like Scotch, and that you studied the Second World War."*

He nodded, an eyebrow raised. Most good scotch didn't have anything to do with World War II except for being bottled shortly thereafter.

"I got this single-malt Scapa for you, distilled next to the Scapa Flow, where..."

"Where the Germans scuttled their fleet in the first war, and the HMS Royal Oak sank after the second!"

"Of course."

"So... shall we have some before dinner?" Eric asked, finding a willing co-conspirator.

"Eh... Pourquoi pas?"

Eric poured out two fingers and raised his glass in a toast.

"It was hard for me this year, Evan," Eric said. *"Very hard. Sometimes, baseball wasn't fun, like it*

should be. It's supposed to be fun!"

"I know, Eric."

"It was hard, without enough players, having to rely on mercenaries. That's not how the Woodchucks used to be. It used to be my friends."

He sighed. I did too; *technically,* I was a mercenary like Matt and the INSEP kids.

"Sometimes it made me think I should stop playing. I have a wife, kids... a house to build."

"But you love it too much," I interjected. "*No? You won't stop playing until they pry the bat from your cold, dead fingers.*" He nodded, laughing at my awkward translation.

"It's true. I love playing with my friends too much. This team, I... I helped build it! I can't just leave it. I can't."

"*Eric... It's been a tough season, I know... and I wish I could have done more to make it better."* I sighed, sipping the Scapa. "*If I had just been a little better, or... if I could pitch, we would have won more games..."* Tears welled in my eyes. "*It could have been different. But all year long, what did we say? What did you tell me the first time we met? 'Our season doesn't start until September.' Remember? 'The playoffs are everything.' Right?"*

He nodded.

"Well here we are in September, and it took a lot of blood, sweat, and blades to get here, but–"

"Blades?" he said, interrupting with sudden laughter.

"*Uh, yeah, you know. Blades. Like, what falls from your eyes when you cry?"*

Eric shook his head.

"*You said* 'lames.' *I think you meant to say* 'larmes.' *But no problem, I understood."*

"Merci," I said, rolling my eyes. *"You know what I mean. It's been hard. We didn't win a lot of games, and sometimes, Matthieu and Matt sucked the joy out of baseball. But things are going to get better, Eric, I promise. Looking at the standings, we just need one win to stay in elite, and we can beat La Guerche or Compiegne. Next year, you'll get a better American, with some good ballplayers coming up from the Cadets... It's going to be better, Eric. This team will survive."*

He nodded again, and raised his glass.

"To one more win, with my American friend: Evan."

We clinked glasses and finished our whiskies. Over dinner, we joked about the time I almost fought Matt in the parking lot, Pierre's unexpected voice change, and Vince's development into a legitimate elite-level starting pitcher. Virginie disagreed with Eric on one thing: Matt's ongoing recalcitrance.

"*After the things he did last year? I couldn't believe they took him back. He begged Jean-Luc to take him back, but Jean-Luc had gone to Cherbourg! So he begged to come back here, and sure, we needed a foreigner, but after he refused to come back for the weekend games against Saint-Lô?"* Virginie shook her head furiously, still upset over the strain the situation had put on Eric. "*Why not fire him right then?"*

"I know, Virginie," I interrupted. "*But we were*

nine, every weekend. We needed the bodies! Not to mention a pitcher."

She looked away.

Some stereotypes are true, and Virginie conformed to those concerning French women; they are beautiful, wise, and powerfully obstinate. I knew with a glance that I wouldn't change her mind anytime soon. She rolled her eyes – like most French women, she had perfected this to an art form, like a Pedro Martinez changeup – and changed the subject.

"*Evan, it was our pleasure to know you this year. You weren't like the Americans we see around here. You had other things in your life besides baseball."*

I cocked my head to the side as if to object, but she interrupted me before I could speak. *"Hey, stop!"* she declared in false outrage. "*You were one of the only things that made the season fun. We want to thank you, because we know that you will be our friend for a long time."*

I accepted the compliment. There was no point in continuing my pretension that I was the typical

American to which they were accustomed, with no distractions other than how they would make it back to the minors back home. I had 48 hours left, so I could drop the façade. They had seen me play 40 games. They knew my future was more MBA than MLB, and that was fine.

I smiled and looked down at my plate.

"*My father made his own calvados,*" Virginie continued. "*In a still he built himself, with apples he picked in our garden. Eric told me that you developed a taste for Calvados, non?*"

I nodded sheepishly. I was supposed to be staying in shape, like any other professional athlete, but I had consumed more than my share of 'calva' since arriving in Normandy. Sue me; calvados was really delicious.

"*When he died a few years ago, he had a dozen bottles left. We split equally among the four children. We only have one bottle left, and we can never make more, so we save it for special occasions. Weddings, births...*" She paused. "*Dinners with true friends. We want to offer you some of Papa's calvados.*" She retrieved a re-used wine bottle from the shelf, its label long stripped from it when it was first refilled with calvados, and poured out three small tumblers as I blinked back tears.

"Not too much," she said with a grin, "*You two have to play well tomorrow.*"

I raised my glass.

"*To the Club of Baseball and Softball of the Woodchucks of Bois-Guillaume!*"[34]

---

[34] Obviously, a literal translation of 'Au Club de Baseball et Softball les Woodchucks de Bois-Guillaume!'

CHAPTER 38: THE LAST TIME

Poke.

Poke.

Poke.

I opened my eyes to see Eric's daughter Marianne nudging me awake on a crisp, cool Sunday morning. Above her, Eric smiled down at me.

"*Are you ready, my friend?*"

I wasn't ready for anything but a cup of strong, black coffee, but I nodded anyway, rubbing the sleep out of my eyes.

"Time's up, let's do this." I mumbled in English.

"*What?*" Marianne said. Inconceivably cute at age

five, her enormous brown eyes blinked, having failed to understand my old anthem from the Reds.

"I said, I'm ready."

I showered quickly, changed, and finished my coffee in the living room. Marianne watched cartoons and danced to the musical numbers, oblivious to the grave importance of our impending confrontation. Maybe she was right, I thought. Maybe the fate of the 2006 Bois-Guillaume Woodchucks didn't amount to a hill of beans... but as the saying goes, it was our hill, goddammit, and they were our beans.

We got to the field before everyone except Aldo, who had already begun combing the basepaths in preparation for the game. I stretched my legs on the Normandy grass, still moist from an overnight shower. Looking up, I saw the Hawks entering through the right-field gate, slouching towards their dugout with the body language of a team that clearly wanted to be somewhere else. Firmly in the elite division's middle class based largely on Piquet's pitching – they were sort of the 1998 Red Sox of France – the relegation tournament held no upside to La Guerche; they had barely missed the final playoff spot for the elite championship, earning a punishment of having to show up dutifully for five weeks to go through the formality of smoking lousy N1A teams to stay in elite.

I had come to France with 12 bats, and one by one, broken all but three: *Kus Emek Bnei Zonot* (an impossibly profane Israeli curse that blended Hebrew and Arabic), *Facta Non Verba* (Deeds, Not Words) and *Audentes Fortuna Juvat* (Fortune Favors the Bold). Swinging the bat, my hands felt slow from a long season, and I just hoped to make it through the last two games without breaking any more, knowing that it would prompt additional snickering from Matthieu.

I led off with a line drive single to center and immediately stole second. With that good start, I wondered if maybe this would be the game we could steal, as Piquet wouldn't pitch until game two.

It wasn't. Matthieu struck out to end the threat, stranding me on third, and Vince fell apart on the mound. We compounded his wildness with atrocious defensive lapses, losing the first game by slaughter rule. It took the wind right out of my sails; it was my last weekend in France and we were rolling over, getting smoked by a good-but-not-great baseball team that wasn't even throwing their ace. It was not how I had envisioned the weekend.

During the between-games sandwich-and-smoke break, I looked around at the usual suspects. There was Zoe, feeding Seb a homemade pasta dish. On the bench was Monique, Aldo's mother, prim and proper with her long skirt and immaculately styled hair, next to Pierre's father, smoking his self-rolled cigarette and staring wild-eyed at the field. I had always dreamed of playing in the big leagues, of doffing my cap towards the fans in a curtain call after my final home run. That wasn't going to happen. My career ended here. These were my fans, and this was the end of the road.

For the last time, I filled out our lineup card, installing myself as the leadoff hitter against the Great Piquet. I walked slowly to home plate, wanting to soak it all in: the soft light burning through the Normandy fog, the air heavy with moisture, even the trademark Piquet sneer from the mound.

Ah yes, I thought. Hello, old friend.

Come get some.

Piquet ran two sliders past me to make it 0-2, but tried to get cute with another one, which I drilled into center for another leadoff single. I made a big turn at first, for once making no attempt to hide my grin as the shortstop tossed the ball to a scowling Piquet. I like this Piquet guy, I thought. I also *owned* him, having hit .444 with an OBP of .700 off him since first facing him in April. Of course, only four of those balls were well hit, and he had probably hastened my firing from Savigny by sawing off two of my bats on Opening Day... but that didn't stop me from declaring victory over the man who I considered the best pitcher in France.

My daydreaming was cut short when Piquet struck out Matt and Matthieu back-to-back to end the inning. We started Quentin, putting him into a tough position. He had only begun to believe in himself, so against an 'ace' like Piquet, the poor kid felt like he had to be perfect, and he wasn't. Shoddy defense behind him left us down 5-1 in the fifth, our only run coming in the third when I worked a walk from Piquet, stole second, and scored on Seb's single to right.

We rallied in the sixth, however, when Piquet tried to sneak a fastball past me inside. I was expecting his sweeping slider – he had a good one, lots of late movement – so I was leaning out over the plate, and the ball struck me on the elbow, not far from the strike zone. Ever the competitor, Piquet immediately barked at the umpire that I hadn't moved, and the pitch was almost a strike! I might have sympathized, but it reminded me of the breaking ball I threw against that damned Rouen Husky at Montigny, who had leaned in gleefully for a cheap HBP. In my mind, stealing a free pass off Piquet finally balanced the scales of justice.

I stole second and scored again on Seb's second RBI single of the game. Matt walked, Matthieu reached on an error, and Aldo singled off a suddenly rattled Piquet to make the game 5-4, taking second base on the throw home. I clapped furiously in the third base coach's box, shouting "*Let's go, Eric!*" as the Quebecois worked his right foot into the batter's box dirt.

Glancing back at me, Eric turned to the umpire and called time, jogging up the baseline to meet me halfway.

"*Evan, they are expecting me to bunt,*" he whispered.

"*Bunt, what are you, nuts?*" I blurted before remembering to keep my voice down. "*Eric, we're down one with two guys in scoring position! There's no WAY we should bunt!*"

"Evan!" he gestured out at the field. "*This is France! And besides, this is the great Antoni Piquet!*" he smirked. "*I think I can do it; I can slash here.*"

I snorted, incredulous. The slash is an aggressive gamble where the hitter squares around as if to bunt – prompting the first and third basemen to charge home plate – before pulling the bat back and trying to smash the ball past helpless fielders, who are suddenly worried about catching a batted ball off the temple. I loved the slash, but had never mustered the courage to call for it in France, because so few Woodchucks could put the ball in play consistently on a normal swing, let alone after the histrionics of a fake bunt.

I locked eyes with Eric, and realized the subtext; he really, really disliked Piquet, and the slash was an opportunity to exact revenge for an ancient (and, I was certain, one-sided) grudge. Over dinner, Eric had described an incident years earlier, where he felt Piquet had played dirty and caused a collision in the basepath. Eric claimed another Woodchuck had pulled him off Piquet in the resulting dogpile, just as he was drawing back to slug the youngster, who for his part had never in six games this year given any indication that he even knew who Eric was. I had no axe to grind with Piquet, so I could count hundreds of reasons *not* to call for a slash, which was basically like throwing a Hail Mary in the third quarter. I looked up to see the umpire waving Eric back to home plate, forcing a rapid decision.

"*Okay, Eric,*" I said. "*You have ONE pitch to try it. If it doesn't work, just slap the ball on the ground to the right side; we'll take one run and a tie ballgame.*"

Stupid, I thought, as Eric jogged back to the batter's box. This was a stupid play, a sure-fire rally killer. Matt would bitch about it 0.4 seconds after it backfired, and I was so tired of his bullshit that I knew we'd get into a screaming match: a crappy ending to the season. As Piquet went into his windup, I cursed myself for agreeing to such an absurd gamble. Eric squared around to bunt, and the third baseman burst forward to field it.

I prayed Eric would foul it off.

As if in slow motion, Eric pulled the bat back into his unorthodox, wide-legged stance. As always, his Quebecois sniper chin jutted forward aggressively, hands high above his shoulders. I cringed.

CRACK!

The ball rocketed off his bat, and for one delirious moment, I thought the ball might leave the Parc des Cosmonautes, a name that suddenly struck me as peculiar. Why, I wondered as the ball arched gloriously over the third baseman's head, did a French baseball team play on a field named after Russian astronauts? THWAP! The ball's collision six inches above the ground against the left field fence snapped me out of my daydreams. Both runners scored standing up as Eric coasted into second wearing the kind of shit-eating grin that only comes from doubling off the wall against your personal, intimate nemesis.

I started laughing.

Hard.

I couldn't help it. I didn't want to show up our opponents – hell, the game wasn't even over, we had only taken a one-run lead with plenty of baseball left – but I never saw that one coming. A guy in his late 30s, suffering most of the season from stomach ulcers and six other injuries, fakes a bunt against the best pitcher in France, 10 years his junior with a lively fastball and no fear of pitching inside, and crushes one off the left field wall to give the Woodchucks a lead. Piquet stomped around the mound angrily – maybe he knew who Eric was after all – and glared at me as I struggled to stifle my laughter in the third base coach's box. My face turned red, and finally I cleared my throat amidst a series of aftershock guffaws. I looked at Eric, tapping my left shoulder, belt, hat, right knee, and nose in a series of fake signals, my jaw somewhere around my waist. He pantomimed a few phony signals back and winked, wearing that same goofy grin.

I motioned to Matt to warm up, knowing one run probably wouldn't suffice. With my spot in the order coming back up, Sylvain took over at third base coach and I jogged to the on-deck circle to warm up, fretting over a possible Hawks comeback. Eric Fournier walked, bringing Vince to the plate. The pizza delivery guy had been swinging a hot bat during the playoffs, and he kept it going by scorching a liner down the left field line, scoring both Erics. The Bois-Guillaume fan base erupted in cheers of "Allez Les Woodchucks!" as Vince gave me a wink and flashed me the Wu-Tang sign.

Suddenly, Piquet had seen enough. He just packed it in. The La Guerche manager had not even crossed the baseline into the field of play before Piquet stormed off the mound to his shortstop position, forcing the manager to make substitutions that addressed the awkward situation of two guys standing at shortstop and no one on the mound. (It wasn't a great look for Piquet, but in his defense, the game meant nothing to La Guerche. They had already won enough games in the tournament to ensure they'd stay in the elite division, so it really only mattered to us.)

I singled in Vince to make it 9-5, and we never looked back. You could put a fork in the Hawks, because they were done the moment Piquet left the game. Their

Goliath bested, they gave in, knowing that they couldn't mount a five-run comeback against the hard-throwing Australian. Matt mowed them down as the field hummed with the anticipation you usually see when a team up 3-0 in the World Series takes a lead late in game four. The crowd – tiny as it was – chanted non-stop, knowing it would witness another rare victory.

On the first pitch of the ninth, Piquet smashed a fastball up the middle to my right. I took one crossover step and laid out, launching myself toward the screaming line drive. In six months in a Woodchucks uniform, I dove for half a dozen balls, always coming *this close* but never quite hauling one in. (The one that ticked off my glove at Saint-Lô might have helped steal a win had I corralled it, a microcosm of our always-close-but-not-quite season.) I extended as far as I could, rolling onto my left side in midair and feeling the ball strain my glove's webbing just before I came crashing to the ground like the Hindenburg. I flopped into a sitting position, displaying the ball in my right hand and wearing a satisfied grin as the crowd shouted "Bravo!"

"You finally got one, mate..." Matt said with a chuckle as I tossed him the ball.

"Goddamn right. Hey, Matt," I responded. "Web gem."

When Matt struck out the final Hawk, I sprinted over to third base, tossing my glove into the dugout. Both teams formed the traditional high-five lines, the Hawks crossing the mound from first base and the Woodchucks from third, and I wanted to be up front.

"Bon match," I said, over and over through the handshake line. "Bon match... bon match..."

After the handshakes, I sat in the dugout, my arm clasped around Eric's shoulder.

"We did it, Eric." I said, almost shouting. "*WE DID IT!"*

"*Good match, coach,"* Vince said, his head cocked back. He reached into his baseball bag for his Lucky Strikes.

"Merci, Vince," I said, laughing. *"Hey... you have a cigarette for me in there?"*

He did a double take, yanking his head back in mock outrage.

"*But Evan, you don't smoke!*"

"When in Normandy, my friend," I said, pulling the cigarette from the pack he offered me. "*One does as the Normans do.*"

Accepting his offer of a light, I leaned back against the dugout feeling suddenly very tired. My head buzzed with nicotine, and I started laughing.

"Eric, I still can't believe you hit that fucking ball off the wall, you son of a bitch."

He laughed with me, winking.

Moments later, a circle of euphoric Woodchucks met just past third base. We had met there every weekend after devastating losses, and for once the group was all smiles. We had hung a loss on the Great Piquet, preserving our right to remain in the Elite division. I addressed the circle, trying hard not to break down in tears.

"My buddies, it has been my grand pleasure to play with you. I was proud to be a Woodchuck, and I loved

wearing this uniform," I said, pulling at my lapel. *"I hope I get to play with you again someday. Now, I have spoken with Eric and Sylvain, and, the team cannot afford to buy us any beer..."*

"Oh, motherfucker!" Vince exclaimed, again in mock disgust.

"...but you should all come over to our apartment, to celebrate!"

We piled into cars to take us down the hill, but not before I snuck out to the first baseline to steal a pillbox full of the Bois-Guillaume infield dirt that rests on my mantel to this day. We stopped on the way to pick up a bottle of vodka and case of beers, and spent the night toasting each other, laughing and drinking and having a good time. Around four in the morning, we finally called it a night, Eric and I crashing on a fold-out couch before he drove me, pie-eyed, to the train station at half past five. On the way, Eric turned to me, surprisingly coherent given the night's festivities.

"Evan, I want to tell you something. I spoke with Sylvain, and we want you to come and play one more

weekend. You're a part of this team, and even if we don't need to win any games, we want you there. To the end, like you said."

I sighed, crestfallen.

"*I... I don't think I can, Eric. I tried. I will call my travel agent, but I-*"

He placed his hand on my shoulder.

"*I understand. I thought you might say that. But if you can, the team will buy your ticket. We would prefer to finish the season with you.*"

There was no chance the team would offer to buy the ticket if they knew how expensive it was, but I said nothing so as not to ruin the moment. He put the car in park. We had arrived at the train station early for my 6:15 train into Paris, just in time for my final flight home.

"*Thank you, Eric. Thank you for everything.*" I shook his hand. "*Wait! One last picture.*"

He grinned and stepped out of the car. I held out my camera and snapped a picture of the two of us, arm-in-arm and grinning happily before the illuminated train station.

"*Goodbye, Eric,*" I said after one last hug.

"*No, no, no, Evan,*" he said. "*See you soon.*"

CHAPTER 39: NOTES FROM THE UNDERGROUND

I called my travel agent the moment I landed; it was no use, as tickets for the following weekend had risen to over $3,000, far more than the team could justify spending. I called Eric to give him the bad news, but he was more upset about Matt, who as I predicted, had used the leverage of the last weekend to extort another €100 out of the club.

On Friday night, instead of flying to France, I donned my Woodchucks' jersey for the final time to attend the retirement party Becky threw for me at a nearby bar. My classmates and I toasted my retirement from professional baseball, drank American beers, and ate hamburgers while I loudly complained about the quality of the bread.

I emailed Eric on Sunday night, eager for news of the team's results against Compiegne. I opened up the following email from Eric on Monday. I ran it through Altavista's Babelfish service. The translation isn't perfect, but I think it works; it'll give you some feel for what it was like for me trying to understand French all summer.

From: Eric

Subject: RE: Ce Weekend

Bonjour Evan, sorry not to have answered. We divided against Compiegne. 1st match: Vince vs. Cuban 47 years old who still launches very well. We manage 18 hits and lead 15-4 but in the 8th I came to help Vince to stop the bleeding but as they had already marked 3 points, we did one 9 2nd handle. Final result: 15-7 for BG. On their side, I do not know how this match was scored, but they made 16 hits! Their ambience was dreadful with unfavourable players and especially their Cuban who yelled all the time, disputed all the time, aims at the head of our players (Aldo and me) and seeks the provocation. In spite of the victory, the moral was not great because it was not an amusing match. For the second match, we had kept Matt and Quentin, and for Compiegne, a left-handed person who never launched a fast ball. We have trouble to strike it but we led 4-0, then 4-3, then 6-3, then 6-6, then 9-6 at the end of the 9th. Arbitration of shit![35] *The referee does not see the interiors of Matt and Matt is irritated. One K wasted, a 2nd, a 3rd. With a runner on base, HBP, which causes the exit of the Cuban coach who approaches the mound towards Matt who goes down from the mound and does not go further. The Cuban enters on the ground and it is the referee and three players of Compiegne that restrain him and that difficult 10 minutes... Thereafter, catastrophe! Passed ball, errors (x2) and 2 runs make 9-8 with a runner on 3rd base. Struck ball left field, a Texas leaguer, Seb moves back from shortstop, Pierre advances from left, and me too from center. Nobody calls for the ball and thus, I have a chance, I call, I divine, I catch the ball but in contact with the ground,*

---

[35] "Arbitration of shit!" ("bad umpiring") became a favorite of my father, who as an attorney, often avails his clients of the arbitration process. He now has something to shout anytime he disagrees with a ruling.

the ball arises! 9-9. Extra inning Matt must leave the mound because 9 innings launched, and Quentin will come. We score a run in the 10th, them too. 10-10 11th inning: Nothing. 12th inning, we score 3 points. 13-10 for BG! Compiegne shouts, howl, bad environment and our young players crack. Quentin gives a walk, HBP, hits and bases full with 13-11. Vince returns to the mound with 1 out. Me, I do not have any more an arm! Ball to Quentin at 3rd base, play at the plate (2nd out) and still 13-11 but Matthieu, which caught 20 innings, throws to 1st base for the double play but throws it into right field and 2 runs score (13-13). Tabarnak! A runner on 2nd base, ball struck to the field centers, I see do or die play, throw it with all what remains with me to the mound, on target, a bounce 3 meters in front of the mound, but Matthieu does not control the ball, escapes it from the glove and victory for Compiegne 14-13. Which is disappointment but still our record of 5-5, we deserved our maintenance in elite. Thank you Evan and see you soon, Eric.

Couldn't have said it better myself.

AFTERWORD: HEY JUDE

About half of what you just read first appeared as blog posts on www.havebatwilltravel.com during the summer of 2006. It had a decent following, 65,000 visitors or so, and got written up in the Boston Globe. Every few months, on holiday breaks from grad school, I would spend a week trying to craft that blog into an early version of this manuscript, adding in the sensitive parts that I couldn't post in real time because people in French baseball were reading it every time I published something new.

That manuscript sat untouched on my hard drive for over a decade.

In the meantime, I'd occasionally reflect on that year

in France and marvel at it, because even today, it doesn't seem real. Sometimes, I think about what might have been. I think that if I had pitched well against La Guerche on opening day, maybe the Lions wouldn't have canned me. Or if I had only thrown three innings instead of five against Bois-Guillaume, maybe I would have avoided my elbow injury and proven myself a reliable second starting pitcher for the Woodchucks. In the end, though, even if I could, I wouldn't change anything. Savigny wanted something I couldn't provide, so I have no regrets that my play revealed that in my month in town. Bois-Guillaume was the right place for me, and besides, the story of getting fired, throwing a no-no as a lame duck, and then getting hired by the team you just blanked is just too perfect. Moreover, the story as it unfolded was mine, it was real, and I lived it the best way I knew how. It was a fair trade; I gave it absolutely every bit of myself and my limited talent, and in exchange, I got great memories and friends I will keep for life.

People ask me what the competition was like, and I just tell them the truth. The best teams in elite were comparable to division III collegiate baseball in the United States – which is to say, pretty damn good baseball[36] – while the worst teams might lose to a top-tier American high school squad. France has gotten better since; apart from a goofball oddity like me, the foreigners used to be former college players or guys who washed out in single A, but in recent years, teams like Rouen have had guys who reached AAA and even sniffed the majors. For example, I think Meurant from Toulouse was the hardest thrower while I was there, and he was probably just a click or two south of 90 mph (Matt wasn't far behind him), but there are guys in France throwing harder now, both foreigners and natives.[37]

As for me, I looked at my own performance in France on three dimensions: baserunning, pitching, and hitting. When it came to baserunning, ego compelled me at the time to fancy myself the fastest base stealer in the league, even acknowledging that there was a guy from Montpellier who might – *might* – have been a half

---

[36] Recall that those division III schools produce some MLB stars on occasion.
[37] Of course, they're also throwing harder in the MLB than they were in 2006, but that's another conversation for another time.

step quicker.

Ok, quarter step. *Maybe.*

Nah, screw it; I was faster than that guy, I was just trying to be diplomatic. If that guy disagrees, he can take it up with the Quiet Storm.

When it comes to pitching, I will confess that it still grates on me that I only pitched that one, measly inning against Saint-Lô, because I felt like I let the Woodchucks down. I sometimes joke that I never allowed an earned run in France, and it's true! But I have to clarify that I only pitched six innings, and only one of them counted after bureaucratic incompetence forfeited my five-inning no-hitter.

At the plate, I calculated my batting stats based on the official scoresheets I had and from my weekly blog reports. I had a .390 batting average, .597 OBP, and .519 slugging percentage for a 1.117 OPS. I stole over 30 bases, getting caught only the one time swiping second at Saint-Lô and once stealing home at PUC, which I note with something of an asterisk because man, I was *safe*. Anyway, that made me an on-base machine and one of the better leadoff hitters in the league, but guys who get on base a lot are a *centime* a dozen in France. In European baseball, they expect the foreigners to hit over .500 and launch a bunch of dingers along the way; they expect you to *dominate*. I brought a lot of things to the table, but pure physical dominance simply wasn't one of them.

When I have told this story, many have pointed out that those numbers don't make sense; how could they fire you if you were hitting nearly .400 and getting on base that much? For a long time, I looked at it the same way, shrugging my shoulders at Savigny canning a guy who pretty clearly did two things as well or better than anyone in the league: get on base, and run like hell thereafter.

I was looking at it the wrong way.

I was just good enough to get paid at the elite level, and even then, it was only because of my nationality; if I had been born Yvan Meaghereau in, say, Alsace, I would just have been another 'pretty good French ballplayer.' None of those 'pretty good' French nationals got paid, so when I say 'hell, I could have helped the

Lions win ballgames,' it's true but it doesn't matter.

There were a handful of Lions every bit as good as me or better, and they constantly chafed when, on the one hand, the Tres Lettres told them 'you're absolutely every bit as good as all these foreigners,' and on the other hand, delivered the unspoken message 'these foreigners get paid but you can't.' That only works if the foreigner getting paid does the big, obvious, observable things that the unpaid French players can't; hit the ball a country mile, or throw a fastball hard enough to crack steel. These are not skillsets that are impossible to find, but they are skillsets I didn't possess. I'll go to my grave knowing intellectually that any team at that level – pointedly, including the Lions – would win more games with a guy like me putting up a 1.117 OPS than they would without him... but it still wasn't enough for a guy like Pierrick to glance over at a guy like me and say 'oh, yeah, that guy deserves to get paid, and I don't.' The margin isn't big enough or visible enough. So when the Lions fired me, it felt irrational and unfair to 2006 Evan Meagher, but 2020 Evan Meagher can see it both ways.

I still consider the season a success, based on the two goals Virginie laid out during my first night in Bois-Guillaume: improve the club atmosphere, and prevent the Woodchucks from being demoted from the elite division. I did my damnedest to improve the ambience, despite the constant headwind of Matt's bellicosity. The guy just had a lot of *anger*, more than any of us could possibly help him deal with, and I spent my summer trying to minimize its impact on the other Woodchucks. I never understood where it came from, and it unfortunately obscured the more likable parts of his personality.

The second goal of staying in elite proved bittersweet, because although our performance in the tournament earned us the right to remain in elite, against all odds and the expectations of the Tres Lettres, club management decided in December that it couldn't survive – organizationally or financially – another year like 2006, barely avoiding forfeits and struggling to field nine ballplayers. The team elected to drop down to the N1A level for the 2007 season, of its own volition. I suppose that after 250 pages, you could read that sentence and think it was all for nothing, that after all that, the Woodchucks dropping down voluntarily instead of being forced out is a distinction without a difference.

I would disagree.

Besides, if you're the kind of person who doesn't see nobility in doing something just to prove that you could do it, Have Bat Will Travel probably wasn't the book for you in the first place.

The Woodchucks played well in 2007 and 2008 in N1A, probably because they had more talented foreigners who weren't constantly bickering at each other. In 2008, they ran roughshod over N1A, led by a guy named Tony Lewis, with whom I shared an unusual kinship; this time, I read *his* blog about French baseball. Tony had been a stud at Missouri State and Drury University, and from what I can tell, he was ten times the ballplayer I had been. He took Bois-Guillaume to the 2008 championship game against Montigny. Like me, Tony fell in love with the club and the town, and if they had won that title, he planned on staying full-time, working odd jobs and bartending while training the youth teams in the offseason, and finding a new field for the team to play on. The neighbors of the Parc des Cosmonautes had always complained to Bois-Guillaume's mayor about foul balls landing in their yards or breaking their windows, finally getting their way in 2010 when they convinced the town to close the field. Tony and Jean-Luc worked mightily to find a new field for the club to play on, but it kept falling through. Without a home field, the Bois-Guillaume club dissolved in 2010, after 25 years of baseball and softball… but I don't see it as tragic. I feel in my bones that Le Club de Baseball et Softball de Bois-Guillaume Woodchucks isn't dead. It's just resting, waiting for me and Tony to make a hundred million dollars so we can re-launch the 'Chucks and restore them to glory.

Getting back to 2006, it has always bothered me that I didn't hit for as much power in France as I did back home. I had just eight doubles and one triple on the season, and only lofted a few balls into Bois-Guillaume's short porch during batting practice. By the end, fatigue played a role, but earlier in the year, I was squeezing the sawdust out of the bat. After getting fired, the pressure of knowing that my next paycheck was only as safe as my ability to get at least three hits each weekend made me tight, and tight muscles don't hit the ball as far as loose ones.

That pressure forever changed the way I look at big leaguers. Having been fired once from a baseball team, I understand on some primal level the uncertainty those guys face, and for me, it excuses at least a *little* bit of what I would previously have perceived as selfishness. As Crash Davis said, the difference between a .300 hitter getting a big contract and a .240 hitter getting fired is just one extra hit a week, one dying quail that drops in or one ground ball that squeaks past a diving infielder. With that kind of job insecurity, I can see how the constant pressure to perform encourages narcissistic, defensive personalities, and how the brief earnings window makes it difficult to turn down anything but absolute top-dollar contracts.

Of course, my story was never really about money. It was about baseball, and I played it as hard as I could, five days a week, wearing through two pairs of baseball pants with all my headfirst slides into second. It was about friends like Kayvon and Chuck, who encouraged me to go overseas, and friends like Fermin, Eric, Aldo, and Seb, who welcomed me once I arrived. It was also about dreams, and how reality all too often crushes them, dissuading you from even trying before you can find it in yourself to pursue them. Candidly, there is no legitimate reason I should ever have drawn a paycheck to play baseball in this world or any other, but I *made* it happen, through sheer force of will and a few lucky breaks.

Usually, that's all it takes.

That's the lesson I think I'd like you to take from all this, Jude. You've probably figured it out by now, but that girlfriend Becky and I made it work. We moved back to San Francisco after grad school and got married in 2011 on the 14th hole at Pebble Beach. Over the years, I always meant to revisit this project, but I was busy building a career.

Then you were born, just six weeks ago as I type these final words, in the crossfire hurricane of global pandemic, nationwide protests, and an unprecedented economic contraction. Have Bat Will Travel was the greatest adventure of my life prior to you coming along, and it seemed only right that with nowhere to go during shelter-in-place, I should finally write up that adventure for you to read someday, in case I'm not around to tell it. Every morning, your mom wakes me up around 3:30 AM, and after feeding, burping, and changing you, I huddle next to you in our shoebox Russian Hill apartment, tapping away at my laptop, trying to get you to stop crying, and removing as many cuss words from the text as I can. (I have to, because your Nonni is still around, and I know that she's gonna read this, cuss words and all.)

There are still more of them than I care to admit, but hey, that's baseball for you, and if you recall your Uncle Jools' words, your dad was a professional baseball player once.

Now eat your greens.

The author and Daniel Kramer in the Reds days before France: together, the Manny Ortez of the San Francisco MABL.

The cake from my going away party; the caption reads 'Le Stud Who Hits Bombs' and it has my face superimposed over that of the Savigny-Sur-Orge Lion.

As a joke, I got cornrows the last weekend before going to France, which now strikes me as a mistake. (I took them out before boarding the plane)

That's me in front of the Arc de Triomphe, having the fateful conversation with Christophe the night before my final game as a Lion, agreeing that I would start and go as long as I could.

Trying to put on a happy face as I pray that the rain will stop long enough to get my final game in as a Lion, against the Bois-Guillaume Woodchucks.

That's me, alone in the dugout in my final game as a Lion.

Vincent was a solid third baseman, strong hitter, and all around really nice guy. I'm glad there's a picture of him encouraging me pitching against Bois-Guillaume, even though we both know it's my last game in the blue-and-white of Savigny.

Slingin' it against the Woodchucks. 5IP, 0H, 0R, 0ER, 2BB, 9K.

Saying my last goodbyes; that's Pierrick on the right with his back turned.

Courtesy of Tony Lewis, that's the Bois-Guillaume field in its usual 'just rained' condition.

The BG helmets, or ‘casques’ as they are known.

That’s Bois-Guillaume’s famed squared-off basepaths, which created not one but two ‘lips’ for infielders to deal with.

Mon ami Quebecois, Eric Coutu. Best teammate a guy could ask for.
(Picture courtesy of Tony Lewis)

Aldo (left) and Seb (right) after a rare win.

Vince, our courageous, soft-tossing lefty.

Seb liked to let it all hang out.

Sylvain always reminded me of Obelix. Just an all-around great guy who worked his tail off for the club.

Left to right that's Eric, Sylvain, and Vince, with Eric's daughter in the foreground. In the background is BG's weird climbing wall, never once observed in use.

It was always a family affair at BG.

Le Woodsmobile: BASK IN ITS GLORY.

The Woodchuck logo had faded a bit, but I still felt it made a statement.

We're about to do our warmups together as a team. That's Pierre on the left.

The humble but beloved Woodchucks clubhouse.

Matt did a number on the Woodsmobile.

Judges scored the round Matt 10, Woodsmobile 8 after his right cross cracked the windshield. The rearview mirror soon fell off, never to be used again.

Courtesy of Tony Lewis, this is the best picture I have of Eric's house. Matt and I would help him out with some manual labor, listen to my iPod, and have a cold beer. In 2013, Bex and I went back and the place had been transformed from a ramshackle scraper into a palace.

Eric and Matt posing in front of Dieppe, on the trip where Eric told us about his PhD thesis on the failed Allied raid there. Of 5,000 Allied troops, about a half dozen made it to the intended rendezvous point (off camera right).

Eric showing us an abandoned German bunker on the beaches above Dieppe.

The Dieppe cemetery; technically Canadian territory, those are all Canadian gravestones.

Courtesy of Tony Lewis, this is the square in downtown Rouen where Joan of Arc was burned. Matt and I would park in the parking structure underneath the square and visit a nearby internet café to keep in touch with friends back home. The Resto Rock was right around the corner.

The famous Formule 1 chain, known and tolerated by all French ballplayers.

The Formule 1 bathrooms and showers were all shared, with access from the hallway, so you'd have strangers in towels waiting in line together in the morning.

Two really tight bunks meant the rooms in Formule 1 were basically the size of American bathroom stalls.

The Formule 1 guests always looked at us like *we* were the weirdos at the communal breakfast.

Saint-Lô had a pretty decent field.

Quentin was our young southerner from INSEP. Here he is pitching against Saint-Lô on the road.

That's Seb catching at Saint-Lô.

The Saint-Lô dugout and stands.

Me and my friend Mark during my short trip home to see Becky in San Francisco.

That's Seb, Vince, and me after the games in Toulouse.

Ladies and Gentlemen, your 2006 Bois-Guillaume Woodchucks.
Top Row left to right: Seb, Quentin, Sylvain, Vince, Eric, me.
Bottom Row left to right: Matthieu, Matt, Aldo, Pierre.

Alex and Jools were great all summer; first they visited me and cheered me up in Rouen, and then they hosted me and Becky in Royal Leamington Spa as we traveled around Europe.

Fresh off my busted nose, Bex and I traveled to Amsterdam, and saw the Stones live.

Years later, this picture of us cliff jumping in Dubrovnik would serve as the 'save-the-date' for our wedding.

Vince getting ready to sling it for all he was worth during the Playdown. Kid played his ass off for us all year.

I decided to shave a Hulk Hogan Fu Manchu moustache for my last weekend of games in the postseason; that's me waiting on the platform to head to Bois-Guillaume for the very last time, having just landed on Saturday morning at Charles De Gaulle after a redeye from Chicago.

That's the night before my last games in Bois-Guillaume, at Eric & Virginie's place. Eric made entrecôtes (ribeye steaks) and trompettes de la mort (trumpets of death mushrooms), and we washed it down with some of Papa's calvados as we recounted the year together. One of my favorite memories of my year in France.

After that last big win against La Guerche, we celebrated in the dingy apartment Matt and I shared and toasted each other until the wee hours.

Matt, Aldo, and Vince throwing up West Coast Ws and other signs during our celebration.

Eric crashed for an hour or two of sleep on our couch and then drove me to make my train home for the very last time. This picture was taken at around 4:30 AM, right in front of the Rouen train station that I visited so many times flying back and forth from Chicago. I shaved the ridiculous Fu Manchu right after that last game in France.

Bex threw me a 'retirement party' at a local bar in Chicago after the season ended.

For his very first game at Fenway, Aldo got to sit on the Green Monster *and* go onto the field. I had to tell him that it's not usually like that.

The author hard at work, juggling baby feeding duties and manuscript editing while on paternity leave during the global pandemic of 2020. Mr. Yuckles looks on in support.

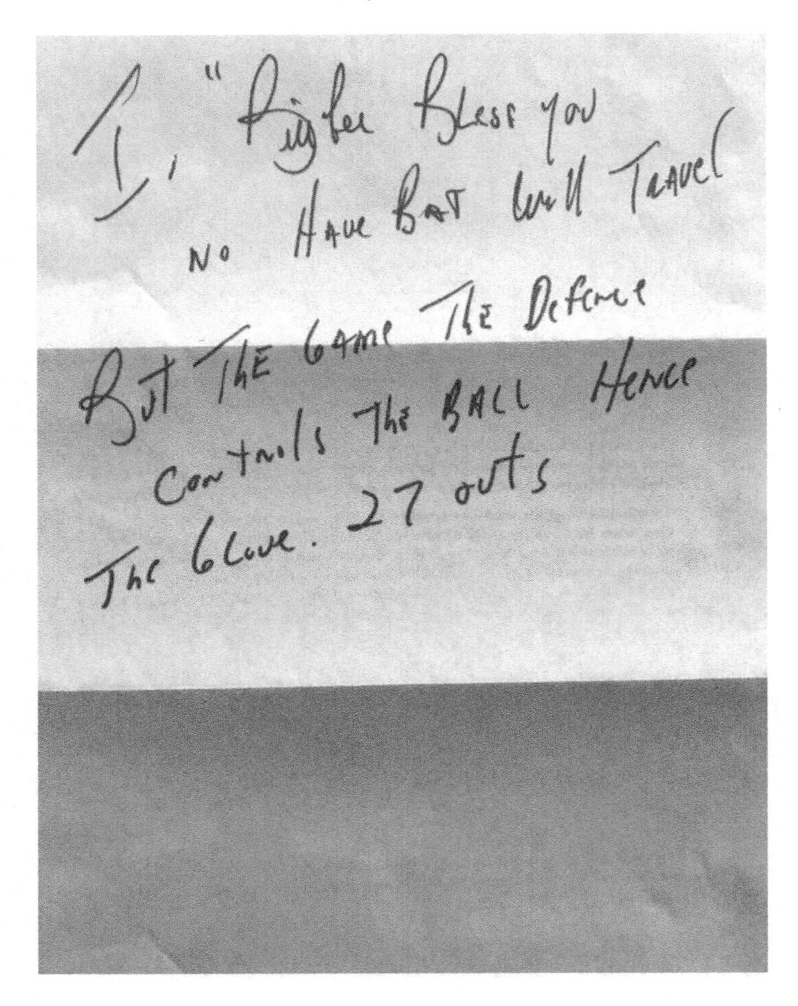

I, "Bill Lee" Bless you
No Have Bat Will Travel
But The Game The Defence
Controls The Ball Hence
The Glove. 27 outs

When I went to publish Have Bat, Will Travel, I discovered that Red Sox legend Bill Lee had written a book called Have Glove, Will Travel. I didn't want to antagonize the legendary Spaceman, so I found his address online and mailed him a letter and self-addressed stamped envelope asking for his blessing to use the name. His response was 100% pure Spaceman, and the original is now mounted on my office wall.

The author many years after the events of this book. From 2014 to 2019, the San Francisco Pacifics won five out of six Bay Area Vintage Base Ball League championship titles, and six out of six Brass Crab trophies, awarded to the best team in the western (San Francisco) division of the BAVBB. As of printing, they remain the only team to win the Treble (league championship, Brass Crab, and Golden Gate Cup championship in the same year), accomplishing the feat in 2017 and 2019.

ACKNOWLEDGMENTS

There are far too many people to thank for their help in this endeavor, but that won't stop me from trying. I would like to offer thanks...

- To Eric, for being a friend, teammate, and comrade-in-arms, and Virginie, for welcoming me into the Woodchucks family. And man, thanks for that calvados, that was something else;
- To Aldo, for showing me what *real* passion for baseball looks like. I don't love the fact that you moved down the road to play for the Huskies after the Woodchucks ceased to exist, but I can overlook it because a guy like you just has to play baseball, period. Why else would you put up with two burly ballplayers crashing on your floor for so long?
- To Seb, for keeping a cool head while others lost theirs, for being a great teammate and friend, and for scoring that implausible run;

- To Sylvain, for doing all the thankless dirty work no one else wanted to do, and doing it with a smile. I'll always think of you as the Obelix of Bois-Guillaume, and hopefully I can buy you a pint of Beamish sometime soon;
- To Vince, for gutting it out every week, for never losing your cool, and for cracking those key base hits during the postseason. Probably had the highest damn WAR on the team, for all the innings you pitched;
- To Pierre, Rafael, Quentin, Christophe, Eric Fournier, and the rest of the Bois-Guillaume Woodchucks. I doubt very much that you could find anyone anywhere in the world as proud of being on a team that won *one* regular season game as I am to have been on the 2006 Woodchucks, and it is entirely because of your friendship and your acceptance. Things will come and go in this world, but I will always and forever be a Woodchuck for life;
- To Aldo's mother Monique, for welcoming me into your home and family; you were the French mother I never had;
- To Carl Hobert, the director of the French department and my cornerbacks coach in high school, famous for launching baseballs at dozing student's heads while

demanding that they conjugate irregular verbs. Everyone in Savigny and Bois-Guillaume consistently commented that I spoke French 'très bien,' with the unspoken implication '...for an American.' I hadn't studied French for almost a decade when I went to France, so Mr. Hobert must have done something right, even though Jose's adorable 5-year-old son in Savigny once turned wide-eyed to his parents to ask them if I was speaking Italian;

- To Jacob, for dragging me out to that Dodgers' game and generally being a mensch;
- To Andrew Wun at Velocity Sports, who got me into shape to take on the world;
- To Tony Lewis, with whom I'll re-launch this club someday. It's been a joy to get to know you and swap stories, and I'm glad *somebody* could lead that motley crew to some honest-to-goodness baseball glory;
- To Troy Nakamura & Greg Moore from USF Baseball – Greg's now at St. Mary's – who showed nothing but love and support for someone who had never attended their program;
- To Fermin, Christophe, and Christian from the Lions, who showed me love and respect, and who I hope weren't put in too awkward a position by me not being the ballplayer Savigny wanted me to be;

- To the rest of the Savigny-Sur-Orge Lions, who I always liked, even if they did drop me like third-period algebra; no hard feelings (on my side at least);
- To Miklos Bankuti & Sierra Peterson, without whose hospitality I would not have been able to pull off the wild back-and-forths during the postseason tournament;
- To Ben Allen, David O'Steen, Kayvon Bina, Parth Raval, David Chang, Justin Parekh, Reza Kermani, and all the other roommates who came and went at the Porn Palace, for putting up with the reckless risk I took installing a batting cage in the backyard, and not freaking out too bad that time I temporarily ruined the floorboards while brewing beer;
- To Sage 'Buttercup' Bray and Aaron 'Abacus' Gubin, my teammates on the five-time defending BAVBB champion San Francisco Pacifics, for reading through this final draft, and to all the other Pax for winning ALL the championships while being the Woodchucks West (i.e., the best damn teammates a guy could ask for);
- To Matt Klinepeter for resurrecting the HBWT website after spammers brought it to its knees;

- To Steve Langone, Antoni Piquet, Roberto Morales, and all the talented pitchers I've ever had the joy of knocking heads with;
- To Joy Tutela, Zach Fleming, and Luke Thomas for all their help and advice;
- To Jools and Alex, for picking me up when I felt down, and for giving me the elusive final line of the book that I could be happy with;
- To Mike and Heide Cygan, for showing up that time at grad school when I was in a pinch and needed Mike to drag the trailer down five levels of parking garage ramp World Strongest Man-style. It has nothing to do with Have Bat Will Travel, but I still wanted to give a shout out for that deus ex machina resolution of a problem when I was really up a creek without a paddle;
- To Marc and Hillary Rubin for bringing me and Becky together, and to Miles, Zach, and Phoebe for showing us that parenthood could be worth it;
- To Christopher Bonzon for his unyielding friendship and cutting-edge medical advice, and to the rest of the Bonzon family – Jeff, Carolyn, Kate, Chip, Amy, Finn, Teddy, and Ben – for being great friends, and most importantly, getting me my first job in finance;

- To Chuck Armstrong and Ryan 'Withers' Conners-Copeland, who gave me the idea of playing in Europe in the first place;
- To Mark Ganek and Sara Neff, for keeping me laughing and choosing the fonts;
- To Jim Shein, for believing in me and encouraging me in all things;
- To Adam Gussow, for his support, inspiration, and the best harmonica playing I've ever heard;
- To Jack Heinz, for inspiring me and not making TOO big a deal about me missing Crim Law classes that fall;
- To Kyle and Adam, my partners in Batter's Box SF and Batter's Box Mobile, who have helped me keep the passion for the game alive; and
- To my parents Judythe and Kieran and my sister Caitlin, for supporting me in all things, even or especially in my most whimsical, unrealistic, and absurd adventures. Because those are the best kind!

And most of all, to Becky, for reasons too numerous to name, but principally because she constantly inspires me to be a better person, husband, and father.

She's *very* good looking, too.

ABOUT THE AUTHOR

Evan Meagher is the 2011 Hot Wing Eating Champion of San Francisco and a CFA charterholder. He holds a BA in Economics and an MA in Organizational Behavior from Stanford University, a JD from the Northwestern University School of Law, an MBA from Northwestern's Kellogg School of Management, and the all-time Over 40 Squat record for the Olympic Club of San Francisco at 501 pounds. After retiring from French baseball, he played on the San Francisco Pacifics of the Bay Area Vintage Base Ball League for nearly a decade, during which they won five BAVBB championships, three Golden Gate Cups, and six Brass Crab trophies. He lives in Boulder, Colorado with his *very* good-looking wife Rebecca, his very adorable son Jude, and his very terrible dogs, Dr. H. Puck Ortiz Spaceman (aka Mr. Yuckles) and Pip Bauer Belichick. In his spare time, he works in finance, and man, what he wouldn't give for another at-bat against Piquet, just for old time's sake.

Made in the USA
Columbia, SC
30 June 2021